T0330177

Economic Thought and the Making of European Monetary Union

Economic Thought and the Making of European Monetary Union

Selected Essays of
Ivo Maes

IVO MAES

*Research Department, National Bank of Belgium, University of
Leuven and Ichec, Brussels, Belgium*

Edward Elgar

Cheltenham, UK • Northampton, MA, USA

Published by
Edward Elgar Publishing Limited
Glensanda House
Montpellier Parade
Cheltenham
Glos GL50 1UA
UK

Edward Elgar Publishing, Inc.
136 West Street
Suite 202
Northampton
Massachusetts 01060
USA

A catalogue record for this book
is available from the British Library

ISBN 1 84064 800 7

Printed and bound in Great Britain by MPG Books Ltd, Bodmin, Cornwall

Contents

List of Figures vii

List of Tables viii

List of Annexes ix

*Foreword by G. Quaden, Governor of the National Bank of Belgium,
    Member of the Governing Council of the European Central Bank* xi

*Foreword by A.W. Coats, Emeritus Professor, University of Nottingham
    and Duke University* xiii

Introduction xv

PART 1: EARLY DEBATES ON EUROPEAN MONETARY
           INTEGRATION 1

1. State and market in post-war integration theory 3

2. Optimum currency area theory and European monetary integration 13

3. Monetary integration debates in the 1970s 29

PART 2: ECONOMIC THOUGHT AT THE EUROPEAN
           COMMUNITY INSTITUTIONS 47

4. The development of economic thought at the European Community
    institutions 49

5. Macroeconomic thought at the European Commission in the 1970s:
   The first decade of the Annual Economic Reports   81

6. Macroeconomic thought at the European Commission in the first
   half of the 1980s   105

PART 3: THE MAKING OF EUROPEAN MONETARY UNION   129

7. EMU from a historical perspective   131

Index   *195*

List of Figures

2.1	A business perception of the impact of EMU	18
2.2	Openness of the European economies	22
3.1	Inflation in the main European countries	31
5.1	Evolution of the European economy	84
5.2	Inflation in Germany and France in the 1960s and 1970s	94
6.1	Main economic indicators for the European Community and the United States	107
7.1	The proposal for a European snake in the Bretton-Woods tunnel	138
7.2	Inflation in Germany and France in the 1960s and 1970s	140
7.3	Exchange rates of some European currencies vis-à-vis the German mark in the 1980s	145
7.4	Interest rate differentials of some European currencies vis-à-vis the German mark in the 1990s	155
7.5	The ERM-crisis: economic fundamentals	156
7.6	Exchange rates of some European currencies vis-à-vis the German mark in the 1990s	157
7.7	Government deficit in the European Union	159
7.8	Key convergence indicators	164
7.9	Inflation convergence in the European Union	165
7.10	Openness of the European economies in 1970 and 1995	169
7.11	Intensity of intra-euro intra-industry trade	169

List of Tables

2.1	Regional net migration in the EC and USA	19
2.2	Shares of intra-industry trade in the intra-Community trade	24
4.1	Institutions of the European Community and staff numbers	50
4.2	Economists at DG II: educational background according to nationality	54
4.3	Economists at DG II: educational background according to age group	55
4.4	Foreign language education in the Community	72
5.1	The Commission of the European Community	85
5.2	A simplified presentation of Directorate-General II (Economic and Financial Affairs)	86
5.3	Typical structure of the Annual Economic Report	89
5.4	Main macroeconomic data	99
7.1	An overview of the functioning of the exchange rate mechanism of the EMS	147
7.2	Cross-border transactions in bonds and equities	149
7.3	Main features of the changeover scenario	160
7.4	Foreign direct investment flows in euro area economies	168

List of Annexes

1.1	Main phases in the process of European integration in the 1940s and 1950s	12
3.1	The European scene	44
3.2	The monetary scene in the 1970s	45
4.1	Structure of the services of the Commission (1994)	77
4.2	A simplified presentation of Directorate-General II (Economic and Financial Affairs) and number of A staff	78
4.3	A succinct chronology of European integration	79
4.4	Participation of non-EC economists in important study groups	80
5.1	Chronology	104
6.1	Main events	126
6.2	Main macroeconomic policymakers at the European Commission	127
7.1	A chronology of European integration	192
7.2	The path to EMU	193

Foreword

G. Quaden

Governor of the National Bank of Belgium, Member of the Governing Council of the European Central Bank

Economic and monetary union (EMU) has been a provisional culmination of the process of European integration. The origins of this process can be traced back to the Second World War, as the devastations of the war resulted in a strong political vision and will to drive European integration forward. During the post-war period then, Europe's economies became more and more interlinked through trade and financial flows. Obviously, the creation of the European Economic Community and the Single Market were important driving forces. Then, economic and monetary union came back on the agenda in the second half of the 1980s, as a next step in the integration process, as the single market would remain incomplete without a single currency. However, a third factor was also indispensable for the realisation of EMU, namely a consensus on a stability-oriented approach to economic policy. A key element of this framework was that price stability should be the fundamental aim of monetary policy. The consensus around this paradigm was a crucial factor behind the remarkable convergence of inflation in the 1980s and 1990s, without which EMU would not have been possible.

This consensus was further reflected in the Maastricht Treaty, as price stability became the ultimate aim of monetary policy, in view of a sustained economic growth. To further safeguard price stability, the European Central Bank, and the national central banks, were given a high degree of independence. However, this autonomy also involved more stringent obligations for the central bank to account for its actions. Indeed, the ultimate foundation of the independence of a central bank is not a law, or even a treaty, but the support by the population at large.

Central bankers have then always to be concerned about explaining and discussing monetary policy, in its various dimensions. A dialogue between the central banks and the academic community is important herein, as it contributes to a more thorough analysis and a better mutual understanding.

The author of this book is very well placed for this, as he lives in both these worlds. This volume offers a very useful contribution to the dialogue between the academic community and the world of European economic policy-making. It analyses the relationship between economic thought and European integration, focusing on economic thought and the policy-making process. By highlighting crucial forces in the integration process, it comes into the area where history borders on, and flows over into, a more prospective analysis.

The essay, written together with Jan Smets and Jan Michielsen, on EMU in an historical perspective, certainly deserves special credit. It not only offers a lucid analysis of the process of European monetary integration, but also provides an intriguing case study on Belgium. It shows that, through creativity and diplomacy, Belgium played a non-negligible part in the creation of EMU. This provides a good indication of the role a central bank of a small country can play in the new world of European economic and monetary union.

Foreword

A.W. Coats

Emeritus Professor, University of Nottingham and Duke University

Serious writers on economic thought and policy are often regarded as either "outsiders" or "insiders", a misleading dichotomy since the two categories frequently overlap in practice. Moreover, some individuals seem able to move effortlessly between the two spheres, and even to inhabit them both without becoming schizophrenic. Ivo Maes admirably exemplifies this "blurring of genres", an expression utilized effectively by the distinguished cultural anthropologist, Clifford Geertz.

Maes's collection of essays demonstrates his singular ability to be both academic - that is, scholary, cautious and conscientiously objective, so far as that is possible - and a successful professional economic researcher within a leading central bank, an environment that may be somewhat more cloistered than the typically frenetic government department.

Ivo Maes's location and nationality are both advantageous from a research standpoint. As a Belgian economist-cum-historian of economics living in Brussels, the city that houses the European Union's major economic institutions, he is ideally placed to study, visit, and understand the nature and functioning of the large and complex organisations that play so prominent a role in the formulation and implementation of European economic policy. He also has excellent opportunities to meet - whether informally or formally - significant numbers of their professional employees. Institutions nowadays feature much more prominently in economic literature than they did two or three decades ago; yet we still have much to learn about their internal operations and structure, and their role in policy-making. Ivo Maes's essays make significant contributions to our knowledge and understanding of these matters. His nationality is also of special value to his research because Belgium, tucked in as it is between France and the Netherlands, has tended to be somewhat neglected, even overlooked, by specialists in international economics. Belgium has neither the Netherlands's powerful intellectual tradition in economics and econometrics nor the political weight of France, in late twentieth century international economic policy negotiations.   Yet arguably the country, through pragmatic and creative proposals, has exercised a disproportionate influence in these matters.

Against this background, Ivo Maes's essays on European monetary integration are of particular value because of the importance of the issues involved, which are so sensitive politically and from the standpoint of national sovereignty.   Here, as elsewhere, Maes's combination of historical knowledge and analytical insight will be helpful to students of all ages and to intelligent laymen seeking to understand how we got where we are.   His essays provide essential background to matters that have figured prominently in the headlines, and will doubtless continue to do so.

Introduction

The quest for economic and monetary union has been one of the core elements of the process of European integration in the post-war period. The essays in this volume provide an analysis of different aspects of the interaction between economic ideas, economic policy-making and the creation of economic and monetary union in Europe. A great deal of attention is given to the interplay between economic ideas and the policy-making process. In this way, the volume aims at contributing to a better understanding of the role of economic ideas in the process of European monetary integration.

The process of European integration is to a large degree a political process, which has its roots in the two world wars and the devastations they caused. The Second World War proved to be a trauma for Europe's political leaders. The Schuman Declaration of May 1950, which provided the basis for the European Coal and Steel Community, stated clearly that "solidarity in production will make it plain that any war between France and Germany becomes not merely unthinkable, but materially impossible". The memory of the wars made for a very strong political will to further European integration, with at its heart a process of Franco-German reconciliation and cooperation.

However, acknowledging the crucial importance of this political dimension does not imply that one should underestimate the importance of economic thought. Economic ideas and beliefs shape the perceptions of policy-makers. Consequently, they play a crucial role in defining vital interests and shaping strategic choices.

At the core of the process of European monetary integration was Europe's quest for exchange rate stability. This was not always easy to understand for American economists, who are generally more in favour of flexible exchange rates. European economists, both policy-makers and academics, much more emphasised the importance of stable exchange rates, especially for the functioning of Europe's internal market and to safeguard the *acquis communautaire*.

Discussions about monetary integration were further shaped by the different economic paradigms and traditions in Europe, especially in France and in Germany, the two main players in the EMU game. The

Franco-German debates on European monetary integration are well known as the controversy between the "monetarists" and the "economists". The "monetarists", with France as a dominant player, were in favour of plans for greater exchange rate stability and exchange rate support mechanisms. They saw a driving role for European monetary integration in the process of economic and, also, political integration of Europe. The "economists", under the leadership of Germany, emphasised the new monetary order to be created. The coordination of economic policies and the convergence of economic performances, especially inflation, were a precondition for EMU. According to their view, monetary union could be only the last and crowning phase in the process of economic integration (coronation theory). The various European projects regarding monetary integration were largely a synthesis of, and a compromise between, these two schools of thought.

The differing views on monetary integration should be situated in the broader French and German conceptions of economic policy-making. In France, there was a long tradition of a more "voluntarist" approach to economic policy-making with an active role for the state in the economy, traditionally characterised as "Colbertism". The "monetarist" ideas, with monetary integration having a leading role in the integration process, fitted into this voluntarist approach. In Germany, ordo-liberalism was very influential in the post-war period. The main objective of economic policy should be to create a framework within which markets could function. The task of monetary policy, the responsibility of an independent central bank, was to assure price stability. In the monetary integration debates, the "economists" stressed the new European monetary order which had to be created and the (convergence) conditions that countries had to fulfill to participate in EMU.

In the beginning, with the formation of the European Economic Community, the Franco-German debates went to the core of economic policy-making. They not only concerned monetary matters, but also the basic mechanisms of economic coordination: planning or the market. Gradually, however, planning and activist Keynesian policies fell into demise. In this, important factors were the stagflation of the 1970s and the failure of demand management policies, both at the international level, e.g. the coordinated expansion of 1978, and at the national level, e.g. the Mitterrand experiment in France in the early 1980s. Gradually, a basic consensus developed on "sound money" policies: stability-oriented, medium-term, economic policies, with an emphasis on the supply side. There were still heated Franco-German debates, like the one on a *gouvernement économique* during the Maastricht Treaty negotiations. But these were now rather at the fringe around a basic consensus on "sound money" policies. The ensuing acceptance of price stability as the ultimate objective of monetary policy was an important factor behind the remarkable convergence of inflation in the 1980s and 1990s, an indispensable condition for the realisation of EMU.

Meanwhile, the formation of the European Economic Community, with the creation of the common market, stimulated a dynamic process of economic integration. Europe's economies became more and more interlinked through trade and financial flows, constraining more and more the autonomy of national policy-makers. This became a fertile ground for economic debate, with economists arguing whether Europe was fit for monetary union. In the second half of the 1980s and in the 1990s, the logic of the integration process, with the loss of national autonomy in policy-making and the need to achieve the single market with a single currency, became important arguments, pointing towards a monetary union.

This volume consists of three parts: "Early debates on European monetary integration", "Economic thought at the European Community institutions", and, "The making of European monetary union". The volume proceeds largely chronologically, beginning with theories of economic integration in the 1950s and 1960s, moving towards thinking among policy-makers in the 1970s and 1980s, and ending with the creation of EMU in the 1990s. It also moves, broadly, from more academic theories, towards economic thought at policy-making institutions, to the unfolding of the process of European monetary integration.

The first part, on the early debates, opens with a chapter on "State and market post-war integration theory". It concentrates on the 1950s, which can be considered as the "Years of high theory" for integration economics, with seminal contributions by Jacob Viner, James Meade and Jan Tinbergen. They considered integration as a dynamic process, with a driving role for market forces, and paid considerable attention to the consequences of economic integration on the structure of government and the organisation of economic policy.

The second chapter, "Optimum currency area theory and European monetary integration" focuses on the debate between Mundell, McKinnon and Kenen in the 1960s. This controversy can be situated in the fixed versus flexible exchange rate discussions of the post-war period and was, to a large extent, centred around the role of the exchange rate in the framework of macroeconomic stabilisation policy. More dynamic elements, like the stimulus a single currency can give to the integration of goods and factor markets, were largely absent.

The third chapter, "Monetary integration debates in the 1970s" considers both contributions by academics and policy-makers. At the core of the paper is the Werner Report and the failure of European Community's first attempt at monetary union. First an analysis is presented of academic reactions to this failure, which were often based on a Phillips-curve framework. Thereafter the focus is on projects of policy-makers to relaunch European monetary cooperation, which culminated in the creation of the European Monetary System.

The second part of the book considers economic thought at the European Community institutions, especially the Commission. It opens with a broad chapter on "The development of economic thought at the European Community institutions". This provides an overview of the development of the European Community and the functioning of its institutions, especially the role of economists at the Commission. At the centre of the chapter is further an analysis of the specificity of economic thought at the European Commission, which is largely a blend of the different European traditions. Initially, German ordo-liberalist thinking and French ideas on indicative planning were very important. Later Anglo-Saxon ideas gained in importance, also due to the internationalisation (or americanisation) of economics in the post-war period.

The fifth chapter "Macroeconomic thought at the European Commission in the 1970s: the first decade of the Annual Economic Reports" contains a crucial case study. It analyses the evolution of economic thought at the Commission, and the factors behind it, from an initial dominance of Keynesian economics toward a more monetarist and supply side oriented approach. It also highlights the shift toward a view of the European economy as a whole, contrasting with the earlier focus on the national economies.

The sixth chapter "Macroeconomic thought at the European Commission in the first half of the 1980s" presents a further case study. It considers the Commission's analysis of Europe's unemployment problem and the debate with the Dornbusch Group in the first half of the 1980s. Moreover, it has an extensive analysis of the distinguishing characteristics of economics at a policy-making institution, like the Commission, compared to academic economics.

The third part of the volume (chapter seven), written together with Jan Smets and Jan Michielsen, considers "EMU from a historical perspective". It presents, first, a historical overview of the process of European monetary integration, paying special attention to the, sometimes heated, debates between the "monetarists" and the "economists". Second, it analyses the reasons for the successful realisation of EMU. It distinguishes between long-term structural factors (such as the strong political will, the growing consensus on stability-oriented policies and the increased integration of Europe's economies) and the specific momentum of the integration process in the second half of the 1980s and the 1990s. Lastly, it considers the role of Belgium. By analysing the role of a small country such as Belgium it illustrates that EMU was not only a Franco-German matter, but a truly multilateral achievement.

This book draws on a of variety of experiences, which are the result of living in different, partly overlapping, worlds and communities. It reflects ideas and approaches, acquired in the policy-making world, especially the National Bank of Belgium, now part of the Eurosystem, as well as shorter stays at the European Commission and the Bundesbank. It also draws on the academic world, both in Belgium, with affiliations at the University of Leuven and Ichec, and more internationally, as a visiting professor at Texas Lutheran College and Duke University. More generally, I very much enjoyed being a "member" of the communities of the history of economic thought and European studies. I am thus indebted to many persons, for their cooperation, comments and insights. I fear however that my expressions of gratitude will, rather necessarily, be incomplete. For those whom I do not mention here, I have tried to express my gratitude at other times, and I would like to say thanks again. However, I also think it appropriate to mention here a few persons by name.

In first instance, I would like to thank very much Guy Quaden, the Governor of the National Bank of Belgium, for his interest and support for this project. His openness certainly stimulates also this broader kind of studies. I hope that it will contribute to strengthening creative and original research at the National Bank of Belgium.

A special word of thanks goes to my co-authors of part three, Jan Smets, Director of the Research Department at the National Bank of Belgium and Commissioner-General for the Euro, and Jan Michielsen, formerly Head of the Foreign and Financial Market Departments at the National Bank of Belgium. Working with them, not only on "EMU from a historical perspective", but also in many other matters, was not only very enriching and stimulating, but also very enjoyable. I am especially indebted to them for sharing with me their profound experience of central banking, policy-making and European negotiations.

I would further like to thank very much Bob Coats, emeritus professor at the universities of Nottingham and Duke. It was both very enriching and enjoyable to participate in his projects on the internationalisation and professionalisation of economics in the post-war period. This has coloured very much my research, especially on economics at the European Community institutions.

Many other persons have further contributed to this project, both in the academic and in the policy-making world. I would like to thank, in alphabetical order, for comments, discussions and insights: F. Abraham. J.-P. Abraham, M. Albert, R. Arena, R. Backhouse, L. Baeck, A.P. Barten, B. Bateman, P. Bekx, K. Bosman, A. Brunilla, E. Buyst, D. Cardon, J.-C. Chouraqui, A. Citzler, A. Cottrell, J. Delors, N. de Marchi, S. Deroose, D. Dinan, M. Emerson, S. England, H. Famerée, M.M.G. Fase, M. Fratianni, F. Froschmaier, G. Grosche, E. Groshen, H. Hagemann, H. Hannoun, D. Hausman, D. Heremans, D. Hodson, D. Howarth, F. Ilzkovitz, O. Issing, A. Italianer, R. Klump, H. Köhler, D. Laidler, A. Lamfalussy, A. Louw, I. Maher, D. Mayes, B. Molitor, F. Mongelli, J.-C. Morel, M. Morgan, M. Mors, J. Mortensen, J. Muysken, S. Ngo-Maï, T. Padoa-Schioppa, C. Panico, J.-P. Patat, J.-C. Paye, A.-M. Peeters, T. Peeters, L. Pench, V. Périlleux, K.-O. Pöhl, J. Polak, L. Quaglia, J.-J. Rey, A. Saether, A. Salanti, P. Santella, A. Sapir, B. Schefold, W. Schönfelder, L. Schubert, H. Schuberth, B. Snoy, C. Spiller, A. Suvanto, G. Tondini, D. Torre, E. Tosi, E. Tower, I. Vaillant, P. Van Cayseele, P. Van den Bempt, P. Van der Haegen, H. Van der Wee, J. Van Ginderachter, V. Van Rompuy, J. van Ypersele, A. Verdun, J. Vignon, H. von der Groeben, K. Weber, M. Wegner, R. Weintraub, P. Werner and C. Willeke.

A special word of thanks goes to the Documentation Service and the secretariat of the Research Department of the National Bank of Belgium, especially to Chris Berghman. They were very helpful, not only on the occasion of this project, but also for many other studies.

Edward Elgar has been a congenial publisher. I would like to say thanks to him, and his colleagues, for their efficiency and help in bringing this project to a successful end.

I would further like to thank the various publishers for their permission to reprint the different articles. More specific acknowledgements are presented at the beginning of every chapter.

While this project was in many instances a social process, there still remains an important dimension of individual responsibility. Neither the National Bank of Belgium nor the Eurosystem, nor any other institution, is responsible for any of the views expressed in this volume. The usual restrictions apply.

Ivo Maes
Brussels, August 2001

PART 1:

Early Debates on European Monetary
Integration

1. State and Market in Post-War Integration Theory*

1.1 INTRODUCTION

During the years following the Second World War, problems of economic integration were widely debated. They were intimately connected to the attempts to build a new order, both on a world and on a regional level, after the destruction of the old regime during the war. It should be no surprise then, that this was also a crucial time in the development of the modern theory of economic integration. The focus of this paper will be on the development of this theory in Europe, where efforts at regional integration were the most intense (see Annex 1.1).

The term "integration" is relatively new in economics. According to Machlup, prior to 1953 the word was not to be found in the subject index of any book on international economics (Machlup, 1976, 62). Machlup considered both general theories of international economics (like Heckscher-Ohlin) and theories of integration among a limited number of countries as falling under the topic of "integration". However, at the end of the 1950s, the term became more closely associated with the idea of regional integration (see Balassa, 1961). In this paper the term "integration" will be used further as regional integration.

* Reprinted from *National and European Markets in Economic Thought*, P. Roggi, L. Baeck and G. Gioli (eds.), Proceedings of the Eleventh International Economic History Congress, Milano, B14, 1994, pp. 83-94, with kind permission from Università Bocconi.

I would like to thank F. Abraham, S. England and the participants of the economics seminar at the University of Limburg, Maastricht, especially J. Muysken, for comments on an earlier draft. The usual restrictions apply.

The paper will focus on three authors: Jacob Viner, James Meade and Jan Tinbergen. Particular attention will be given to the role of the state and the market in their theories. Economic integration always involves an interplay of state and market forces. Through integration, a greater market is created, as impediments to free movement of goods, people and capital are abolished. However, the state has a role in this process. Two questions are important: When is government intervention appropriate? and, At what level of government should this take place?

1.2   VINER'S ANALYSIS OF CUSTOMS UNIONS

A discussion of the origins of modern integration theory has inevitably Jacob Viner's book *The Customs Union Issue* (1950) as a starting point. His work constituted both a breaking point with the past, and the paradigm for further research.

Jacob Viner was mainly an academic economist and spent most of his time at the universities of Chicago and Princeton. His book *The Customs Union Issue* was a project of the Carnegie Endowment. The purpose was to make available information on customs unions in order to help solve post-war problems. His study contains a wealth of information on customs unions, especially the German *Zollverein*. Viner's work focuses on the market for goods and on tariffs as the main barrier to trade. In his definition, the complete elimination of tariffs between the member states and the introduction of a common external tariff are the essential conditions for a customs union (Viner, 1950, 5). He pays particular attention to the compatibility of a customs union with the "most-favoured nation" principle. However, his work is best known for his analysis of the economic aspects of a customs union.

As Viner remarks, most economists, both protectionists and free traders, have been favourable to customs unions. He, however, questions whether the formation of a customs union will necessarily be a movement in the direction of free trade. He sees the basic issue (Viner, 1950, 44) thus:

> The primary purpose of a customs union, and its major consequence for good or bad, is to shift resources of supply, and the shift can be either to lower- or to higher-cost sources, depending on circumstances.

Viner analyses the impact of the customs union on trade flows, introducing the concepts of "trade-creation" and "trade-diversion". In the case of trade-creation there is a shift from domestic supply to supply from the customs partner. This will increase economic welfare as higher-cost domestic sources of supply are replaced by lower-cost imports from the customs partner. In the case of trade-diversion, there is a shift in supply from a non-member country to a member country. This has a welfare cost as lower-cost sources of supply are replaced by higher-cost supplies in the partner country.

Basically, a customs union will be welfare creating when the trade-creating effects outweigh the trade-diverting effects. However, Viner also discusses "administrative economies" and terms of trade effects of a customs union, (Viner, 1950, 55-65) and he was also aware of the influences of economies of scale (Viner, 1950, 44).

When considering the role of state and market, one can say that Viner regards a customs union as a governmental decision to take part in a bigger market. This implies that a national state loses part of its sovereign rights. It can no longer impose a tariff against the partner countries and it has to share decision-making power on the common external tariff.

Given these governmental decisions on the setting-up of a customs union, Viner sees market forces as having a driving role in the integration process, leading to a greater coordination of economic policies. These market forces can even be so strong that they can push towards a uniformity of rates of excise taxes (Viner, 1950, 61).

However, this need for harmonisation of policy in a customs union makes Viner very sceptical about the future of new customs unions, given the increase of government intervention in the economy. He writes (Viner, 1950, 136):

> Two neighbouring countries contemplating complete customs union today must therefore contemplate also the necessity of harmonising their general patterns of economic controls, which would involve a much more complete degree of economic unification than would a representative nineteenth-century customs union.

In a certain sense, Viner's words can be considered as prophetic. The Treaty of Rome, by means of which the European Economic Community was created, emphasises tariff unification. However, nearly three decades later, a new drive towards the "internal market" had to be launched, focusing on the remaining barriers in the Community. These barriers were, to a large extent, linked to government intervention in the economy.

1.3 THE CONTRIBUTION OF JAMES MEADE

James Meade's involvement with economic integration was not only theoretical, but also more practical. From 1937 to 1940, he worked in

Geneva for the League of Nations. During the Second World War, he was brought into the Economic Section of the British Cabinet Office where he participated in the elaboration of both the monetary and the trade aspects of the post-war world economic order. In fact, he was the main author of the British proposals for an international commercial union (see Vines, 1987, 411).

Meade's analysis of economic integration was only a small part of his work on international economics, for which he received the Nobel Prize in 1977. His main contributions to integration economics in the 1950s were *Problems of Economic Union* (Meade, 1953) and *The Theory of Customs Unions* (Meade, 1955). He also made some applied studies on the Belgium-Luxembourg Economic Union (Meade, 1956a) and Benelux (Meade, 1956b).

In analysing an economic union between countries and the transfer of sovereignty necessary for the functioning of this single integrated market, Meade clearly started from the "subsidiarity principle", according to which a function should be allocated to the lowest level of government, unless welfare gains can be reaped by assigning it to the next higher level (Van Rompuy et al., 1991, 111). As Meade wrote (1953, 6):

> What are the minimum economic powers which they must surrender to the supranational or union authority? What is the maximum range of economic functions that they can properly retain for their own national governments?

In his discussion of economic union, Meade distinguishes three elements: commercial policy or a customs union, movements of labour and capital and balance-of-payments adjustment.

Meade was especially interested in the welfare aspects of a customs union, "whether this removal of barriers to trade between the two partner countries is likely to lead to a more or to a less economic use of the world's economic resources" (Meade, 1955, 14).

As Meade admits himself (1955, 33), his work on customs unions is basically a critical analysis of Viner's concepts of trade-creation and -diversion. His basic criticism is that Viner's analysis is most suitable to situations "where all elasticities of demand are zero and all elasticities of supply are infinite" (Meade, 1955, 36), i.e. supply curves are horizontal and demand curves vertical. Meade then refines the analysis, introducing negatively inclined demand curves and cost curves which could be upward sloping or downward sloping (in the case of economies of scale).

The formation of a customs union has important effects on the role of the national state in the economy. Meade discusses trade policy, state industries and fiscal policy.

For trade policy, it is obvious that the government has to surrender all instruments to the union. Meade notes (1953, 15) that the state has also to "forsake those rather less overt devices which are, nevertheless, equally destructive of international trade", especially domestic regulations.

When state trading is used as an alternative means of restricting imports, it has no place in the union. However, when there are economies of scale or external effects, government intervention can be appropriate. This intervention should not impede the functioning of the single market.

Also the scope of fiscal policy will be more limited, as taxes or subsidies affect trade flows when they fall on the production or consumption of particular commodities.

Meade's conclusion shows the logic of the integration process (1953, 27):

> The union authorities will have to concern themselves very deeply with what are often considered to be purely domestic issues both of economic welfare and of national defence. Otherwise the objective of the large integrated market risks frustration.

Meade further discussed whether economic efficiency could be improved by adding freedom of factor movements to freedom of trade in goods (Meade, 1953, 56). He was critical of the Stolper-Samuelson analysis that free trade would equalise factor prices. He concluded that movements of labour and capital were desirable to make the most economic use of the union's resources as well as for easing balance of payments adjustments in the union (Meade, 1953, 73). However, he was very concerned about the problems that free movement of labour and capital could create for independent national policies, particularly in the areas of distribution policy, stabilisation policy and differences in demographic trends and policies.

First, differences in national policies for the redistribution of income and property could create conflicts with a free movement of factors of production. The single market rules out direct controls and interventions. The government can still influence distribution by fiscal measures. However when these create a divorce between the actual rewards of factors of production and their market value they will induce movements which are economically unjustified.

Second, differences in the stance of stabilisation policy can cause capital movements and balance of payments disequilibria.

The third problem concerns the migration of labour. Meade develops a Malthusian line of thought whereby uncontrolled births in one part of the union could lead to overpopulation in the union as a whole.

Mead also paid a lot of attention to the balance of payments implications of integration. His starting point was that "in the modern world the methods of import licensing and exchange control have become the normal method of adjustment of balances of payments" (Meade, 1953, 29). As this method would be excluded with a customs union, Meade investigated whether there were practicable alternatives for adjusting balances of payments. In Meade's view disequilibria in the balance of payments could be tackled by a combination of three instruments: domestic stabilisation policies, variations of exchange rates and accommodating capital flows, especially international reserves.

In this context, Meade considered whether complete integration could solve the balance of payments problems of a union. Meade distinguished five elements which ease balance-of-payments adjustments in a single country (Meade, 1957, 385):

- a greater mobility of goods, labour and capital. Hereby, Meade clearly anticipated the Mundell (1961) and McKinnon (1963) arguments for an optimum currency area (see Maes, 1992);
- a single common currency and banking system;
- a single government and thus a stabilisation policy for the country as a whole;
- a single external policy;
- transfers towards regions with structural problems.

Forming an economic union with not only free movement of goods, but also free movement of labour and capital and balance-of-payments adjustment would require an extensive harmonisation of economic policy and transfer of significant powers to a supra-national government. Meade concluded (1953, 83) that "it is no accident that in the federal democratic states ... more and more economic power is passing from the member-states to the central union".

Meade is an advocate of greater integration in the Western world, both for economic and political reasons. However he thought that, in the 1950s, integration should be limited to the markets for products. In his view, divergences were still too great to proceed to an integration of factor markets and a single currency.

1.4   TINBERGEN'S INTERNATIONAL ECONOMIC INTEGRATION

Like Meade, Tinbergen was an adviser to the League of Nations at Geneva during the second half of the 1930s. From 1945 to 1955, he was director of the Central Planning Bureau of the Netherlands. As such he was involved in the elaboration of Benelux and the European common market. Tinbergen's main book on the topic was *International Economic Integration* (1954).

The book is divided into two parts. The first, "The Essence of International Economic Relations Between Autonomous States", analyses the nature of international economic relations in a world of autonomous governments. The topics treated concern: current transactions, factor movements, financial transactions and the balance of payments. The second part, "International Economic Integration", goes into the question of to what degree these international relations should be deliberately regulated in an integrated world.

For Tinbergen, economic integration concerns the regulation of international relations. As such it is in essence a question of the organisation of economic policy (Tinbergen, 1954, 95, original italics):

> Integration may be said to be the creation of the most desirable structure of international economy, removing artificial hindrances to the optimal operation and introducing deliberately all desirable elements of co-ordination or unification. The problem of integration therefore forms part of a more general problem, namely that of the *optimum economic policy*.

A crucial question in the organisation of economic policy is the degree of centralisation. This is intimately connected with the question of economic integration (Tinbergen, 1954, 98): "Which functions in international economic life should be subject to central control and which should be left to individual countries, enterprises or persons?"

The appropriate degree of centralisation of instruments of economic policy depends on the spillover effects they provoke, "their effect on the well-being of each of the countries concerned" (Tinbergen, 1954, 98). In general, Tinbergen argues, there is a strong case for decentralisation as it gives more freedom to the economic agents. The strongest arguments for centralisation apply to instruments with important spillover effects, be they supporting or conflicting.

Tinbergen discusses integration in three areas: stabilisation policy, trade policy and international payments. Most famous is his discussion of trade policy. Tinbergen is somewhat sceptical about the free trade doctrine that the elimination of import duties and quantitative restrictions would lead to an optimum division of labour between nations. He considers this as only the negative part of a policy of complete integration (Tinbergen, 1954, 117). In his view, a number of positive measures are necessary for integration (Tinbergen, 1952, 149):

- measures to eliminate other distortions between markets, e.g. differences in indirect taxes and rules;
- supervision of the elimination of trade barriers;
- a stable macroeconomic environment;
- measures to supplement the forces of free competition, e.g. cooperation schemes to obtain the most efficient concentration of production in certain sectors.

To conclude his discussion of international integration, Tinbergen (1954, 142) goes into the question of which agencies of international economic cooperation would be appropriate. He remarks that this is ultimately connected with the "problem of political integration".

1.5   CONCLUSION

The early post-war period were "Years of High Theory" for integration economics. Major contributions came from Jacob Viner, James Meade and Jan Tinbergen. They elaborated and refined the theory of economic integration to a high degree.

Jacob Viner's analysis became paradigmatic for customs-union theory. He questioned whether a customs union would increase economic welfare, distinguishing between trade-creation and trade-diversion. Meade both refined and extended Viner's model. He criticised Viner's analysis of a customs union, building a more general model. Meade also extended the analysis to an economic union, comprising not only free trade of goods but also movements of factors of production and balance-of-payments adjustments. Thereby he produced a marvellous analysis of the conditions for an economic and monetary union.

When considering the role of the state and the market in their theories of integration, it is important to remark that most economists in the early post-war period, particularly Meade and Tinbergen, believed in the "public interest" notion of government. They were in favour of government intervention to supplement the working of market forces. This is clearly reflected in their theories of economic integration. Most famous is Tinbergen's distinction between negative and positive integration: positive policy measures are necessary to create a truly integrated and functioning market. Negative measures, for example, the abolition of tariffs, are not sufficient.

Viner, Meade, and Tinbergen paid considerable attention to the consequences of economic integration on the structure of government and the organisation of economic policy. Viner emphasises market forces as having a driving role in the integration process, pushing for an harmonisation of national economic policies. Meade's analysis of the role of the state starts from the subsidiarity principle. However, he is also very aware of the logic of the integration process, leading towards a greater harmonisation of economic policy. Tinbergen considers further the question of what integration means. For him integration is essentially a question of optimising the organisation of economic policy. To investigate the appropriate degree of integration he uses a relatively simple, but very powerful, analysis of the spillover effects of the instruments of economic policy.

REFERENCES

Balassa, B. (1961), Toward A Theory of Economic Integration, *Kyklos,* XIV, 1-17.

Machlup, F. (1976), A History of Thought on Economic Integration, *Economic Integration: Worldwide, Regional, Sectoral. Proceedings of the Fourth Congress of the International Economic Association,* London: Macmillan, pp. 61-85.

Maes, I. (1992), Optimum Currency Area Theory and European Monetary Integration, *Tijdschrift voor Economie en Management,* XXXVII, 137-152.

McKinnon, R. (1963), Optimum Currency Areas, *American Economic Review,* 717-725.

Meade, J. (1953), *Problems of Economic Union,* London: Allen & Unwin.

Meade, J. (1955), *The Theory of Customs Union,* Amsterdam: North-Holland.

Meade, J. (1956a), The Belgium-Luxembourg Economic Union, 1921-1939, *Princeton Essays in International Finance.*

Meade, J. (1956b), Benelux: The Formation of the Common Customs, *Economica,* XXIII, 201-213.

Meade, J. (1957), The Balance-of-Payments Problems of a European Free-Trade Area, *Economic Journal,* 379-396.

Mundell, R. (1961), A Theory of Optimum Currency Areas, *American Economic Review,* 657-665.

Van Rompuy, P., F. Abraham and D. Heremans (1991), Economic Federalism and the EMU, *European Economy,* Special Edition No. 1, 109-135.

Tinbergen, J. (1952), On The Theory of Economic Integration, reprinted in Klaassen H.L. et al. (eds.), (1959), *Selected Papers,* Amsterdam: North-Holland, pp. 138-151.

Tinbergen, J. (1954), *International Economic Integration.* Amsterdam: North-Holland.

Viner, J. (1950), *The Customs Union Issue,* New York: Carnegie Endowment for International Peace.

Vines, D. (1987), Meade, James Edward, in Eatwell J. et al. (eds.), *The New Palgrave,* III, London: Macmillan, pp. 410-417.

Annex 1.1 - Main phases in the process of European integration in the 1940s and 1950s

1947	June	Announcement of the "European Recovery Programme" by US Secretary of State, George Marshall
1948	January	Establishment of Benelux
	April	Foundation of the Organisation of European Economic Cooperation (OEEC)
1949	April	Foundation of the North Atlantic Treaty Organisation (NATO)
	May	Foundation of the Council of Europe
1950	May	Schuman Declaration
	July	Foundation of the European Payments Union (EPU)
	October	Idea of a European Defence Community (EDC) is launched
1952	July	Establishment of the European Coal and Steel Community (ECSC)
1954	August	French National Assembly rejects the ECD Treaty
1958	January	Establishment of the European Economic Community (EEC) and the European Atomic Energy Community (EAEC)
1960	May	Establishment of the European Free Trade Association (EFTA)

2. Optimum Currency Area Theory and European Monetary Integration*

2.1 INTRODUCTION

Traditionally, the theoretical literature on monetary integration has been dominated by the theory of optimum currency areas[1][2]. This analysis has its origins in a debate, during the 1960s, between Mundell, McKinnon and Kenen about the criterion which delineates the optimal domain of a currency area.

This paper will analyse and assess this debate with the hindsight of not only thirty years of theoretical developments, but also the recent process of European monetary integration. Particular attention will be given to both the relevance and limitations of optimum currency area theory for understanding the actual process of monetary integration in Europe.

* Reprinted from *Tijdschrift voor Economie en Management*, June 1992, 137-152, with kind permission from the K.U.Leuven.

I would like to thank F. Abraham, P. Bekx, E. Buyst, A. Citzler, A.W. Coats, M. Morgan, E. Tower, P. Van Caysele, R. Weintraub, an anonymous referee and, especially, N. de Marchi for useful comments and suggestions. The usual restrictions apply.

[1] It should be noted that an optimum currency area differs from a monetary union. An optimum currency area is characterised by fixed exchange rates and convertibility of currencies. A monetary union also implies complete liberalisation of capital transactions and integration of financial markets (cf. Committee for the Study of Economic and Monetary Union, 1989, 14).

[2] See, for instance, Gandolfo, 1986, Ch. 18, Rivera - Batiz and Rivera - Batiz, 1985, Ch. 17 and Wood, 1986, 3.

While this paper highlights the economic mechanisms at play, one caveat is certainly necessary. Monetary integration implies in essence an important transfer of sovereignty from the national states to a central authority. National states lose, to a large extent, their responsibilities in the field of monetary and exchange rate policy. It implies that monetary integration has an important political dimension.

2.2   MUNDELL'S SETTING OF THE AGENDA

2.2.1 Background

Mundell's paper "A Theory of Optimum Currency Areas" (Mundell, 1961), can be situated in the exchange rate controversy of the post-war period. The Bretton-Woods System of fixed exchange rates was increasingly criticised during the 1950s. Two basic arguments were advanced in favour of flexible exchange rates[3]:

- exchange rate changes are the more appropriate instrument for correcting current account imbalances;
- flexible exchange rates give countries more freedom to pursue their own domestic macroeconomic policy objectives[4].

In his optimum currency area paper Mundell cautioned against the practicability of a floating exchange rate system. He opens his "Concluding Argument" by stating that: "The subject of flexible exchange rates can logically be separated into two distinct questions. The first is whether a system of flexible exchange rates can work effectively and efficiently in the modern world economy ... The second question concerns how the world should be divided into currency areas" (Mundell, 1961).

In his article Mundell assumes that this first condition is met so that floating rates function efficiently. He focuses his paper on the second question, the appropriate domain of a currency area.

---

[3]   In this paper, in line with the optimum currency area approach, irrevocably "fixed" exchange rates are compared with purely "flexible" exchange rates. Naturally, these polar cases may not be the relevant comparison for policy decisions.

[4]   Further theoretical developments and the experience of floating exchange rates since the 1970s showed rather that floating exchange rates do not insulate economies, but that they alter the form of interdependence, see Kenen, 1988 and Krugman, 1989.

2.2.2 The "Optimum" Currency Area

Mundell, in line with the optimal exchange rate debate, investigates the stabilisation argument for flexible exchange rates[5]. He distinguishes three policy objectives: full employment, price stability and external balance. His concern is the cost, mainly in terms of unemployment, that a common currency area can cause when the economy is confronted with a shock.

Mundell first discusses the case where demand shifts from the products of country B to the products of country A. A depreciation of the currency of country B would restore external balance, relieve unemployment in country B and contain inflation in country A. "This is the most favourable case for flexible rates based on national currencies" (Mundell, 1961).

Thereafter, he considers a continent which is divided into two countries, the United States and Canada, with a floating exchange rate between them. But the continent is also divided in two regions, which do not correspond to the countries: the East which produces cars and the West which produces lumber (Mundell, 1961). More fundamentally, however, a region is defined in terms of factor mobility: mobile internally but immobile externally (Mundell, 1961).

A shift in demand from cars to lumber would cause unemployment in the East, inflationary pressures in the West and payments imbalances between the two regions. The flexible exchange rate system will correct payments imbalances between the two countries but not between the two regions. Moreover, unemployment will persist in the East and inflationary pressures in the West. Mundell concludes then that the case for flexible exchange rates is "in logic, a case for flexible exchange rates based on regional currencies, not on national currencies. The optimum currency area is the region" (Mundell, 1961). This forms the basis for Mundell's famous criterion that a high degree of internal factor mobility demarcates an optimal currency area.

Mundell's criterion has been the subject of many discussions and controversies. Thereby it is important to distinguish between labour and capital mobility (cf. Fleming, 1971).

---

[5] In his optimum currency area article Mundell, when considering aggregate demand management, does not distinguish (with a minor exception, p. 664) between fiscal and monetary policy and the different effects they have on the external balance (the classic "Mundell-Fleming" contribution, see Mundell, 1962 and Fleming, 1962). He also assumes, in line with the then dominating Keynesian paradigm, stable prices and wages.

Ingram (1959) argued that capital mobility is crucial for an optimum currency area[6]. He stressed that capital flows can play a vital equilibrating role in balance-of-payments adjustment. However, Corden (1972) argues that this is only a temporary solution. "Banks, governments, or branches of firms cannot borrow indefinitely, other than to finance productive investments" (Corden, 1972)[7]. This suggests that the role of capital flows is more limited to easing the burden of adjustment, by allowing long-term adjustment to be spread out in time (cf. Willett and Tower, 1980).

Also labour mobility as a factor of adjustment has been criticised. Corden (1972) argued not only that labour mobility is generally low, but also that it is not desirable. In his view social and economic costs are inflicted on the workers who migrate, to the benefit of those who remain employed[8].

2.2.3   Fixed Exchange Rates or One Currency?

There is a certain ambiguity in Mundell's article whether a currency area refers to fixed exchange rates or a common currency (with one central bank and a single monetary policy).

Mundell stresses the functions of money as a unit of account and medium of exchange, which become more valuable the wider a currency is accepted: "Money is a convenience and this restricts the optimum number of currencies. In terms of this argument alone the optimum currency area is the world, regardless of the number of regions of which it is composed" (Mundell, 1961).

Also, he develops the argument that there is an important asymmetry in the adjustment mechanism between a single currency area and a currency area with several currencies and fixed exchange rates.

A shift of demand from region B to region A will cause unemployment in B and inflationary pressures in A. If country A (e.g. Germany) follows strict monetary policy to combat inflation, then the whole burden of adjustment will be thrown on B. "The policy of surplus countries in restraining prices therefore imparts a recessive tendency to ... a currency area with many separate currencies" (Mundell, 1961). This contrasts with a single currency

---

[6]   See also Ingram 1960 and 1973. Ingram has been criticised by Pfister 1960. Also Scitovsky stresses the equilibrating role of capital movements, see Scitovsky, 1957 and 1967.

[7]   The equilibrating role of capital flows has been questioned, as the determinants of capital movements are very complex (see Fleming, 1971, 472 and Tower and Willett, 1976, 52).

[8]   For an overview of criticisms of labour mobility see, e.g., Ishiyama, 1975, 349.

area where "the pace of inflation is set by the willingness of central authorities to allow unemployment in deficit regions" (Mundell, 1961).

This nicely foreshadows the "deflationary bias" argument put forward against the European Monetary System[9]. It can further explain the Bundesbank's insistence on an independent European Central bank committed to price stability (Pöhl, 1990).

But while Mundell develops these crucial distinctions between a single currency and fixed exchange rates, there are other passages where he does not make this distinction. So for instance his famous definition of an optimum currency area as "a domain within which exchange rates are fixed" (Mundell, 1961). Also in other instances he equates a single currency and fixed exchange rates (e.g. p. 660).

An explanation could be that Mundell was mainly concerned about the traditional macroeconomic objectives: full employment, stable prices and external balance. To attain these objectives he investigated the merits of fixed versus flexible exchange rates.

However, recent research would stress the distinction between a single currency and fixed exchange rates (cf. Bertola, 1988 and Commission of the European Communities, 1990). Some crucial differences concern:

- transaction cost: a single currency eliminates costs from currency conversion and hedging. These savings on transaction cost could amount to 0.3% to 0.4% of the GDP of the European Community (Commission of the European Community (1990)). However, this study does not take into account the costs of introducing the single currency;
- transparency of prices: as goods and services would be priced in the same currency, this would further strengthen the integration of goods and factor markets;
- credibility: a single currency gives from the outset maximum credibility to a monetary union as it makes exit from the union very difficult[10], something of crucial importance for long-term investment decisions. A rough indication of the importance of credibility can be found in business perceptions of monetary union: opinions on the

---

[9]   See, e.g., Giavazzi and Giovannini, 1988. However, this argument is not new. See, e.g., Balogh, 1950, 302 and Meade, 1957, 385. Also, Keynes criticised the Bretton-Woods system for being asymmetrically severe toward countries in deficit, cf. Solomon, 1977, 13.

[10] The temptation for time-inconsistency is significantly reduced (cf. De Grauwe, 1989 and Kydland and Prescott, 1977).

prospects for the business climate become much more positive when a
single currency complements the single market (see Figure 2.1);
- external benefits: only with a single currency can a monetary union
lead to a recasting of the role of currencies on the international scene.

To conclude, a single currency would not only lead to a more thoroughgoing
integration in the monetary field, but also stimulate and deepen integration in
other areas. Monetary integration is part of a more general integration
process.

Figure 2.1 - A business perception of the impact of EMU

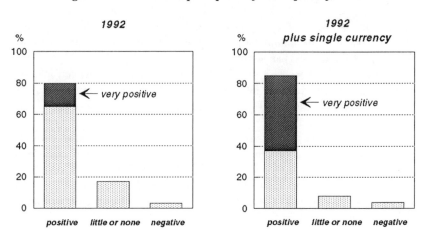

Source: Business survey undertaken for the Commission of the European
Communities by Ernst and Young, Commission of the European
Communities, 1990, 10.

2.2.4   Assessment

Mundell basically regards the demarcation of an optimum currency area as a
trade-off between the convenience of money and the stabilisation function of
exchange rate changes.

Mundell's identification of internal mobility of factors of production as
important for the demarcation of an optimum currency area is not new. Both
Meade and Scitovsky singled out factor mobility as a determinant of a single

currency area[11]. But they also considered the free movement of goods and a central monetary and fiscal authority as important elements conducive to a single currency area. Such a central fiscal authority, with interregional solidarity through the federal social security and tax system, is very important in most existing federal states.

Also, Mundell's contribution is narrower in dimension compared to Meade and Scitovsky. They both situated a single currency area in a more general analysis of economic integration.

The implications of Mundell's theory for the actual process of monetary integration in the European Community are more complex. Capital mobility is becoming very high among the countries of the European Community, especially with the 1992 programme, leading to the formation of a European financial market. Labour mobility is much lower in Europe than in the United States (see Table 2.1). The 1992 programme comprises several measures to stimulate the free movement of people. But, due to cultural and linguistic factors, workers will remain less mobile in Europe. However, empirical evidence for the United States suggests that labour mobility is less important than capital mobility for the adjustment process (Eichengreen, 1990).

Table 2.1 - Regional net migration in the EC and USA

(average rates per annum, % of population)

	1970-1979	1980-1985
EC (64 regions)	0.4	0.2
USA (50 states + DC)	0.8	0.7

Source: Commission of the European Communities, 1990, 151.

Note: Numbers represent total net migration movements across regional boundaries, and thus include movements to or from regions from other Member States and third countries as well as movements between regions within a country. The figure shown is the average of the absolute values of the net migration balance for its regions.

---

[11] See Meade, 1957, 385 and Scitovsky, 1957 and 1958. See also Friedman, 1953, 193, fn 16. However, one could remark that Mundell has also been working on the interrelation between factor mobility and international trade (Mundell, 1957) but he does not consider this in his optimum currency area framework.

2.3   McKINNON'S CONTRIBUTION

2.3.1   Background

McKinnon also situates optimum currency area theory in the "extensive literature on the relative merits of fixed versus flexible exchange rates" (McKinnon, 1963).   He credits Mundell for putting the currency area question on the agenda.   He accepts Mundell's idea of factor mobility as determining an optimum currency area, but he wants to supplement it with an openness criterion.   He defines openness as the ratio of tradable to non-tradable goods.

McKinnon further defines optimum as "a single currency area within which monetary-fiscal policy and flexible external exchange rates can be used to give the best resolution of three (sometimes conflicting) objectives" (McKinnon, 1963).   The three objectives are the same as with Mundell: full employment, price stability and external balance.

McKinnon's focus is especially on the price stability objective.   This assumes "that any capitalist economy requires a stable-valued liquid currency to insure efficient resource allocation" (McKinnon, 1963).

2.3.2   The Openness Criterion

McKinnon basically argues that, for an open economy, the exchange rate is not an appropriate instrument of macroeconomic policy.   Not only is it not very effective in correcting external imbalances, but it also endangers the stability of the price-level.   He then challenges Mundell's basic (explicit) assumption that changes in the exchange rate are effective.

A depreciation of the currency would increase the prices of tradables (both exportables and importables).   This would, given the high ratio of tradables to non-tradables, lead to an important increase in the domestic price-level.

Also, in a highly open economy, flexible exchange rates become less effective as an instrument to improve the trade balance.   "In the extreme case where the economy is completely open ... the only way the trade balance can be improved is by lowering domestic expenditures ... Changes in the exchange rate will necessarily be completely offset by internal price-level repercussions with no improvement in the trade balance" (McKinnon, 1963)[12].

The above argument is reinforced by the probable absence of money illusion in an open economy: "A devaluation would be associated with a large domestic price-level increase and hence money illusion would not be much help in getting labor to accept a cut in real wages" (McKinnon, 1963)[13].

However, one assumption is crucial for McKinnon's analysis: that price stability prevails in the outside world (cf. Corden, 1972 and Ishiyama, 1975). If the international economy were unstable, flexible exchange rates could fulfil a very useful "insulation" function, also in small open economies. This highlights the importance of identifying the source of the disturbance which affects the economy.

2.3.3 The Monetary Dimension

For McKinnon the monetary dimension is of the utmost importance, something which has rather been neglected in the ensuing literature. He devotes about half of his article to a section: "Monetary Implications of the Model". He admits that this makes the notion of optimality "complex and difficult to quantify precisely, so what follows does not presume to be a logically complete model" (McKinnon, 1963).

McKinnon focuses on the liquidity properties of money. He emphasises the importance of stable money to promote economic growth: "the process of saving and capital accumulation in a capitalistic system is greatly hampered unless a suitable numéraire and store of value exists" (McKinnon, 1963).

However, there is, just as with Mundell, a certain ambiguity whether he is concerned with fixed exchange rates or a single currency. Basically, he considers them as more or less equivalent. In his introduction he discusses "a single currency system, or - what is almost the same thing - a fixed exchange rate system with guaranteed convertibility of currencies" (McKinnon, 1963). But the ambiguity is very nicely illustrated in one passage where, at the same

---

12 As Ishiyama (1975, 350) has remarked, a similar conclusion holds when one measures the openness of the economy by the percentage of imports to national income (the percentage of trade instead of tradables). Following trade multiplier analysis, the more open the economy, the less severe the drop in income necessary to correct a payments deficit. Expenditure-reducing policies are then more appropriate than expenditure-switching policies.

13 An argument also used by Mundell (1961, 663). See also Orcutt (1955, 6).

time, he more or less equates fixed rates with a single currency and highlights some crucial differences between the two:

> To maintain the liquidity value of individual currencies for small areas, a fixed exchange rate system is necessary. In addition, capital movements among small areas are more needed to promote efficient economic specialisation and growth than free capital movements among large, economically developed areas. Contractual arrangements for such movements are greatly facilitated by a common currency. These arguments give us some insight into why each of the fifty states in the United States could not efficiently issue its own currency, aside from the inconvenience of money changing (McKinnon, 1963).

2.3.4 Assessment

McKinnon's contribution is an attempt to refine and complement Mundell's optimality criterion for a currency area. His theoretical framework, for which he follows Mundell, can be situated in the optimal exchange rate debate. Mundell focuses on factor markets and on the conditions which render exchange rate adjustments superfluous.

Figure 2.2 - Openness of the European economies

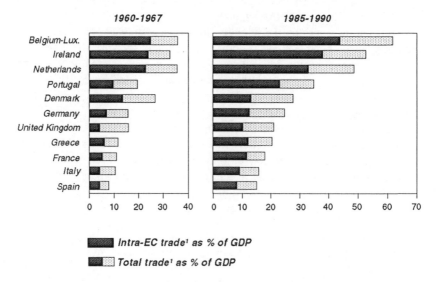

Intra-EC trade[1] as % of GDP

Total trade[1] as % of GDP

Source: Eurostat.
   [1] *Average of merchandise imports and exports.*

McKinnon, on the contrary, focuses in the goods market and on the conditions which make exchange rate adjustment ineffective. Integration of goods markets (i.e. highly open economies) is then a factor conducive to a single currency area, as already mentioned by Meade.

McKinnon's openness criterion is of special importance for small open economies, like Belgium and the Netherlands (see Figure 2.2). These countries have a policy of anchoring their currencies to the German mark. The inflationary consequences of devaluing their currency against the German mark and the resulting loss of the competitive advantage of the devaluation, have been a major reason for this policy choice.

McKinnon also pays extensive attention to the monetary dimension. His main preoccupation is the maintenance of the liquidity properties of money. But, as with Mundell, there is a certain ambiguity whether an optimum currency area is about a single currency or fixed exchange rates.

2.4   KENEN'S DIVERSIFICATION CRITERION

Kenen credits Mundell with the first explicit formulation of the optimum currency area question (Kenen, 1967)). He accepts that mobility of factors of production is a criterion that delineates an optimum currency area[14]. But in his view product diversification is more appropriate as a criterion: "diversity in a nation's product mix, the number of single-product regions contained in a single country, may be more relevant than labor mobility" (Kenen, 1967)[15].

Kenen focuses on payment imbalances, supposing that they have their origins in disturbances in individual exports. If a country has a diversified export sector, "the law of large numbers will come into play ... Its aggregate exports, then, are sure to be more stable than those of an economy less thoroughly diversified" (Kenen, 1967)[16]. More diversified economies are then less vulnerable to external shocks and have the least need for flexible rates to maintain external balance.

Kenen himself admits two caveats:

- his argument does not apply when changes in export demand arise from business-cycle swings (Kenen, 1967);

---

[14] Flanders calls this "the Mundell-McKinnon-Kenen consensus" (Flanders, 1967, 103).

[15] The diversification argument was already advanced by Orcutt, 1955.

[16] Kenen also remarks that sufficient occupational mobility is a necessary condition for domestic stability.

- a diversified economy may have a rather small marginal propensity to import (Kenen, 1967)[17].

Kenen's contribution further illustrates the complexity of determining an optimum currency area. His diversification criterium would favour monetary union in Europe, as the different economies of the European Community are generally characterised by a diversified industrial structure (see Table 2.2). However, the 1992 programme could lead to a greater concentration of industry (Krugman, 1991). This could make Europe less suitable as an optimum currency area.

Also in Kenen's paper there is an ambiguity whether an optimum currency area comprises a single currency or fixed exchange rates.

Table 2.2 - *Shares of intra-industry trade in the intra-Community trade*
(as % of total intra-Community trade)

Country	1970	1980	1987
Belgium-Luxembourg	0.69	0.76	0.77
Denmark	0.41	0.52	0.57
Germany	0.73	0.78	0.76
Greece	0.22	0.24	0.31
Spain	0.35	0.57	0.64
France	0.76	0.83	0.83
Ireland	0.36	0.61	0.62
Italy	0.63	0.55	0.57
Netherlands	0.67	0.73	0.76
Portugal	0.23	0.32	0.37
United Kingdom	0.74	0.81	0.87

Source: Buigues, Ilzkovitz and Lebrun, 1990, 41.

---

[17] Kenen's criterion may then appear the opposite of McKinnon's, as also argued by McKinnon, 1967. However, when intra-industry trade is prevalent a diversified economy may at the same time be a very open economy. Typical examples of open and diversified economies are Belgium and the Netherlands.

2.5   GENERAL ASSESSMENT

Starting from Mundell's original insights, the theory of optimum currency areas grew more and more complex.   It became recognised that monetary integration entailed both costs and benefits.

The main cost is the abandonment of the exchange rate as an instrument of adjustment.   The costs of giving up this instrument depend on (a) the size and nature of the shocks which can affect the balance of payments and (b) the ease with which the economy can adjust (price and wage flexibility, factor mobility, interregional transfers).

Benefits are mostly related to the introduction of a common currency and the stimulus this provides for further integration.   These benefits depend also on the design of the monetary union, e.g. independence and responsibility of the central bank, role of budgetary policy, instruments for social cohesion (for an overview of these issues, see Maes, 1991).

Moreover, both costs and benefits should be weighted against one another.   This highlights the political dimension of monetary integration, as weighting implies inevitably values judgments[18].

A question which remains rather mysterious is why the literature on monetary integration has been so dominated by Mundell's optimum currency area theory.   A question which is even more pertinent given the early high quality contributions of Meade and Scitovsky, but which have found much less resonance in the literature.   An unequivocal answer does not seem possible.   Nevertheless, several elements can be advanced:

- Mundell's contribution has to be situated in the fixed versus flexible exchange rate controversy, the dominating debate in the domain of international monetary economics in the 1960s.   The contributions of Meade and Scitovsky were more situated in the field of integration economics, a much less prominent and glamorous area;
- the word "optimum" has always had a special attraction for economists.   However, one could rather argue that the word "optimum" is a misnomer for a theory which emphasises a single criterium to determine an "optimum" currency area;
- the importance of Mundell and Chicago in the field of international monetary economics in the 1960s.   In effect, Kenen's paper was

---

[18]   As noted by Cooper, optimality can call for a more complex array of jurisdictions, cf. Cooper, 1976, 135.   For an overview of further developments, cf. Ishiyama, 1975, Robson, 1987, Ch. 9 and Tower and Willett, 1976.   For an application of the "cost-benefit" approach to the actual process of European monetary integration, see Commission of the European Communities, 1990.

presented at a conference in Chicago, organised by Mundell. And, as H. Johnson has remarked: "it is by now no secret that the problems (of the conference) were defined to follow very closely the work of Robert A. Mundell, our convenor" (Johnson, 1967).

2.6   CONCLUSION

The optimum currency area debate between Mundell, McKinnon and Kenen can be situated in the fixed versus flexible exchange rates controversy in the post-war period. It was Mundell who put the question on the agenda, even if the idea was not new.

Mundell defines an optimum currency area basically in terms of internal factor mobility. This could pose a problem for European monetary integration, as labour mobility is rather low in Europe. However, the 1992 programme, with the creation of a European financial area and several measures to stimulate the free movement of people, contributes to a greater mobility of factors of production, making Europe more suitable as an optimum currency area.

McKinnon challenged Mundell's (explicit) assumption that flexible exchange rates function effectively. Analysing a small open economy, he demonstrated that a devaluation is not very effective in correcting payments imbalances and, moreover, would damage price stability. This has been a major argument for small open economies like Belgium and the Netherlands to anchor their currencies to the German mark.

Kenen focused on the nature of external shocks. A high degree of product diversification diminishes the need for exchange rate flexibility, as product-specific shocks would average out. This would argue for monetary union in Europe, as countries in the European Community are typically characterised by a diversified industrial structure.

The optimum currency area debate centred then around the role of exchange rate policy in the framework of macroeconomic stabilisation policy. The focus was on the cost giving up the exchange rate as an instrument of adjustment.

Attempts were also made by Mundell and McKinnon to analyse the advantages of a single currency, but these were less successful. They were not always clear whether they were discussing a single currency area or a fixed exchange rate zone. Later research has shown the crucial differences between the two, especially the stimulus that a common currency can provide for the integration of goods and factor markets.

REFERENCES

Balogh, T. (1950), Problems of Western Unification, *Bulletin of the Oxford Institute of Statistics,* 12, 299-314.

Bertola, G. (1988), Factor Flexibility, Uncertaintly and Rate Exchange Regimes, in De Cecco M. and A. Giovannini. (eds.), *A European Central Bank?*, Cambridge: Cambridge University Press, pp. 95-119.

Buigues, P., F. Ilzkovitz and J.-F. Lebrun (1990), The Impact of the Internal Market by Industrial Sector, *European Economy*, Special Edition.

Commission of the European Communities (1990), One Market, One Money, *European Economy*, 44, Oct.

Cooper, R. (1976), Worldwide Regional Integration: Is There an Optimal Size of the Integrated Area?, Cooper R. (1986), *Economic Policy in an Interdependent World*, Cambridge: MIT Press, pp. 123-136.

Corden, W. (1972), Monetary Integration, *Essays in International Finance*, Princeton University, April.

De Grauwe, P. (1989), *International Money*, Oxford: Clarendon Press.

Eichengreen, B. (1990), One Money for Europe? Lessons from the U.S. Currency Union, *Economic policy*, 10, April, 118-187.

Flanders, J. (1967), Comment: The Currency Area Problem, Mundell R. and Swoboda A., (eds.), *Monetary Problems of the International Economy*, Chicago: University of Chicago Press, pp. 101-105.

Fleming, M. (1962), Domestic Financial Policies Under Fixed and Under Floating Exchange Rates, *IMF Staff Papers*, 9, Nov., 369-380.

Fleming, M. (1971), On Exchange Rate Unification, *Economic Journal*, Sept., 467-488.

Friedman, M. (1953), The Case for Flexible Exchange Rates, *Essays in Positive Economics*, Chicago: University of Chicago Press, pp. 157-203.

Gandolfo, G. (1986), *International Economics*, Berlin: Springer-Verlag.

Giavazzi, F. and A. Giovannini (1988), The Role of the Exchange-Rate Regime in a Disinflation, in Giavazzi F. and M. Miller, (eds.), *The European Monetary System*, Cambridge: Cambridge University Press, pp. 85-111.

Ingram, J. (1959), State and Regional Payments Mechanisms, *Quarterly Journal of Economics*, Nov., 619-632.

Ingram, J. (1960), Reply, *Quarterly Journal of Economics*, 74, Nov., 648-652.

Ingram, J. (1973), The Case for European Monetary Integration, *Princeton Essays in International Finance*, April.

Ishiyama, Y. (1975), The Theory of Optimum Currency Areas: A Survey, *IMF. Staff Papers*, July, 344-383.

Johnson, H. G. (1967), The "Problems" Approach to International Monetary Reform, in Mundell R. and A. Swoboda, (eds.), *Monetary Problems of the International Economy*, Chicago: University of Chicago Press, pp. 393-399.

Kenen, P. (1967), The Theory of Optimum Currency Areas: An Eclectic View, in Mundell R. and A. Swoboda, (eds.), *Monetary Problems of the International Economy*, Chicago: University of Chicago Press, pp. 41-60.

Kenen, P. (1988), *Managing Exchange Rates*, London: Chatham House Papers.

Krugman, P. (1989), *Exchange-Rate Instability*, Cambridge: MIT Press.

Krugman, P. (1991), *Geography and Trade*, Gaston Eyskens Lectures, Cambridge: MIT Press.

Kydland, F. and E. Prescott (1977), Rules Rather than Discretion: the Inconsistency of Optimal Plans, *Journal of Political Economy*, June, 473-491.

Maes, I. (1991), Monetaire Integratie, *Economisch en Sociaal Tijdschrift*, June, 189-216.

McKinnon, R. (1963), Optimum Currency Areas, *American Economic Review*, Sept., 717-725.

McKinnon, R. (1967), Discussion: The Currency Area Problem, Mundell R. and A. Swoboda, eds., *Monetary Problems of the International Economy*, Chicago: University of Chicago Press, p. 112.

Meade, J. (1957), The Balance-of Payments Problems of a European Free-Trade Area, *Economic Journal*, Sept., 379-396.

Mundell, R. (1957), International Trade and Factor Mobility, *American Economic Review*, 47, 3, June, 321-335.

Mundell, R. (1961), A Theory of Optimum Currency Areas, *American Economic Review*, Sept., 657-665.

Mundell, R. (1962), The Appropriate Use of Monetary and Fiscal Policy for Internal and External Stability, *IMF Staff Papers*, 9, March, 70-79.

Orcutt, G. (1955), Exchange Rate Adjustment and Relative Size of the Depreciating Bloc, *Review of Economics and Statistics*, Feb., 1-11.

Pfister, L. (1960), State and Regional Payments Mechanisms: Comment, *Quarterly Journal of Economics*, 74, Nov., 641-648.

Pöhl, K.-O. (1990), Plaidoyer pour une Politique Monétaire Indépendante, *Le Monde*, 18 Janvier.

Rivera-Batiz, F. and L. Rivera-Batiz (1985), *International Finance and Open Economy Macroeconomics*, London: Macmillan.

Robson, P. (1987), *The Economics of International Integration*, 3ed., London: Unwin & Hyman.

Scitovsky, T. (1957), The Theory of the Balance of Payments and the Problem of a Common European Currency, *Kyklos*, X, 1, 18-44.

Scitovsky, T. (1958), *Economic Theory and Western European Integration*, London: Allen & Unwin.

Scitovsky, T. (1967), The Theory of Balance-of-Payments Adjustment, *Journal of Political Economy*, Aug., 523-531.

Solomon, R. (1977), *The International Monetary System 1945-1976: An Insider's View*, New York: Harper & Row.

Tower, E. and T. Willett (1976), The Theory of Optimum Currency Areas and Exchange - Rate Flexibility, *Special Papers in International Economics*, Princeton.

Willett, T. and E. Tower (1970), The Concept of Optimum Currency Areas and the Choice Between Fixed and Flexible Exchange Rates, in Halm G., (ed.), *Approaches to Greater Flexibility of Exchange Rates*, Princeton: Princeton University Press, pp. 407-415.

Wood, G. (1986), European Monetary Integration?, *Journal of Monetary Economics*, 329-336.

3. Monetary Integration Debates in the 1970s*

3.1 INTRODUCTION

In the monetary field, the 1970s were an eventful period. Plans for European monetary union were launched at the Hague Summit of December 1969. However, exchange rate volatility increased, with the demise of the Bretton-Woods System and the turbulent history of the European currency snake as prime examples. The creation of the European Monetary System would, gradually, mark a return to more exchange rate stability in the European Community. In this context monetary integration debates flourished. They provide a rich topic for research.

In this paper the focus will be on the role of the state and the market in these monetary integration debates. When analysing the role of the state it is appropriate to distinguish between two types of functions of the state: the creation of an institutional framework in which economic agents can function and policies which the state execute (Maes, 1994). It is also important to keep in mind that monetary integration involves a very important transfer of sovereignty: the transfer of monetary policy, i.e. the setting of interest and

* A more extended draft of this essay is forthcoming, in French, as "Débats sur l'Intégration Monétaire Européenne dans les Années Soixante-dix: Le Rôle de l'Etat et du Marché", in Torre D., S. Ngo - Maï and E. Tosi, (eds.), *Intégration Européenne et Institutions Economiques,* Bruxelles: De Boeck.

I would like to thank J. Delors, S. Deroose, M. Emerson, J. Michielsen, S. Ngo-Maï, T. Peeters, D. Torre, E. Tosi and P. Werner for interesting comments and suggestions. The usual restrictions apply.

exchange rates, from national institutions to a supra-national European institution.

The events and debates of the 1970s illustrate the driving role which institutions can play in the process of European integration if they are in tune with political and economic circumstances. The Werner plan proposal of 1970 to create an Economic and Monetary Union proved to be out of tune, especially because the required degree of economic policy convergence was not feasible. However, the European Monetary System, contrary to many expectations, turned out to be a driving force in the process of European monetary integration. Its flexible character permitted it to weather many storms. However, it contributed also to a greater convergence, both of economic policy and performance, an essential condition for the formation of an economic and monetary union. This illustrates the role which institutions can play, if they are in tune with the functioning of markets and the economic policies pursued.

3.2   BACKGROUND: THE EUROPEAN SCENE

At the Hague Summit of December 1969 an ambitious programme to relaunch European integration was established, comprising both a widening of the Community, enlargement and a deepening, economic and monetary union (annex 3.1). This was made possible by the coming to power of new political leaders in France and Germany. In 1969 General de Gaulle resigned and Pompidou was elected as president in France. He, and his finance minister Giscard d'Estaing, followed a more pro-European policy. The other major event was the formation of a new government in Germany, a Social Democrat-Free Democrat coalition, with Willy Brandt as chancellor. The Brandt government supported European integration, one of the reasons was the need for a counterbalance to its Ostpolitik.

The further widening of the Community in the 1970s and 1980s would be quite successful, but would also absorb a lot of energy and dominate the European scene. After difficult negotiations, the United Kingdom, Ireland and Denmark joined the European Economic Community in January 1973. However, after the electoral defeat of the conservative government, the new Labour government asked for a renegotiation of the terms of accession. After a positive referendum on the new terms in June 1975, the United Kingdom stayed in the Community. In June 1979, however, the conservative government of Mrs Thatcher asked for a reduction of the British budget contribution. Discussions continued for several years, and would only be resolved at the June 1984 Fontainebleau Summit. Meanwhile, Greece had become a member of the Community and accession negotiations had started with Portugal and Spain.

Of fundamental importance in the monetary union project was the Werner Report of October 1970. This contained both a blueprint for economic and monetary union and a plan for its realisation by stages. The European Community started on this path. In March 1972, the European snake was established, an exchange rate arrangement to limit fluctuations between the currencies of the Community.

The monetary union project quickly ran into difficulties. The international environment became very hostile with the collapse of the Bretton-Woods system and the first oil price shock of October 1973. It would lead to a serious worsening of the Europe's economic performance in the 1970s: inflation rose and economic growth slowed down: Europe's stagflation crisis had started[1].

Figure 3.1 - Inflation in the main European countries
(annual percentage changes)

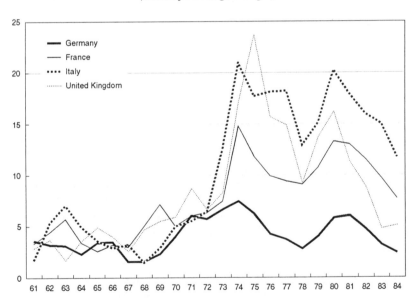

Source: European Commission.

---

[1] For an overview of the European Commission's analysis of the economic situation in the 1970s, see Maes, 1998.

Moreover, Europe's governments reacted very differently to the crisis. For German policy-makers, the oil shock was mainly an inflationary shock, to be contained with restrictive policies. The French considered it, in first instance, as a deflationary shock and followed more expansionary policies. So, differences in inflation rates soared, making fixed exchange rates unsustainable. The European snake had then a turbulent existence: there were several realignments of parities and many currencies dropped out (Annex 3.2). From March 1976 onwards, after the second French departure, it was generally considered as a de facto German mark zone.

The idea of a monetary union was relaunched by Roy Jenkins, the president of the European Commission, especially in his famous Florence speech (Jenkins, 1977). A less ambitious monetary integration project was proposed by Helmut Schmidt, the German chancellor, and Valéry Giscard d'Estaing, the French president, in a joint initiative. This was submitted at the European Council of Copenhagen in April 1978 and would lead to the creation of the European Monetary System in March 1979. Their motives were, to a large part, political, in which uneasiness with the Carter administration in the United States played a not unimportant role (Ludlow, 1982 and Dell, 1994).

3.3   THE WERNER REPORT

After the Hague Summit, a committee, under the chairmanship of the Luxembourg prime minister Pierre Werner, was set up to elaborate a plan for the creation of an economic and monetary union. The Group submitted its final report in October 1970 (Council-Commission of the European Communities, 1970, hereafter referred to as Werner Report). This report formed the basis for further discussions and decisions. It contained a programme for the establishment, by stages, of an economic and monetary union by 1980.

In the Werner Report attention was first focused on the final objective of economic and monetary union. Thereafter, the realisation by stages was elaborated.

In the background of the Report loomed a basic ambiguity concerning the crumbling Bretton-Woods system. On the one hand, the unease with the Bretton-Woods system was one of the driving forces for European monetary integration. On the other hand, the European attempt to narrow exchange rate fluctuations took the framework of the fixed exchange rate system of Bretton-Woods for granted.

3.3.1 The Final Objective

The Report first presented a very general picture of economic and monetary union: "Economic and monetary union will make it possible to realise an area within which goods and services, people and capital will circulate freely and without competitive distortions, without thereby giving rise to structural or regional disequilibrium" (Werner Report, 9).

To assure the cohesion of economic and monetary union two elements were necessary: transfers of responsibility from the national to the Community level and a harmonisation of the instruments of economic policy in various sectors.

On the institutional plane, this implied, following the Report, the existence of two Community institutions, a centre of decision for economic policy and a Community system for the central banks. However, the Report did not elaborate very much on these structures.

The Werner Report underlined the fundamental political significance of transfers of responsibility to the Community level. It is also considered that economic and monetary union was realisable in the next ten years, "provided the political will of the Member States to realise this objective, solemnly declared at the Conference at The Hague, is present" (Werner Report, 14).

3.3.2 The Stages towards Economic and Monetary Union

The Werner Report proposed a plan in three stages to attain economic and monetary union. This gradualist approach towards economic and monetary union was laid down by the heads of state and government at the Hague Summit and was typical for the process of European integration. As Werner notes: "Cette approche graduelle restait dans la ligne fonctionnelle qui a caractérisé la construction européenne dès ses débuts ... Depuis ces débuts la Communauté connaît l'antinomie de ces polarités: le gradualisme de sa méthode d'une part, l'indivisibilité de l'économie de l'autre" (Werner, 1977, 8).

The Report did not lay down a precise timetable for the whole of the plan. Rather it wanted to maintain a measure of flexibility, while concentrating on the first phase.

It proposed that the first stage would commence on 1 January 1971 and cover a period of three years. The main elements were: (a) a reinforcement of procedures for consultation and policy coordination; (b) a further liberalisation of intra-Community capital movements and steps towards an integrated European capital market; (c) a narrowing of exchange rate fluctuations between Community currencies.

Of the second stage the Report noted that it "will be characterised by the promotion on a number of fronts and on ever more restrictive lines of the action undertaken during the first stage" (Werner Report, 28).

The Report also proposed to establish a European Fund for Monetary Cooperation, as a forerunner of the Community System of Central Banks. However, it was left open whether this would be in the first or second stage.

Of fundamental importance in the Report was the concept of "parallel progress". This notion formed a compromise between the "monetarists" (emphasising greater exchange rate stability and European exchange rate support mechanisms, with France as an important advocate) and the "economists" (emphasising the coordination of economic policies and economic convergence, led by Germany). This notion enabled the Werner Group to present a unanimous Report (Tsoukalis, 1977, 101).

3.3.3   An Assessment of the Report

The first attempt at monetary union was not very successful. The Marjolin Report aptly summarised the overall development between 1969 and 1975: "if there has been any movement it has been backward" (CEC, 1975, 1). Main reasons were the turbulent international environment, the priority given to national policy objectives and the French (Gaullist) resistance against supra-national institutions[2]. However, there were also weaknesses in the Report itself, especially that it "paid relatively little attention to institutional matters" (Baer and Padoa-Schioppa, 1988, 53). In their further analysis, Baer and Padoa-Schioppa (1988, 57) discuss four important intrinsic weaknesses of the Werner Report: (a) insufficient constraints on national policies. The Werner Report was too much based on voluntary agreements and guidelines; (b) institutional ambiguities. It was not always clear who was responsible for which decision; (c) an inappropriate policy conception. The Report was based on a very high degree of confidence in the ability of policy instruments to affect policy goals in a known and predictable way. This was typical for the, then dominating, hydraulic Keynesian paradigm (Coddington, 1983); (d) a lack of internal momentum. The Werner Report did not envisage an interactive process in which the implementation of certain steps would trigger

---

[2]   Pompidou got angry at reading the Report, while Maure Schumann remarked: "Il ne faut pas compromettre l'union économique et monétaire des Six par un fatras institutionnel prématuré" (Werner, 1991, 132).

market reactions that in turn would necessitate further steps towards economic and monetary union.

3.4 THE ACADEMIC DEBATE

The Werner Report was followed by intense discussions, both among policy-makers as in academic circles. In this section the focus will be on the more academic debate. Discussions were very wide ranging, covering many areas. Here the two most salient questions will be considered: the feasibility of the economic and monetary union and the introduction of a common European currency.

3.4.1 Feasibility of Economic and Monetary Union

Many distinguished economists (e.g. Corden, 1972 and Johnson, 1972) expressed their scepticism with respect to the feasibility of the Werner Report.

Macroeconomic discussions in the early 1970s took typically place in a "Phillips-curve World" (De Grauwe, 1975), which assumed a stable relationship between inflation and unemployment[3]. Differences in inflation between countries can then be traced to three main factors: (a) the position of the Phillips curves (trade-union aggressiveness, structural factors affecting unemployment, etc.); (b) the rates of productivity growth; (c) the preferences of the governments between unemployment and inflation.

In this type of world, inflation rates between two countries will only be equal by accident. Every country has then a "national propension to inflation" (Magnifico, 1971, 13). Of crucial importance hereby is the economic policy choice of the government.

Differences in inflation rates would then lead to payments imbalances, which were incompatible with fixed exchange rates: "The principal danger involved in participating in a fixed rate area arises from the certainty, in the absence of perfect competition in product and factor markets, that developments would occur from time to time that pushed the relative cost levels of the participating countries out of line and even some that tended to push them progressively further and further out of line" (Fleming, 1971, 467).

Monetary union would force a country to accept a trade-off between unemployment and inflation which it considered as suboptimal. The country

---

[3] This would later be challenged, see, e.g., De Grauwe et al., 1975, 12.

would be forced to sacrifice its internal balance in order to preserve balance-of-payments equilibrium.

Proponents of monetary union mainly focused their attention on two points: (a) the importance of factor mobility, especially capital mobility, as an adjustment mechanism (Ingram, 1973). However, also this approach, with the "monetary-fiscal policy mix", is not without weaknesses (Corden, 1972, 31); (b) the importance of a differentiated regional policy (Magnifico, 1971, 13 and Study Group, 1973, 13).

3.4.2   A Common European Currency

One of the bolder ideas being launched during the debates in the 1970s was the creation of a (parallel) common European currency (Magnifico, 1971, Mundell, 1973 and Study Group, 1973).

Three main arguments were advanced in favour of the creation of a common European currency (Study Group, 1973, 19): (a) the exchange rate arrangement would be easier to operate if a common European currency was available and could be used as a common intervention medium; (b) it would serve to counterbalance the dollar; (c) political and prestige considerations.

However, even proponents were conscious of certain dangers which the introduction of a (parallel) common European currency would cause (Meade, 1973, 92): (a) it could render speculation between European currencies easier; (b) private use of a European currency might lead to uncontrolled monetary expansion or contraction; (c) a too rapid and generalised use, leading to a de facto monetary integration, could create regional problems.

The boldest proposal was certainly the so-called "All Saint's Day Manifesto" (Basevi et al., 1975) signed by nine economists from eight European countries, favouring a market-led approach to monetary union. The basic idea was, with one reform, to attain two objectives: a single European currency and the eradication of inflation. The Manifesto recommended that the central banks of the European Community would issue a European parallel currency with a constant purchasing power, called the "Europa". Initially, the central banks would issue Europa's only against their national currencies, on demand of the economic agents. This new currency would compete with national currencies in all monetary functions.

Independent experts, many of them involved in the All Saint's Day Manifesto, elaborated a weaker version of the parallel currency approach in the so-called "Optica Reports" (Basevi et al., 1976 and 1977), for the European Commission. However, these ideas were not really influential among policy-makers. Rather, as remarked by a well placed observer, ministry of finance officials and central bankers turned "wild" at these proposals.

3.5 DEBATES AMONG POLICY-MAKERS

The crisis in the world economy and the monetary turbulences were major causes of concern to policy-makers in Europe. Several proposals were formulated to contribute to greater exchange rate stability in Europe. To a large extent, they were a continuation of the earlier debates between "monetarists" and "economists". Here two proposals will be considered: the Fourcade plan (aiming at a strengthening of the institutional framework of the exchange rate mechanism) and the Duisenberg plan (aiming at more policy coordination).

3.5.1 The Fourcade Plan

On 16 September 1974 Jean-Pierre Fourcade, the French finance minister, presented a communication on new initiatives in the monetary field. One of the main points was a change in the institutional framework of the Community exchange rate mechanism. As such the Fourcade plan can be clearly situated in the "monetarist" tradition.

The snake would continue to exist, but would be complemented by a "welcoming mat" for the other Community currencies (Fourcade, 1974, 22). This could be done by allowing European currency rates to fluctuate according to reference rates, which could be adjusted and temporarily suspended. The reference rates and fluctuation margins would be defined in relation to a European monetary unit of account, a new unit of account that would be derived from a basket of various European currencies. So, as some observers noted, the Fourcade plan would create "a kind of boa around the snake" (van Ypersele and Koeune, 1985, 44). Moreover, it was intended that the use of the European unit of account would contribute to a more symmetrical system. In the snake, the intervention obligations were formally symmetrical. However, as the loss of reserves constitutes a more effective constraint on a weak currency country, the burden of adjustment falls, de facto, on the weak currency country.

The Fourcade plan also provided for a consolidation and extension of intra-Community credit mechanisms. In the longer term, the creation of a European Monetary Cooperation Fund, with its own means of intervention, was proposed.

3.5.2   The Duisenberg Plan

In July 1976 the Dutch finance minister, Wim Duisenberg, presented certain proposals to improve the coordination of economic policy and the management of exchange rates. The big novelty was the proposal of target zones for the non-snake currencies. They could function as guideposts for the management of exchange rates, but that was not their main purpose. As argued by Oort, the Dutch Treasurer-General and main author of the plan, the target zones "are primarily intended to serve as a trigger for consultation and, it is hoped, for coordination of economic policy in general" (Oort, 1979, 208). The plan can then be situated in the "economist" tradition of improving economic policy convergence.

   The target zones would be defined in terms of effective exchange rates, i.e. trade weighted averages of exchange rates. This would have a double advantage: they would reflect international competitive positions and would be less likely to create unrest in the exchange markets. The snake would be maintained and would participate as an entity in the system of target zones.

   The target zones were primarily intended as a framework for meaningful discussion: they could serve as a concrete trigger for and a focus of consultation. Gradually, countries should be willing to accept stronger policy commitments.   However, the policy obligations were very clearly asymmetrical: "In no case should a country be asked, induced, or forced to adopt policies that add to domestic inflation" (Oort, 1979, 210).

3.6   THE EUROPEAN MONETARY SYSTEM

The technical monetary debates in the 1970s would provide an important input in the debates among policy-makers when they prepared for the creation of the European Monetary System. This is not the place to go into the technical functioning of the EMS. Here, the main debates, surrounding the creation of the EMS, will be presented[4].

3.6.1   The Feasibility of the EMS

At its creation, there was a lot of scepticism whether the EMS would survive for a long period, given the divergencies of the economic situation (Trezise,

---

[4]   For an overview of the functioning of the EMS, cf. Giavazzi and Giovannini, 1989, Giavazzi et al., 1989 and Ungerer, 1997.

1979). Proponents of the EMS countered with two main arguments (van Ypersele, 1979).

Firstly, the EMS would have to be accompanied by a greater convergence of the European economies and a strengthening of economic policy coordination. It was intended that the divergence indicator, the main novelty in the exchange rate system, would play an important role, as a trigger for policy coordination[5]. Moreover, the divergence indicator should also contribute to a more equilibrated adjustment process, making the EMS a more symmetrical system, in contrast to the snake. In practice however, the divergence indicator has played no significant role and the German mark quickly functioned as the anchor of the System.

Secondly, the EMS should be a flexible system, with realignments of exchange rates. It would be necessary to "avoid the rigidity of the Bretton-Woods system and to de-dramatise exchange rate adjustments" (van Ypersele, 1979, 9). During its first years the EMS has certainly operated in a flexible manner, with several realignments. However, parity adjustments were not de-dramatised, but were often traumatic experiences for policy-makers. These devaluation drama's, together with the realisation of the limited margin of manoeuvre for national economic policies, would give the exchange rate mechanism of the EMS a disciplinary function (Giavazzi and Pagano, 1988). It so contributed to coordination and convergence of economic policy, especially after 1983.

3.6.2 An Inflationary Bias

At the time of the creation of the EMS, there was a fear that divergencies in inflation rates would continue. This would then lead to speculation, forcing the Bundesbank to intervene, increasing the money supply and inflation in Germany (van Ypersele, 1979, 13). As time has progressed, this criticism has certainly receded.

However, the inflationary bias discussion is important to understand the interactions between the institutional set-up of an exchange rate system and the policies, which will be pursued. Three main elements contributed to the absence of an inflationary bias:

---

5   The indicator of divergence is constructed as an index. The maximum divergence is reached when an EMS currency is simultaneously at its upper (or lower) bilateral margin against all other participating currencies: 100% of the potential margin around its ecu central rate. When a currency reaches a "divergence indicator" of 75%, the country is presumed to take adequate measures.

- in the set up of the EMS, the obligation to intervene when the fluctuation margins were reached, was a much more effective constraint on economic policy than the much vaguer obligation to consult or take measures when the divergence indicator was surpassed;
- it is easier for a strong currency country to sterilise interventions than for a weak currency country. So, the weak currency country has to take most of the burden of adjustment in terms of policy adjustment;
- the Bundesbank had obtained that, in the case of interventions which endangered price stability, it could temporarily suspend interventions. It invoked this clause during the 1992-1993 ERM crisis.

3.6.3   A Deflationary Bias

A lot of criticism has focused on the, supposed, deflationary bias of the EMS. It was argued that countries with higher inflation rates would be forced to adopt more restrictive policies, which would be detrimental to growth. Also, it was feared that a strong German mark would pull up the other Community currencies against third countries.

Proponents of the EMS responded that possible deflationary effects of more restrictive policies would be temporary. Moreover, they argued that greater monetary stability would reduce uncertainty and so encourage business confidence and investment.

The deflationary bias debate is certainly not easy to evaluate. In a very thorough and balanced assessment, Gros and Thygesen (1992, 156) argue that: "the view of an inherent deflationary bias in the EMS seems questionable". Moreover, they conclude that the EMS has been an important shock absorber mechanism and has provided a stable framework for a coordinated response to outside shocks.

3.7   CONCLUSION

A monetary union involves a very important transfer of sovereignty: the transfer of monetary policy, i.e. the setting of interest and exchange rates, from a national institution to a supra-national European institution.

During the 1970s, proposals were advanced, especially the All Saint's Day Manifesto, to get to monetary union through a market led approach. These proposals were never accepted by policy-makers, who have a, not unjustified, aversion to leaving monetary matters to the market. However, these parallel currency proposals brought the idea of a European currency unit to the foreground. On the whole, market forces have been important in the process of monetary integration, mainly as a constraint on the state and policy-makers.

When considering the role of the state, it is important to distinguish between two types of functions of the state: the institutional one, the creation of a framework in which economic agents can function, and policies, which the state executes. This brings one right in the middle of the monetary integration debate among European policy-makers in the 1970s: the discussions between the "monetarists" and the "economists". The "monetarists" argued that an exchange rate system will by itself stimulate a deeper coordination of national policies. The "economists" argued that a harmonisation of national economic policies is a precondition for any institutional form of monetary integration.

Events in the 1970s firstly seemed to favour the economist thesis, when the snake was gradually dismantled, under the influence of divergent economic policies and foreign exchange market turmoil. However, new proposals were launched, leading to the creation of the European Monetary System. In the design of the EMS, lessons were learned from earlier exchange rate arrangements and monetary integration debates. The EMS was a flexible system, whereby exchange rates could be adapted. Moreover, it evolved through time. Gradually, with policy-makers realising the limitations of activist economic policies, it became more instrumental in policy coordination.

The events and debates of the 1970s highlight also the driving role which institutions can play if they are in tune with political and economic circumstances. The Werner plan proposal for a European Monetary Union proved to be out of tune. The supranational institutions which it proposed were politically unacceptable, especially for the Gaullists in France. Also, from a more economic point of view, it supposed a too important degree of convergence to be feasible.

The European Monetary System, contrary to many expectations, turned out to be a driving force in the process of European monetary integration. Its flexible character permitted it to weather many storms. However, it contributed also to a greater convergence, both of economic policy and performance, an essential condition for the formation of an economic and monetary union. So the EMS, through contributing to exchange rate stability and convergence, was an essential building block for Europe's economic and monetary union.

REFERENCES

Baer, G. and T. Padoa-Schioppa (1988), The Werner Report Revisited, in Committee for the Study of Economic and Monetary Union, *Report on Economic and Monetary Union*, Luxembourg, April 1989.

Basevi, G. et al. (1975), A Manifesto for European Monetary Union and Monetary Reform, *The Economist*, Nov. 1.

Basevi, G. et al. (1976), *Towards Economic Equilibrium and Monetary Unification in Europe* (Optica Report 1975), CEC, Brussels.

Basevi, G. et al. (1977), *Inflation and Exchange Rates: Evidence and Policy Guidelines for the European Communities* (Optica Report 1976), CEC, Brussels.

Coddington, A. (1983), *Keynesian Economics. The Search for First Principles*, London: Allen & Unwin.

Commission of the European Communities (1975), *Report of the Study Group "Economic and Monetary Union, 1980"* (Marjolin Report), Brussels, March.

Council-Commission of the European Communities (1970), *Report to the Council and the Commission on the Realisation by Stages of Economic and Monetary Union in the Community*, Werner Report, Luxembourg, October.

Corden, W. (1972), Monetary Integration, *Essays in International Finance*, Princeton University, no. 93, April.

De Grauwe, P. (1975), Conditions for Monetary Integration - A Geometric Interpretation, *Weltwirtschaftliches Archiv*, 634-645.

De Grauwe, P., D. Heremans and E. Van Rompuy (1975), Towards European Monetary Union, *Memo from Belgium*, no. 170.

Dell, E. (1994), Britain and the Origin of the European Monetary System, *Contemporary European History*, Vol. 3, no. 1, March, 1-60.

Fleming, M. (1971), On Exchange Rate Unification, *Economic Journal*, Sept., 467-488.

Fourcade, J.-P. (1974), A Communication by the President of the Council, *Bulletin*, EC, 9, 21-23.

Giavazzi, F. and A. Giovannini (1989), *Limiting Exchange Rate Flexibility: The European Monetary System*, Cambridge: MIT Press.

Giavazzi, F., S. Micossi and M. Miller, (eds.), (1989), *The European Monetary System*, Cambridge: Cambridge University Press.

Giavazzi, F. and M. Pagano, (1988), The Advantage of Tying One's Hands: EMS Discipline and Central Bank Credibility, *European Economic Review*, 1055-1082.

Gros, D. and N. Thygesen (1992), *European Monetary Integration*, London: Longman.

Ingram, J. (1973), The Case for European Monetary Integration, *Princeton Essays in International Finance*, no. 98, April.

Jenkins, R. (1977), Europe's Present Challenge and Future Opportunity, *Bulletin*, EC 10-1977, 6-14.

Johnson, H. (1972), Problems of European Monetary Union, in Johnson H., *Further Essays in Monetary Economics*, London: Allen & Unwin, pp. 312-324.

Ludlow, P. (1982), *The Making of the European Monetary System*, London: Butterworth.

Magnifico, G. (1971), European Monetary Unification for Balanced Growth: A New Approach, in Magnifico G., *European Monetary Unification*, (1972), London: Macmillan, pp. 1-42.

Maes, I. (1994), State and Market in Post-war Integration Theory, in Roggi P. et al., (eds.), National and European Markets in Economic Thought, *Proceedings of the Eleventh International Economic History Congress*, B16, Milano, pp. 83-94.

Maes, I. (1998), Macroeconomic Thought at the European Commission in the 1970s: The First Decade of the Annual Economic Reports, *Banca Nazionale del Lavoro Quarterly Review*, Dec., 387-412.

Meade, J. (1973), European Monetary Union, in Study Group on EMU, *European Economic Integration and Monetary Unification*, Brussels, pp. 89-98.

Mundell, R. (1973), Why Europa?, in Study Group on EMU, *European Economic Integration and Monetary Unification*, Brussels, pp. 110-122.

Oort, C.J. (1979), Managed Floating in the European Community, in S.I. Katz, (ed.), *US-European Monetary Relations*, Washington D.C.: American Enterprise Institute, pp. 192-219.

Study Group on Economic and Monetary Union (1973), *European Economic Integration and Monetary Unification*, Commission of the European Communities, Brussels.

Trezise, P. (1979), Political Commitment: The Central Question, in P. Trezise, (ed.), *The European Monetary System. Its Promise and Prospect*, Washington D.C.: The Brookings Institution, pp. 1-4.

Tsoukalis, L. (1977), *The Politics and Economics of European Monetary Integration*, London: Allen and Unwin.

Ungerer, H. (1997), *A Concise History of European Monetary Integration*, Westport: Quorum Books.

van Ypersele, J. (1979), Operating Principles and Procedures of the European Monetary System, in P. Trezise, (ed.), *The European Monetary System: Its Promise and Prospect*, Washington D.C.: The Brookings Institution, pp. 5-23.

van Ypersele, J. and J.-C. Koeune (1985), *The European Monetary System. Origins, Operation and Outlook*, European Perspectives, Brussels: CEC.

Werner, P. (1977), *L' Europe Monétaire Reconsidérée*, Lausanne: Centre de Recherches Européennes.

Werner, P. (1991), *Itinéraires Luxembourgeois et Européens*, Luxembourg: Editions Saint-Paul.

Annex 3.1 - The European scene

1969	December	Hague Summit (agreement, in principle, on enlargement and monetary union)
1970	October	Werner Report
1972	March	Establishment of the Snake
1973	January	Accession of Denmark, Ireland and the United Kingdom
1974	April	United Kingdom demands renegotiations of terms of accession
1975	June	British referendum supports renegotiated terms
1976	July	Start accession negotiations with Greece
1978	October	Start accession negotiations with Portugal
1979	February	Start accession negotiations with Spain
	March	Establishment of the EMS
	June	First direct elections to the European Parliament United Kingdom argues for a reduction of its budget contribution
1981	January	Accession of Greece
1984	June	Fontainebleau Summit (agreement on the budget)

Annex 3.2 - The monetary scene in the 1970s

1969	December	Hague Summit: EMU becomes a Community objective
1970	October	Werner Report
1971	August	Nixon announces the suspension of the dollar into gold
	December	Smithsonian agreement (new central rates and wider fluctuation margins)
1972	April	EEC narrows margins of fluctuation to 2.25% (EEC "Snake" in Smithsonian "tunnel")
	May	Accession of the United Kingdom, Ireland and Denmark
	June	United Kingdom, Ireland and Denmark leave EEC snake
	October	Danish krone rejoins the snake
1973	February	Italian lira drops out of snake
	March	End of Bretton-Woods system: floating of snake against US-dollar. German mark revalued
	June	Revaluation of German mark
	September	Revaluation of Dutch guilder
	October	First oil shock
1974	January	French franc drops out of EEC snake
1975	July	French franc rejoins EEC snake
1976	March	France drops out of EEC snake
1979	March	Creation of the European Monetary System
	September	Revaluation of German mark and devaluation of Danish krone
	October	Second oil price shock. Tightening of monetary policy in US
	November	Devaluation of Danish krone
1981	March	Devaluation of Italian lira
	November	General realignment
1982	February	Devaluation of Belgian franc and Danish krone
	June	General realignment
1983	March	General realignment

PART 2:

Economic Thought at the European Community
Institutions

4. The Development of Economic Thought at the European Community Institutions*

4.1 INTRODUCTION

This paper is an attempt at a "rational reconstruction" of the development of the economic thought at the European Community institutions[1]. A basic problem that one encounters is that the European Community is a very special construction, an entity "*sui generis*" as lawyers like to say. It is neither a federation, nor an intergovernmental organisation, but rather something between the two.

It is an intergovernmental organisation to the degree that changes in the Treaties governing the Community have to be approved by all countries, after an intergovernmental conference. However, within the areas designated in

---

* Reprinted from The Post-1945 Internationalisation of Economics, Coats, A.W., (ed.), (1996) *History of Political Economy*, Annual Supplement, 245-276, with kind permission from Duke University Press.

I would like to thank F. Abraham, A.W. Coats, S. Deroose, M.M.G. Fase, F. Ilzkovitz, A. Italianer, M. Mors, J. Mortensen, A. Saether, P. Van der Haegen and J. Van Ginderachter for comments on previous drafts. The usual disclaimers apply.

[1] In this paper the term "European Community" is used. The Maastricht Treaty institutes the "European Union", which not only comprises the "Community" but also the intergovernmental cooperation on foreign and defence policy and justice and interior policy. Here the term "European Community" is preferred as the focus of this paper is on economic matters.

the Treaties, it can exercise sovereign powers and, through time, the influence of the Commission (its executive) has been growing.

Delineating the development of economic thought at the Community institutions is then not easy. It should certainly comprise the development of ideas at the Commission. However, this will not suffice. National initiatives and study groups with representatives of the different countries have played an important role in the development of the Community and the thinking at its institutions. In this paper, a more encompassing approach, taking into account the work of important study groups, is taken.

The paper starts with an overview of the institutions of the Community, with a special focus on the role of economists in the Commission, in sections 1 and 2. Economic thought at the Community institutions is, to an important extent, centred around the notion of integration, which is the topic of the third section. Then the development of economic thought at the Community institutions, in relation to the actual process of integration, is presented. This is followed by an overview of elements of continuity and change and an assessment of the international influences.

4.2   THE INSTITUTIONS OF THE COMMUNITY

The major institutions of the European Community are the Parliament, the Council, the Commission and the Court of Justice[2] (Table 4.1).

Table 4.1 - *Institutions of the European Community and staff numbers*
Budget 1995

Parliament	3 827
Council	2 379
Economic and Social Committee and Committee of the Regions	661
Commission	19 667
Court of Justice	837
Court of Auditors	458

Source: Official Journal of the European Communities 369, 37, 31 December 1994, 153.

---

[2]   Smaller institutions are the Economic and Social Committee and the Court of Auditors. With the Maastricht Treaty, a Committee of Regions was created. For an overview, see Noël, 1993.

The European Parliament consists of the representatives of the people of the member states. Since 1979, it has been elected by direct universal suffrage. The Parliament has advisory and supervisory powers; however, its supervisory powers are limited to the Commission, and not to the Council. The Parliament has to approve the budget of the Community. It has certain legislative powers, which were extended with the Maastricht Treaty. The Council is made up of representatives of the governments of the member states. It is the main decision-making institution of the Community. Since 1974 there have also been regular meetings of the Heads of State or Government (the "European Council") where the general guidelines for the development of the Community are set out. The Commission consists of 20 members, appointed by agreement between the member governments. They have to act in complete independence and in the general interest of the Community. It has three main functions: (a) guardian of the Treaties, to ensure that the provisions of the Treaties and the decisions of the institutions are properly implemented; (b) executive arm of the Community; (c) initiator of Community policy. The Commission has the sole right to present proposals and drafts for Community legislation. The Court of Justice ensures that the implementation of the Treaties is in accordance with the rule of law.

As the Commission is the largest Community institution and as it has a crucial role in the initiation and execution of Community policy, the functioning of the Commission and the role of economists therein will be analysed in greater detail in the next section.

4.3 THE FUNCTIONING OF THE COMMISSION AND THE ROLE OF ECONOMISTS

The term "Commission" is used both for the College of the Commission, the body of 20 Commissioners, as for the services of the Commission, the administration.

While the College of the Commission is a collegiate body, each Member has a special responsibility for some part of the institution's work and for the services dealing with these areas. Each Commissioner has a personal staff, called a cabinet, which works directly with him[3].

The services of the Commission consist of the Secretariat-General, 22 Directorate-Generals and some specific services (see Annex 4.1 for an overview). Important posts in the administration (director-general, deputy director-general and director) are allocated according to a quota system by

---

3   For an insight in the functioning of the Delors cabinet, see Ross, 1994.

nationality. There is a remarkable continuity in the occupation of senior positions by nationality. Thus the director-general of DG VI (Agriculture) has typically been a Frenchman, the director-general of DG IV (Competition) a German, etc. The higher the position, the greater the possibility that a vacancy will be filled by somebody from outside the Commission, with the appropriate nationality. The lower the position, the less important these influences. However, even at junior positions, there is a very important concern for "equilibria", so that the different countries of the Community should be represented.

The Commission administration is certainly more heterogeneous than national administrations, as diversity is one of the main characteristics of the European Community. This diversity, in terms of nationality, language, political opinion, trade union membership, etc., is naturally reflected in the Commission and contributes to a more complex and heterogeneous informal structure and "enterprise culture". Generally, personnel are often together with people of the same nationality or language. There are also different "networks". One of the most famous was certainly the Delors network. As Grant (1993, 104) remarked: "Any official who is French, socialist and competent, with a useful area of expertise, is almost certain to be invited into the Delors network. Anyone with a couple of those qualities would be seriously considered, as long as one of them is competence". Another network, of a very different nature, is the so-called, "Brugge network", of the graduates of the College of Europe, a famous graduate school in European studies in the Belgian town of Bruges, who keep excellent contacts among each other.

An economist in the Commission can fulfil a job as a general administrator or as a "professional economist". The need for specialist economic expertise by the Commission is clearly recognised, as there are special recruitment competitions for economists. However, economists in the Commission seem, qua methodology and worldview, to be a more heterogeneous group than economists at international institutions like the IMF or the World Bank, where many graduated from American universities. This compares with a still more important diversity among European universities qua economic methodology and Weltanschauung. So, as a general rule, British economists are more free market oriented and Frenchmen more activist. Germans are typically more concerned with questions of economic order and policies necessary for the functioning of a free market economy (e.g. competition policy).

A prime place for professional economists is DG II - Economic and Financial Affairs (see Annex 4.2), which can be considered as the economic research department of the Commission. In DG II, attention is given to both macroeconomic issues (mainly directorates, A, National economies, C, Surveillance of the Community economy, D, Monetary matters and F, International economic and financial matters), as well as to sectoral aspects of Community policy (mainly directorates B, Economic service and E, Financial instruments and capital movements). An important outlet for the results of their analysis is "European Economy", a publication of the services of the Commission. Inside the Commission administration, the economists of DG II have a reputation of being a relatively homogeneous group, free market oriented and fairly conservative.

To get a better idea of economists at DG II and their educational background, I organised a short survey. Of the 130 A staff (university graduates) 74 replied[4]. As far as I can judge the sample seems representative. A few important features of the survey are (Table 2):

- 47 out of 74 economists studied abroad (64%). It is an indication of the existence of a kind of mutual attraction between people who studied abroad and international institutions;
- 28 economists had a Ph.D. (38%), while a few others were still working on it. 21 of them had studied abroad, not necessarily for their Ph.D.;
- the Belgians are very well represented, 11 out of 74; elements of explanation are the relatively high Commission salaries and the location of DG II in Brussels;
- economists from the Southern countries (Italy, Spain and Greece) are fairly well represented and have mostly studied abroad. This could be an indication of a lack of well-qualified positions for persons with an advanced education in these countries.

To obtain a better insight in the internationalisation and Americanisation process a classification according to age group, distinguishing between European and American universities, is presented (Table 3). A few remarks:

- one clearly notes the internationalisation process: younger economists were more likely to have studied abroad than older economists;
- DG II economists had a clear preference for studying in a "foreign" European country than in America. However, the American share is slightly higher among younger economists;

---

4   Not all the A staff at DG II are economists. However, the number of non-economists is rather limited.

- among the European countries, Belgium was the most popular (13), due to the attractiveness of the College of Europe in Brugge (8 graduates). Then followed the United Kingdom (10), France (9) and Italy and Germany (4 each);
- among the American universities, the University of Chicago was the most popular, with 3 graduates in the sample.

Table 4.2 - *Economists at DG II: educational background according to nationality* *

Country	Economists	Studied abroad*	Ph. D.
Belgium	11	4	1
Denmark	4	1	0
France	6	4	4
Germany	17	13	10
Greece	5	5	1
Ireland	3	1	1
Italy	8	7	2
Netherlands	5	3	3
Portugal	2	1	0
Spain	8	7	4
United Kingdom	5	1	2
Total	*74*	*47*	*28*

Source : Based on a survey of the A staff of DG II; 74 out of 130 replied.
* *Studied abroad: a European country different from the country of origin, or the USA or Canada; not always leading to a degree.*

Other services which, to different degrees, use specialist economic expertise are the Statistical Office, DG I (External Relations), DG III (Industry), DG IV (Competition), DG V (Employment, Industrial Relationships and Social Affairs), DG VI (Agriculture), DG VII (Transport), DG VIII (Development), DG XIII (Telecommunications, Information Industries and Innovation), DG XV (Internal Market and Financial Institutions), DG XVI (Regional Policies), DG XVII (Energy) and DG XXIII (Enterprises' Policy, Distributive Trades, Tourism and Social Economy[5]).

---

[5] I have the impression that, in comparison to other international organisations (Coats, 1986), relatively more economists in the European Community work as general administrators than as economic experts.

Table 4.3 - Economists at DG II: educational background according to age group*

	Total	Studied abroad	Studied in America*	Studied in a "foreign" European country	Ph. D.
50 and above	16	9	3	6	9
40 - 49	19	9	3	7	5
below 40	39	29	12	20	14
Total	*74*	*47***	*18*	*33*	*28*

Source: Based on a survey of the A staff of DG II; 74 out of 130 replied.

*   *America = USA and Canada.*

** *The total number of economists who studied abroad is lower than the sum of America and "foreign" European countries, as there are 4 people who studied both in America and in a "foreign" European country.*

In general, however, the Commission services are administrative and legally oriented. Typical is that, until recently, there were only a few economists in DG IV (Competition), which was dominated by lawyers. During recent years there has been a tendency to use more economists, especially in services related to the internal market and external relations. The commissioners Cockfield and Brittan, both British, played a stimulating role in this. The growing use of economic expertise is also reflected in a greater economic input in policy preparation in these areas.

A not atypical career for an economist in the Commission is to start in DG II. After some years, there comes a move to another DG or a cabinet, where he or she will become the economic specialist. Later, he will move further to a more administrative job, higher up in the hierarchy, if his career goes well[6]. However, even for so-called "professional economists" there are some important differences between economics at the Commission and academic economics[7]. The reason is that the Commission is a policy-oriented institution, where certain qualities of academic economics are less useful.

---

6 A not atypical phenomenon in a government service, cf. Coats, 1981, 10.

7 I draw here largely on the comparison which George Baldwin makes between academic economics and economics in the World Bank, in Coats, 1986, 116.

Instead, other characteristics are at a premium:

- being a good team member, also with non-economists. There are limits to "independent originality". As remarked by one observer: "Economists working in government service have a vested interest in promoting consensus on basic issues of economic analysis. Academics, on the other hand, while they must ride with the tide, have a vested interest in differentiating their product" (Marris, 1986, 109);
- quick judgment, as there is less time for in-depth analysis of problems;
- good communication skills: writing clear and accessible papers and achieving consensus in meetings. This can be different from "academic brilliance";
- emphasis on empirical work, with special attention to the methodology of the statistics.

Hereby, one should stress that "skills in communication and the art of persuasion are generally at a premium in international agencies, given their limited powers" (Coats, 1986, 167). However, also to have an impact inside a multinational (and multilingual) organisation, communication and negotiation skills are more important than in national organisations[8]. Marris' remarks about the OECD apply equally well to the European Commission: "'good economics" merges almost imperceptibly into the art of persuasion', (Marris, 1986, 113).

Economists at the Commission can really work as economists and some have been offered certain positions because of their specialist economic expertise. However, it was mostly stressed that decisions were political compromises. A not unimportant function of economists then is to produce arguments which justify political decisions. This primacy of politics leads sometimes to frustrations among economists[9].

Recently economists have been taking a more important role in the preparation of Community policy in certain areas. Examples are competition policy and environmental policy, where, under the influence of economists, there is a greater concern for the costs and benefits of alternative instruments to attain certain objectives.

---

[8]   As also remarked by Delors, cf. Hay, 1989, 17.
[9]   An example is certainly the Common Agricultural Policy.

4.4   SOME REMARKS ON THE NOTION OF INTEGRATION

As expressed in the preamble to the Maastricht Treaty, the purpose of the European Community is to stimulate the process of European integration. However, the notion of integration is difficult to define.

As Tinbergen remarked, economic integration concerns the regulation of international relations. As such it is in essence a question of the organisation of economic policy:

> Integration may be said to be the creation of the most desirable structure of international economy, removing artificial hindrances to the optimal operation and introducing deliberately all desirable elements of co-ordination or unification. The problem of integration therefore forms part of a more general problem, namely that of the *optimum economic policy*. (Tinbergen, 1954, 95, original italics).

A crucial question in the organisation of economic policy is the degree of centralisation. This is intimately connected with the question of economic integration: "Which functions in international economic life should be subject to central control and which should be left to individual countries, enterprises or persons?" (Tinbergen, 1954, 98).

The appropriate degree of centralisation of instruments of economic policy (containing both elements of coordination and harmonisation) depends on the spillover effects they provoke, "their effect on the well-being of each of the countries concerned" (Tinbergen, 1954, 98). In general, Tinbergen argues, there is a strong case for decentralisation as it gives more freedom to the economic agents. The strongest arguments for centralisation apply to instruments with important spillover effects.

This corresponds to the "subsidiarity principle" which is actually a fundamental criterion by which to judge the appropriateness of Community action. It is enshrined in the Maastricht Treaty. This subsidiarity principle states that "functions should be allocated to the lowest level of government, unless welfare gains can be reaped by assigning it to the next higher level" (Van Rompuy et al., 1991, 111).

European integration is a very important political decision as it implies a transfer of sovereignty, from the Member State to a supranational authority. This means that there is a transfer of decision-making to common institutions and a corresponding limitation of the areas of decision-making remaining with the individual State (Louis, 1990, 11).

With the formation of the European Community the emphasis is on a concept of sovereignty, consistent with sovereignty being divisible.

Transfers of sovereignty are not to be seen in quantitative terms, like surrendering territory. Rather, the focus is on partial transfers of jurisdiction: power and responsibility for certain broad areas are transferred from the Member State to the Community (Louis, 1990, 13).

The integration process can have two dimensions: deepening and widening. Deepening implies a more thoroughgoing integration, bringing more areas into the sphere of the Community and strengthening its institutions. Widening entails opening the Community to new members (Maes, 1991). In this paper, the widening of the European Community will not be analysed. However, one should remark that different rounds of enlargements have made the European Community more heterogeneous, both from an economic and social point of view as from a more political view. With respect to the deepening of economic integration, different phases can be distinguished (Balassa, 1961). They are characterised by an increasing transfer of sovereignty from the national state to the supranational authority:

- free trade area: tariffs and quotas are abolished among the participants; there is no common external trade policy;
- customs union: conditions of a free-trade area plus a common external trade policy;
- common market: not only free movement of goods and services (customs union) but also free movement of factors of production (labour and capital);
- economic union: characteristics of a common market and also a harmonisation of economic policy;
- economic and monetary union: not only an economic union, but also fixed exchange rates and a coordination of monetary policy, and eventually a common currency.

4.5   A BRIEF HISTORICAL OVERVIEW

4.5.1   Toward a European Economic Community[10]

The Second World War marked a turning point in European history. It was a catastrophe that led to an almost complete collapse of Europe. It also discredited the previous international order, based on the nation-state.

---

[10] For a succinct chronology of European integration, see Annex 4.3.

In this atmosphere, initiatives at European integration flourished. Crucial was the Schuman Declaration which laid the basis for the European Coal and Steel Community. The gist of the proposal was explained in these terms:

> the French Government proposes to take action immediately on one limited but decisive point ... to place Franco-German production of coal and steel under a common High Authority, within the framework of an organisation open to the participation of the other countries of Europe ... The solidarity in production thus established will make it plain that any war between France and Germany becomes not merely unthinkable, but materially impossible; ... this proposal will build the first concrete foundation of a European federation which is indispensable to the preservation of peace

In 1951 France, Germany, Italy, Belgium, Luxembourg and the Netherlands signed the Treaty of Paris that established the European Coal and Steel Community.

The next step was the formation of the European Economic Community and the European Atomic Energy Community in 1958. The European Economic Community provided for the creation of a common market (with free movement of goods, services, labour and capital), several common policies, the coordination of economic policy and the establishment of institutions to improve social and regional cohesion. The objective of the European Atomic Energy Community was to strengthen cooperation in the nuclear industry. However, with the coming to power of De Gaulle in France in 1958, it was increasingly marginalised as it came too close to the heart of France's national sovereignty: the nuclear "*force de frappe*" (Pinder, 1991, 10) [11].

For a better understanding of the philosophy behind the Community and the Treaties it may be useful to give a short overview of the major differences in economic paradigms and national interests in France and Germany, the two crucial countries. Economic policies in France and Germany in the first decades following the war were based on quite different conceptual frameworks, even if both were embedded in a social market economy.

France followed a more dirigiste economic policy (Schor, 1993, 6). Key elements were the nationalisation of crucial sectors of the economy and a policy of indicative planning. In 1945 firms in the credit, energy and transport sectors were nationalised. In 1947 the first plan was launched, under the instigation of Jean Monnet. It determined the main orientations of

---

[11] This is somewhat ironic, as it was just France which had been pushing for the EAEC (Monnet, 1976, 627).

the economy and, while providing incentives, it remained indicative. While it can be situated in the French tradition of "colbertism", the French planning office was also a spearhead of Keynesianism in France, with the national accounts at its heart (Rosanvallon, 1987, 40).

In Germany, economic policy was more market-oriented, under the inspiration of Ludwig Erhard (Erhard, 1943). The main task of economic policy was to create a secure and unobtrusive legal and financial framework within which markets could operate efficiently (Lipschitz and Mayer, 1988, 370). Following this "Ordnungspolitik" the main tasks of economic policy are: (a) monetary policy: ensure the stability of prices and the currency. A strong and independent central bank is appropriate; (b) fiscal policy: rather limited tasks for the government; (c) structural policy: has a more passive role. Competition policy is emphasised. As concerning differences in national interests, one can remark that Germany was a more industrial country, while in France the agricultural sector was relatively more important.

From this background it is easier to understand the blueprint and the equilibria in the Treaties. The creation of a common market was strongly favoured by the Germans. In line with ordo-liberal thinking competition policy was an important feature of the common market. The common agricultural policy and the European Atomic Energy Community were due more to French inspiration.

4.5.2 A Blueprint for Monetary Union

Monetary union was not one of the original objectives of the European Economic Community. The chapters on macroeconomic policy in the Treaty of Rome were rather sketchy. Two factors can, to a large extent, explain this emphasis. Firstly, the international monetary system, established at Bretton-Woods, provided a stable monetary framework for the Community. Secondly, the creation of a customs union was already considered to be a far-reaching objective.

At the Hague Summit of December 1969 an ambitious programme to stimulate European integration was adopted. Several factors contributed to the change in atmosphere which placed economic and monetary union in the centre of attention:

- the successful completion of the customs union and, somewhat less satisfactorily, the common agricultural policy before the end of 1969.

A new thrust forward seemed necessary to maintain the momentum and even to avoid retrogression;

- disenchantment with the central place of the American dollar in the Bretton-Woods system. There was a sentiment, especially nourished by the French, that the Community needed its own "monetary individuality" (Bloomfield, 1973, 11);
- fear about the future of the fixed exchange rate system, also in the European Community. The May 1968 events in France contributed to severe exchange crises, leading to a devaluation of the French franc and a revaluation of the German mark in 1969. The Community feared that further exchange rate instability could lead to the disintegration of the customs union and the demise of the common agricultural policy.
- the coming to power of new political leaders. In 1969 General de Gaulle resigned and Pompidou was elected as president in France. He, and his finance minister Giscard d'Estaing, followed a more pro-European policy. The other major event was the formation of a new government in Germany by the Social Democrats and the Free Democrats with Willy Brandt as chancellor. The Brandt government supported the EMU project, one of the reasons was the need to counterbalance its Ostpolitik (recognition of the German Democratic Republic).

At the Hague Summit the Heads of State and Government requested the Council to draw up a plan with a view to the creation of an economic and monetary union. A committee, chaired by the Luxembourg Prime Minister Pierre Werner, produced a report by October 1970 (Council-Commission of the European Communities, 1970, hereafter referred to as Werner Report). It contained a program for the establishment by stages of an economic and monetary union by 1980.

The Werner Report first presented a very general picture of economic and monetary union: "Economic and monetary union will make it possible to realise an area within which goods and services, people and capital will circulate freely and without competitive distortions, without thereby giving rise to structural or regional disequilibrium" (Werner Report, 9). A monetary union is more closely defined as implying "total and irreversible convertibility of currencies, the elimination of margins of fluctuation in exchange rates, the irrevocable fixing of parity rates, and the complete liberation of movements of capital" (Werner Report, 10). The establishment of a single currency for the Community is not considered necessary, even though it would stress the irreversible character of the monetary union. To assure the functioning of the economic and monetary union two elements are necessary: transfers of responsibility from the national to the Community level and a harmonisation of the instruments of economic policy in various sectors. On the institutional plane, this implied the existence of two Community organs: a centre of decision for economic policy and a Community system for the central banks. However, the Report did not elaborate very much on these structures.

The Werner Report also underlined the fundamental political significance of the transfer of responsibilities to the Community level: "These transfers of responsibility and the creation of the corresponding Community institutions represent a process of fundamental political significance which entails the progressive development of political cooperation. The economic and monetary union thus appears as a leaven for the development of political union which in the long run it will be unable to do without" (Werner Report, 26).

The Werner Report proposed three stages on the path to economic and monetary union. It did not lay down a precise timetable for the whole of the plan. Rather it wanted to maintain a measure of flexibility, while concentrating on the first phase. Its main elements were: (a) a reinforcement of procedures for consultation and policy coordination; (b) a further liberalisation of intra-Community capital movements and steps towards an integrated European capital market; (c) a narrowing of exchange rate fluctuations between Community currencies. Of the second stage the Report noted that it "will be characterised by the promotion on a number of fronts and on ever more restrictive lines of the action undertaken during the first stage" (Werner Report, 28).

Of fundamental importance in the Werner Report is the concept of "parallel progress". This notion formed a compromise between the "monetarists" (favouring a narrowing of exchange rate fluctuations, mainly represented by France) and the "economists" (emphasising the coordination of economic policies, and led by Germany). This notion enabled the Werner Group to present a unanimous Report (Tsoukalis, 1977, 101).

The Werner Report formed the basis for a first attempt at economic and monetary union in the early 1970s. However, it was not very successful, as noted in the Marjolin Report: "if there has been any movement it has been backward" (Commission of the European Communities, 1975, 1). Two factors played an important role in the failure of the Werner Report: changes in the international environment and lack of political will.

The early 1970s saw the final collapse of the Bretton-Woods system. Exchange rate instability increased dramatically, increasing also the tensions between the European countries. Pressures were further exacerbated by the oil price shock of October 1973. The lack of political will became very clearly apparent with the oil shock of October 1973. Policy-makers, thinking in terms of Phillips curves as a theoretical framework, concentrated on national objectives, while policy harmonisation and coordination were put aside. It led to growing divergencies among the economies of the Community.

The 1970s and early 1980s can be seen as a period of stagnation. The main accomplishment was the creation of the European Monetary System in March 1979. It was to a large degree a Franco-German initiative with the German chancellor (Helmut Schmidt) and the French president (Valérie Giscard d'Estaing) as the main architects[12]. The aim of the European Monetary System was much more limited than the earlier attempt at monetary union. The objective was to create a zone of monetary stability. Changes in exchange rates would still be possible, but subject to mutual consent.

On the whole, the EMS has functioned better than most experts had expected. The basic reason was a major change in the conception of economic policy at the end of the 1970s and the early 1980s: away from a policy of fine-tuning and towards a stability oriented policy (Baer and Padoa-Schioppa, 1988, 58).

4.5.3 The Delors Decade

Before Jacques Delors became president of the European Commission at the beginning of 1985, he toured the Member states, discussing ideas to relaunch European integration. A renewed campaign for a European internal market emerged as the most favoured option, as it fitted in with the general tendency towards deregulation, which had received a strong impetus with the Reagan presidency in the United States (Colchester, 1988, 6).

Delors sensed there was a favourable constellation of forces to push forward European integration. Lord Cockfield, the British commissioner for the Internal Market, prepared the famous "White Paper" (Commission of the European Communities, 1985), which identified existing barriers and presented a program of policy measures to remove them. A list of nearly three hundred directives was drawn up to eliminate these barriers and unify the European market. Moreover, a hectic timetable was laid out, to have these directives adopted by the end of the next commission's reign, December 1992.

---

[12] For a fascinating overview of the origins of the EMS, see Ludlow, 1982.

The 1992 programme was adopted by the Community. It became a Treaty obligation with the adoption of the Single European Act in 1986, the first major revision of the founding Treaties of the Community. The Act extended greatly the scope of the Community and simplified the decision-making process. The Act constituted an early and crucial triumph for the 1992 project. It further contributed to the renewed momentum of the Community. Moreover, the internal market programme was also part of a more general economic policy strategy of the Commission, aimed at improving the microeconomic foundations of the economy (Mortensen, 1990, 31). Other important elements of this strategy were wage moderation, budgetary consolidation and increasing the flexibility of markets.

The European Community continued on this élan. At the summit meeting of Hanover in June 1988, economic and monetary union was brought back on the agenda. The heads of State or Government decided to set up a Committee with the task of studying and proposing concrete steps leading towards economic and monetary union. This Committee, mainly composed of central bank governors and chaired by Jacques Delors, produced its report in April 1989 (Report on Economic and Monetary Union in the European Community, hereafter referred to as Delors Report). The Delors Report became crucial as a reference and anchor point in further discussions, just as the Werner Report had been nearly two decades ago. The report basically revolved around two issues: firstly, what economic arrangements are necessary for a monetary union to be successful? Secondly, what gradualist path should be designed to reach economic and monetary union? (Padoa-Schioppa, 1990, 22).

In defining the necessary conditions for a monetary union, the Delors Report referred back to the Werner Report. On the institutional level, the Report proposed the creation of a "European System of Central Banks". To attain economic and monetary union the Committee proposed three stages. However, it underlined the indivisibility of the whole process: "the decision to enter upon the first stage should be a decision to embark on the entire process" (Delors Report, 31).

The Committee's three phases, in contrast to the Werner Report's emphasis on the first stage, were all worked out in considerable detail. These stages imply, from an institutional and legal point of view: the preparation of a new Treaty (first stage), the creation of a new monetary institution (European System of Central Banks, second stage), and the transfer of responsibilities to this new institution (third stage). From an economic and monetary point of view, these stages entailed an increased convergence and a closer coordination of economic policy.

The procedure to revise the Treaties formally started in December 1990 with the opening of two intergovernmental conferences, one on economic and monetary union and one on political union. These conferences were concluded in December 1991, at the Maastricht Summit of the heads of State or Government. The new Treaty was, after long discussions, ratified by the Member States in the second half of 1993.

The Treaty of Maastricht marks a step forward for the European community on a par with the Treaty of Rome. It creates a so-called European Union, which is based on three pillars. The first is the old Community, but with greatly extended responsibilities. The main element is economic and monetary union. The Treaty specifies the future monetary constitution of the Community, including the Statute of the European Central Bank. To strengthen the economic and social cohesion of the Union a cohesion fund will be set up. Also, the path to economic and monetary union was specified. Crucial is the fixing of a deadline, 1 January 1999 at the latest, for the third phase (the irrevocable fixing of the exchange rates or the introduction of the ecu). The second pillar is for foreign and security policy. The third concerns cooperation on such topics as immigration, asylum and policing. These pillars are intergovernmental, in which the commission, parliament and court have a more restricted say.

Looking back one can notice a hectic and thoroughgoing integration process in the 1980s and the beginning of the 1990s. Two important factors contributed to this deepening process. Firstly, the logic and momentum of the integration process, whereby integration in one area sets in motion forces which induce integration in other areas (e.g. from one market to one money). Secondly, the power of federalist forces, aiming at European integration. Essential was the strongly pro-European attitude of France and Germany, which together constituted a powerful axis. Important also was the increased role of the European Commission under the leadership of Jacques Delors.

4.6   CHANGE AND CONTINUITY

Economic thought at the European Community institutions evolves, in essence, around the process of economic integration. It is closely related to economic policy, as one of the main aims is to develop an appropriate strategy to stimulate the integration process in the European Community. This has some important implications:

- it is a highly "political economy" theory, as integration implies a transfer of sovereignty from the national to the European level. The

political economy dimension comes to the foreground as different
countries have different ideas on how to pursue European integration.
These differences among countries are based on differences in both
national interests and economic thought;
-   the development of economic thought is largely a function of the
    actual situation, the quest for an appropriate strategy and the need to
    support the integration process with well documented studies. When
    the internal market program was elaborated, the Commission
    produced a report "The Economics of 1992" (CEC, 1988), on the
    impact of completing the internal market. In 1990, just before the
    start of the intergovernmental conference on economic and monetary
    union, she published a report "One Market, One Money" (CEC,
    1990), on the potential benefits and costs of an economic and
    monetary union.

In considering these past decades of development of economic thought at the
European Community institutions one observes some important continuities,
especially the tension between the logic of integration and the attachment to
national sovereignty, and the recurring debate between "monetarists" and
"economists" about the appropriate strategy towards monetary union. The
most important shift occurred at the end of the 1970s with the move from a
more activist to a more structural and stability-oriented conceptual
framework.

4.6.1   The Tension between the Logic of Integration and the Attachment to National Sovereignty

Starting a process of integration sets in motion forces which push for a
further deepening of integration. This is something which was noted early in
the theory of economic integration[13.] For example, the formation of a
customs union will limit the scope of fiscal policy in a participating country,
as taxes and subsidies affect trade flows. The quest for monetary integration
in the Community was to a large extent motivated by the desire to
consolidate and extend the achievements of the common market and the
common agricultural policy (Giavazzi and Giovannini, 1989, 12).
    However, the attachment to national sovereignty was a crucial element in
the failure of several attempts at integration:

---

[13]   Examples are Viner, 1950, 136 and Meade, 1953, 27, see also Maes, 1994.

-   the plans for the European Defence Community were rejected by the French parliament;
-   the European Atomic Energy Community was marginalised by De Gaulle as it was too close to France's nuclear *force de frappe*;
-   a crucial element in the failure of the Werner Report was the priority given to national policy objectives after the first oil shock;
-   the common market was eroded in the 1970s and first half of the 1980s as countries favoured their own companies through subsidies and government contracts;
-   the ratification of the Maastricht Treaty was seriously delayed as some countries, especially Denmark and the United Kingdom, were reluctant to accept a new transfer of sovereignty.

This tension between sovereignty and integration is also reflected in discussions on the concept of subsidiarity and its application.

4.6.2   The Strategy of Monetary Integration

In the discussions about how to proceed with monetary integration, it is customary to discern two basic approaches: the "monetarist" and the "economist". These terms have a very specific content in the monetary integration debate, which is very different from their use in other contexts.

According to the "monetarists", monetary integration will have a stimulating effect on the integration process. The stabilising of exchange rates will induce a convergence of economic policies and performances. Monetary integration will stimulate economic and political integration. These views were mostly held in France, Italy, and at the European Commission.

It is noteworthy that in the European Commission monetary matters were to a large extent the responsibility of French and Italian officials. Also the member of the Commission responsible for monetary matters was often French: e.g. R. Barre, F.-X. Ortoli, J. Delors, Y.-T. de Silgy. The director general of DG II "Economic and Financial Affairs" was typically Italian: e.g. U. Mosca, T. Padoa-Schioppa, M. Russo, A. Costa, G. Ravasio and the director for "Monetary Matters" was mostly French: e.g. F. Boyer de la Giroday, J.-P. Mingasson, J.-F. Pons, H. Carré. There were also moments of close cooperation between the Commission, France and Italy on monetary integration, as during the discussions of the Delors Committee on economic and monetary union. So Delors asked Ciampi and de Larosière, the governors of the Banca d'Italia and the Banque de France, to speak on his behalf during the meetings of the Committee (Grant, 1994, 123).

An important figure was Tommaso Padoa-Schioppa, who was director-general of DG II at the end of the 1970s and the early 1980s. At that period he got to know Delors, who was then chairman of the economic and monetary committee of the European parliament. After his stay in Brussels, Padoa-Schioppa returned to the Banca d'Italia. When Delors became president of the Commission, he requested a report by a study group, chaired by Padoa-Schioppa, on the implications of the internal market for the future of the Community (Padoa-Schioppa, 1987). It contained a warning that the liberation of capital movements was inconsistent with the prevalent combination of exchange rate stability and national autonomy of monetary policy. According to Grant (1994, 199), Padoa-Schioppa was the man who convinced Delors that the time was ripe for a push for Economic and Monetary Union.

The "economists" emphasise the differences among countries in inflation, productivity, government finances. They stress that a convergence of economic performances and economic policy is a necessary condition for monetary integration. Without sufficient convergence the fixing of the exchange rate could break down or lead to important regional problems. Monetary integration can only be the crowning act of a process of economic integration. These ideas were most prominent in Germany, especially at the Bundesbank (Bundesbank, 1994, 26).

Proposals for monetary integration in the Community were typically a compromise and synthesis of these two positions:

- of fundamental importance in the Werner Report is the notion of "parallel progress" in the development of both monetary unification and the harmonisation and unification of economic policies (Werner Report, 26). This notion enabled the Werner Group to present a unanimous report (Tsoukalis, 1977, 101);
- the exchange rate mechanism of the European Monetary System should form the basis of a system of fixed exchange rates, which portrays a monetarist signature. However, the fixity of exchange rates is diluted through the existence of margins of fluctuation and the possibility of realignments;
- the Maastricht Treaty contains several deadlines. The most important is 1 January 1999 as the ultimate date for the third and final phase of monetary union (article 109J). This makes the transition to a monetary union as irreversible as possible. However, at the same time, the so-called "convergence criteria" concerning inflation, public

finance, exchange rates and long term interest rates have to be satisfied (also article 109J).

4.6.3   The Shift from a More Activist to a More Stability Oriented Economic Policy

At the end of the 1970s a shift occurred in Europe from a more activist policy towards a strategy based on medium-term stability, market-oriented policies and emphasis on measures enforcing the supply side of the economy. The shift was apparent in all major European countries. The clearest break was in the United Kingdom with the election victory of Margret Thatcher in 1979. In Germany a more conservative government was formed in 1982 under Helmut Kohl. However, a major change in fiscal policy had occurred already in 1981 under his socialist predecessor, Helmut Schmidt. In France the change occurred somewhat later, given the election victory of Mitterrand in 1981. After 18 months of a rather disastrous experiment in "policy activism", the socialists reoriented their economic policy in a much less interventionist way.

An important element in this reformulation of economic policy strategy in the early 1980s was the failure of macroeconomic policy coordination at the end of the 1970s. At the G7 Bonn summit in May 1978, a coordinated macroeconomic strategy at a worldwide level, under the pressure of the American president Jimmy Carter, was drawn up. The more expansionary budgetary policy in 1979 and 1980 coincided with an economic recovery, working pro-cyclically. This created a severe trauma, especially in Germany, which was confronted with a balance-of-payments deficit, and also in international institutions like the OECD and the European Commission, which were important advocates of policy coordination. It raised the issue of the efficiency of economic policy, especially at these international institutions. It made economists much more sceptical about possibilities for fine-tuning policy.

This shift towards a more stability-oriented stance of economic policy was also clearly reflected in the economic thought at the institutions of the European Community:

-   in both the Delors Report and the Maastricht Treaty, price stability was emphasised as the overriding goal of monetary policy, which had to be carried out by an independent central bank. These ideas were not mentioned in the Werner Report when monetary policy was discussed (e.g. Werner Report, 13 and 21);

- both the Delors Report and the Werner Report emphasise that monetary policy has to be centralised in the monetary union, under the responsibility of a European central bank. The Werner Report also proposed the creation of a "centre of decision for economic policy", which will exercise "a decisive influence over the general economic policy of the Community" (Werner Report, 12);
- a smaller budget for the Community was proposed. In a recent report of a study group an EC budget of 2% of Community GDP is considered capable of sustaining economic and monetary union (CEC, 1993, 6). This contrasts with the earlier MacDougall Report, which considered an EC budget of 5% to 7% of EC GDP necessary for a monetary union (CEC, 1977, 20). This shift reflects both a different politico-economic paradigm, with a more limited role for the government in economic life, as a smaller role for the Community, given the attachment of national states to their sovereignty and the application of the subsidiarity principle;
- a new view on industrial policy, which had figured prominently on the policy agenda of the Community in the 1970s, as a way to complement the internal market. Hereby special attention was given to sectors confronted with problems (CCE, 1973, 17 or CEC, 1977, 48). In the 1980s and 1990s, the emphasis is on a more "horizontal" industrial policy, where the creation of a favourable environment for firms is encouraged, as well as on competition policy (CEC, 1989, 62).

Even more important for the development of the Community was the way that a further push towards integration fitted into this new conceptual framework. The completion of the internal market, with its elimination of the remaining barriers to a free flow of goods, services, persons and capital, was compatible with the deregulation strategy being pursued in the various European countries. Macroeconomic policy in the countries of the Community became more stability oriented, as policy-makers realised the illusory nature of the trade-off between inflation and unemployment. This orientation fitted in with a policy of stable exchange rates and a move towards a monetary union.

4.7   THE INTERNATIONALISATION INFLUENCE

It is not easy to assess the international or American influence in the thinking at the European Community institutions, as many different elements play a role (Coats, 1992, 5). As the economic thought at the European Community institutions is already a kind of international thought, it seems appropriate here to focus on the Americanisation tendency and to contrast this with a "European economics".

One could argue that the American influence has been increasing during the last decades. This has been especially so for form and method (quantification and use of the English language), relatively less in matters of substance. Mathematisation and quantification, which several observers consider as typical for the American style of economics (Portes, 1987, Kolm, 1988, Baumol, 1995 and Mayer, 1995), have become more important in studies of the European Commission. Also, in practice, English is becoming more and more the dominant language in the Community institutions. The main reason is that English is the second language of most Europeans, with the exception of the British and the Irish (Table 4.4).

Several factors contribute to this growing Americanisation:

- academic economics in Europe is becoming more like academic economics in America (Frey and Eichenberger, 1993, Klamer, 1995). So the intellectual environment, wherein economists at the European Community institutions work, is becoming more Americanised. It implies also that economists who are newly recruited, both as administrators or as consultants, are nowadays thinking more along American lines;
- more young Commission economists have studied abroad, especially at American universities (Table 4.2);
- with the 1973 enlargement, the United Kingdom became a member of the Community. This has certainly contributed to a more Anglo-Saxon trait in the economic thinking at the European Community institutions, as British economists are, in general, more in touch with American economics than continental economists (Backhouse, 1996);
- the OECD has a very important role in the transatlantic transmission of economic ideas. It fulfils a "bridging role" between American and European officials, both during meetings and informal contacts;
- American economists also pay attention to the functioning of the European economy. Their analyses have, in differing degrees, an impact on the thinking of European economists and at the Commission;
- there are also very direct influences, like the contribution of non-EC experts to studies undertaken by the European Community (see Annex 4.4).

Table 4.4 - Foreign language education in the Community
(percentage of pupils in general secondary education learning
English, French or German as a foreign language, 1991-1992)

Country	English	French	German
Holland	96	65	53
Germany	93	23	-
Denmark	92	8	58
Spain	92	10	0.3
France	84	-	27
Belgium (Flemish)	68	98	22
Italy	61	33	3
Belgium (French)	58	1	6
Portugal	55	25	0.4
United Kingdom	-	59	20
Ireland	-	69	24

Source: Eurostat, The Economist, 14-1-1995, 25.

Summarising then, one could argue that the American influence is increasing, especially in respect of form and method (quantification, English language). However, economics at the Community institutions retains a somewhat different character. Important is its emphasis on certain conditions necessary for the functioning of a free market economy, like competition policy, the need for wage moderation for a process of sustainable and balanced growth, etc. These are mainly elements of (German) ordo-liberal thinking, coupled with a more activist (French) attitude towards economic policy. This rather differentiates economic thought at the Community institutions from a more noninterventionist (American) economics, notwithstanding many influences and interactions. These elements go to the core of the economic thought at the European Community institutions. The quest for monetary integration in Europe is something that meets with scepticism and criticism among American economists, who attach more importance to the exchange rate as an adjustment mechanism. In the economic thought at the European Community institutions the role of the exchange rate as an adjustment mechanism is relativised (e.g. concern with the loss of effectiveness of the exchange rate instrument in very open economies, dangers of overshooting and misalignment). Moreover, the dangers of volatile exchange rates for the functioning of the internal market and the process of European integration are emphasised.[14]

4.8   CONCLUSION

Economic thought at the European Community institutions is, to a large extent, centred around the notion of economic integration. The "political economy" dimension is prominent, as integration implies a transfer of sovereignty from the national to the European level. This political economy dimension comes even more to the foreground as different countries have different ideas on how to pursue European integration, based on both differences in national interests and in economic thought.

When analysing the development of economic thought at the European Community institutions one can discern some important continuities, especially the tension between the logic of integration and the attachment to national sovereignty, and the recurring debate between "monetarists" and "economists" about the appropriate strategy for monetary integration. The most important shift occurred at the end of the 1970s, with the move from a more activist towards a more structural and stability oriented conceptual framework.

Economic thought at the institutions of the European Communities has undergone important international (American) influences, both directly (e.g. studies of American economists on the European economy, participation of non-EC economists in important study groups) and indirectly (recruitment of American trained economists, influences of American economics on academic economics in Europe). However, economic thought at the European Community institutions has also some characteristics which differentiate it from American economics, such as a greater concern for conditions for the functioning of a free market economy. Competition policy, price stability, moderate wage developments etc. are important. Moreover, Europe's quest for exchange rate stability is met with more scepticism and criticism on the other side of the Atlantic.

---

[14]   An example is Feldstein's criticism of EMU in The Economist (Feldstein, 1992), which provoked reactions in defense of EMU from numerous European economists, like De Grauwe, Giovannini, Gross, Steinherr, Thygesen, etc. (see also Salmon, 1995).

REFERENCES

Backhouse, R. (1996), The Post - 1945 Internationalisation of Economics, Britain, in Coats, A.W. (ed.), The Post - 1945 Internationalisation of Economics, *History of Political Economy*, Annual Supplement, 33-60.

Baer, G. and T. Padoa-Schioppa (1988), The Werner Report Revisited, in Committee for the Study of Economic and Monetary Union (ed.), *Report on Economic and Monetary Union*, Luxembourg, April 1989, pp. 53-60.

Balassa, B. (1961), Toward a Theory of Economic Integration, *Kyklos*, XIV, 1-17.

Baumol, W. (1995), What's Different about European Economics?, *Kyklos*, Vol. 48, No 2, 187-191.

Bloomfield, A. (1973), The Historical Setting, Krause B. and W. Salant, (eds.), *European Monetary Unification and its Meaning for the United States*, Washington: Brookings, pp. 1-30.

Bundesbank (1994), Die Zweite Stufe der Europäischen Wirtschafts- und Währungsunion, *Monatsbericht*, Januar, 25-44.

Coats, A.W. (1981), Introduction, Coats A.W., (ed.), *Economists in Government*, Durham: Duke University Press, pp. 3-26.

Coats, A.W. (ed.), (1986), *Economists in International Agencies*, New-York: Praeger.

Coats. A.W. (1992), The Post - 1945 Global Internationalization (Americanization?) of Economics, mimeo.

Colchester, N. (1988), A Survey of Europe's Internal Market, *The Economist*, July 9.

Commission des Communautés Européennes (1973), La Réalisation de l'Union Economique et Monétaire, *Bulletin des Communautés Européennes*, Supplément 5/73.

Commission of the European Communities (1975), *Report of the Study Group "Economic and Monetary Union 1980"*, Marjolin Report, Brussels, March.

Commission of the European Communities (1977), *Report of the Study Group on the Role of Public Finance in European Integration*, Brussels, April.

Commission of the European Communities (1985), *Completing the Internal Market*, White Paper from the Commission to the Council, Luxembourg.

Commission of the European Communities (1988), The Economics of 1992, *European Economy*, no. 35, March.

Commission of the European Communities (1989), The Community Economy at the Turn of the Decade, *European Economy*, no. 42, Nov., 25-104.

Commission of the European Communities (1990), One Market, One Money, *European Economy*, no. 44, Oct.

Commission of the European Communities (1993), Stable Money - Sound Finances, *European Economy*, no. 53.

Committee for the Study of Economic and Monetary Union (1989), *Report on Economic and Monetary Union in the European Community*, Delors Report, Luxembourg.

Council - Commission of the European Communities (1970), *Report to the Council and the Commission on the Realisation by Stages of Economic and Monetary Union in the Community*, Werner Report, Luxembourg, October.

Erhard, L. (1943), Wirtschaftspolitische Erfordernisse nach Beendigung des Krieges, W. Stützel et al., (eds.), *Grundtexte zur Sozialen Marktwirtschaf* (1981), Gustav Fischer Verlag, pp. 15-18.

Feldstein, M. (1992), Europe's Monetary Union, *The Economist*, June 13.

Frey, B. and R. Eichenberger (1993), American and European Economics and Economists, *Journal of Economic Perspectives*, Vol. 7, no. 4, 185-193.

Giavazzi, F. and A. Giovannini (1989), *Limiting Exchange Rate Flexibility: The European Monetary System*, Cambridge: MIT Press.

Grant, C. (1994), *Delors - Inside the House that Jacques Built*, London: Nicholas Brealy.

Hay, R. (1989), *The European Commission and the Administration of the Community*, European Documentation.

Klamer, A. (1995), A Rhetorical Perspective on the Differences between European and American Economists, *Kyklos*, Vol. 48, No. 2, 231-239

Kolm, S.-C. (1988), Economics in Europe and in the U.S., *European Economic Review*, Vol. 32, No. 1, 207-212.

Lipschitz, L. and T. Mayer (1988), Accepted Economic Paradigms Guide German Economic Policies, *IMF Survey*, Nov. 28, 370-374.

Louis, J.-V. (1990), *The Community Legal Order*, 2^e ed., Commission of the European Communities.

Ludlow, P. (1982), *The Making of the European Monetary System*, London: Butterworths.

Maes, I. (1991), The European Community in the 1990s: Deepening or Widening?, *Global Forum Series*, Occasional Paper no 92-2, Center for International Studies, Duke University.

Maes, I. (1994), State and Market in Postwar Integration Theory, Roggi P. et al. (eds.), *National and European Markets in Economic Thought*, Proceedings of the Eleventh International Economic History Congress, Milan, pp. 83-94.

Marris, S. (1986), The Role of Economists in the OECD, Coats A.W., (ed.), *Economists in International Agencies*, New-York: Praeger, pp. 98-114.

Mayer, T. (1995), Differences in Economics: Europe and the United States, *Kyklos*, Vol. 48, No. 2, 241-249.

Meade, J. (1953), *Problems of Economic Union*, London: Allen & Unwin.

Monnet, J. (1976), *Mémoires*, Paris: Fayard.

Mortensen, J. (1990), *Federalism vs. Co-ordination. Macroeconomic Policy in the European Community*, Brussels: CEPS.

Noël, E. (1993), *Working Together - The Institutions of the European Community*, European Documentation.

Padoa-Schioppa, T. (1987), *Efficiency, Stability, Equity*, Oxford: O.U.P.

Padoa-Schioppa, T. (1990), *Financial and Monetary Integration in Europe: 1990, 1992 and Beyond*, Occasional Paper no. 28, Group of Thirty.

Pinder, J. (1991), *European Community*, Oxford: Oxford University Press.

Portes, R. (1987), Economics in Europe, *European Economic Review*, Vol. 31, No. 6, 1329-1340.

Rosanvallon, P. (1987), Histoire des Idées Keynesiennes en France, *Revue Française d'Economie*, Vol. 4, No. 2, 22-56.

Ross, G. (1994), Inside the Delors Cabinet, *Journal of Common Market Studies*, Vol. 32, No. 4, 499-523.

Salmon, P. (1995), Three Conditions for Some Distinctiveness in the Contribution of Europeans to Economics, *Kyklos*, Vol. 48, No. 2, 279-287.

Schor, A.-D. (1993), *La Politique Economique et Sociale de la Ve République*, Paris: P.U.F.

Study Group on Economic and Monetary Union (1973), *European Economic Integration and Monetary Unification*, Commission of the European Communities, Brussels.

Tinbergen, J. (1954), *International Economic Integration*, Amsterdam: Elsevier.

Tsoukalis, L. (1977), *The Politics and Economics of European Monetary Integration*, London: Allen and Unwin.

Van Rompuy, P., F. Abraham and D. Heremans (1991), Economic Federalism and the EMU, *European Economy*, Special Edition, No. 1, 109-35.

Viner, J. (1950), *The Customs Union Issue*, New York: Carnegie Endowment for International Peace.

Annex 4.1 - Structure of the services of the Commission
(1994)

Cabinets
Secretariat-General
Forward looking unit
Legal Service
Spokesman's Service
Consumer Policy Service
Task Force "Human resources, education, training and youth"
Translation Service
Joint Interpretation and Conference Service
Statistical Office

DG	I	Economic External Relations
DG	IA	Political External Relations
DG	II	Economic and Financial Affairs
DG	III	Industry
DG	IV	Competition
DG	V	Employment, Industrial Relationships and Social Affairs
DG	VI	Agriculture
DG	VII	Transport
DG	VIII	Development
DG	IX	Personnel and Administration
DG	X	Audiovisual Affairs, Information, Communication and Culture
DG	XI	Environment, Nuclear Safety and Civil Protection
DG	XII	Science, Research and Development Joint Research Centre
DG	XIII	Telecommunications, Information Industries and Innovation
DG	XIV	Fisheries
DG	XV	Internal Market and Financial Institutions
DG	XVI	Regional Policies
DG	XVII	Energy
DG	XVIII	Credit and Investments
DG	XIX	Budgets
DG	XX	Financial Control
DG	XXI	Customs Union and Indirect Taxation
DG	XXIII	Enterprises' Policy, Distributive Trades, Tourism and Social Economy

Euratom Supply Agency
Security Office

Annex 4.2 - A simplified presentation of Directorate-General II (Economic and Financial Affairs) and number of A staff (December 1994)

Staff of the DG   18

Directorate A: National economies   17
1.   Member States I: Denmark, Germany and France
2.   Member States II: Greece, Ireland and United Kingdom
3.   Member States III: Benelux and Portugal
4.   Member States IV: Spain and Italy

Directorate B: Economic Service   18
1.   Economic aspects of integration and evaluation of external policy
2.   Evaluation of the Structural Funds and social and agricultural policies
3.   Evaluation of competition and research and development policies; internal market and industrial affairs
4.   Evaluation of transport, environment and energy policies

Directorate C: Surveillance of the Community economy   22
1.   Evaluation and surveillance of the Community economy
2.   Surveillance of budgetary situations
3.   Economic forecasts
4.   Econometric models

Directorate D: Monetary matters   18
1.   Monetary union: institutional, legal and financial matters
2.   ECU
3.   EMS, national and Community monetary policies
4.   International aspects of monetary union

Directorate E: Financial instruments and capital movements   16
1.   Coordination with the EIB and development of financial instruments
2.   Analysis of financial circuits and instruments, including the EIB
3.   Financial integration and capital movements

Directorate F: International economic and financial matters   21
1.   Central and Eastern Europe including the newly independent states
2.   Other European countries and the international environment
3.   International financial matters

Total   130

Annex 4.3 - A succinct chronology of European integration

1950	May	Schuman declaration
1952	July	Establishment of the European Coal and Steel Community (ECSC)
1954	August	France rejects the European Defence Community (EDC)
1958	January	Establishment of the European Economic Community (EEC) and the European Atomic Energy Community (EAEC)
1969	December	The Hague Summit. Monetary union becomes an objective of the Community
1973	January	The United Kingdom, Ireland and Denmark become members of the European Community
1979	March	Establishment of the European Monetary System (EMS)
1985	March	European Council agrees on an internal single market by December 1992
1987	January	Single European Act
1988	June	European Council relaunches the monetary union project
1991	December	Agreement on the Maastricht Treaty
1993	November	Maastricht Treaty ratified
1994	January	Start of Phase 2 of Economic and Monetary Union

Annex 4.4 - Participation of non-EC economists in important study groups

Study Group on Economic and Monetary Union October 1973	R.A. Mundell
Study Group on the Role of Public Finance in European Integration April 1977	R. Mathews (Canberra) W. Oates (Princeton)
Efficiency, Stability, Equity September 1987	P. Krugman (MIT)
One Market, One Money October 1990	P. Kenen (Princeton) R.E. Baldwin (Geneva and NBER) R. Lyons (Columbia and NBER) R. Bryant R. Portes
Stable Money-Sound Finances 1993	F. Schneider (Linz) C. Walsh (Adelaide) T. Courchene (Kingston, Ontario) H. Blöchliger (Basle) R. Frey (Basle)

5. Macroeconomic Thought at the European Commission in the 1970s: The First Decade of the Annual Economic Reports*

5.1   INTRODUCTION

The 1970s were a period of economic turmoil, marked by the breakdown of the Bretton-Woods system, two oil price shocks, stagflation and important changes in economic theories and beliefs. The purpose of this paper is to analyse the shifts in macroeconomic thought in the 1970s at the European Commission, an institution which has become increasingly important in shaping policy formulation at the European level[1].

In the analysis of these shifts in macroeconomic thinking, special attention is given to elements which are specific for policy institutions. One of the purposes of this paper is to contribute to a better understanding of how

---

*   Reprinted from *Banca Nazionale del Lavoro Quarterly Review*, no. 207, December 1998, 387-412, with kind permission from Banca Nazionale del Lavoro.

    I would like to thank F. Abraham, B. Bateman, E. Buyst, A.W. Coats, A. Cottrell, S. Deroose, M. Emerson, F. Froschmaier, D. Heremans, F. Ilzkovitz, A. Louw, J. Mortensen, P. Van den Bempt, M. Wegner and participants at seminars at the European Society for the History of Economic Thought (Marseille), LATAPSES - Sophia Antipolis, the Bank of Finland and the History of Economics Society (Montréal) for comments and discussions. The usual restrictions apply.

[1]   The further evolution of macroeconomic thought at the European Commission, in the first half of the 1980s, is analysed in Maes, 2000.

economic thought changes at policy institutions, as compared to academic institutions.

The analysis will focus on the Annual Economic Reports, the main macroeconomic policy document of the Commission.   These Annual Economic Reports consisted of two main parts: a description of the economic situation and policy recommendations.   This implies that the economic theories and paradigms are less explicit and more hidden, compared to traditional academic economic texts.   Consequently, a history of the Annual Economic Reports involves a greater degree of "rational reconstruction". This is even more so as the economic thought behind the Reports was more heterogeneous, as the Reports were a compromise between different persons and tendencies.

The paper opens with a description of the origins of the Reports in the process of European monetary integration.   The next sections go deeper into the policy conception of the Reports and how this policy conception changed through time.

5.2   BACKGROUND: FROM THE GOLDEN SIXTIES AND MONETARY INTEGRATION PLANS TO STAGFLATION

At the beginning of the 1970s, economic thought among economic policy-makers was still dominated by the experience of the "golden sixties": strong economic growth, stable prices and the success of Keynesian demand management.   European economic integration also thrived in the 1960s, especially with the successful completion of the common market.   The launching of the monetary union project, at the Hague Summit of 1969, reflected this atmosphere.

The Annual Economic Reports of the European Community were a by-product of this first attempt at monetary union in the Community in the early 1970s.   The blueprint for the monetary union project can be found in the Werner Report (Council-Commission of the European Communities, 1970), which contained a plan for the establishment of an economic and monetary union by 1980 (see Annex 5.1).

The Werner Report first discussed the essential characteristics of an economic and monetary union.   It envisaged two poles of decision making: a centre of decision for economic policy and a Community system for the central banks.

Thereafter, it specified the main elements of the stages towards monetary union: (a) a reinforcement of procedures for consultation and policy coordination;   (b)   a   further   liberalisation   of   intra-Community   capital movements and steps towards an integrated European capital market; (c) a narrowing of exchange rate fluctuations between Community currencies.

Of fundamental importance in the Werner Report is the concept of "parallel progress" (Tsoukalis, 1977, 101). This notion formed a compromise between the "monetarists" (arguing that a narrowing of exchange rate fluctuations would induce a convergence of economic policies and performances and so stimulate economic and political integration, mainly represented by France) and the "economists" (emphasising the differences in economic performance of the different economies and the need for convergence and policy coordination as a prerequisite for monetary unification, led by Germany).

The first phase of economic and monetary union started on 1 January 1971. The Annual Economic Report had a pivotal role in the coordination of economic policy in the Community. It was installed by the "Council Decision of 22 March 1971 on the strengthening of the coordination of short-term economic policies of the Member States of the European Economic Community" (Conseil, 1971)[2]. The purpose of this directive was to strengthen and improve the coordination procedures in order to achieve a high degree of convergence of the economic policies pursued by the Member States.

However, Europe's first attempt at monetary union was not very successful. The breakdown of the Bretton-Woods System in the early 1970s and the first oil shock of 1973 made for an unfavourable international environment. More fundamentally, divergencies about policy priorities between the European countries, especially France and Germany (see Wegner, 1985), came to the surface and led to wide differences in inflation rates and exchange rate turmoil in Europe.

The breakdown of the Bretton-Woods System implied further that economic policies, especially monetary policy, did not have to be geared any more in function of the exchange rate against the dollar. This implied that policy makers had to find a new nominal anchor for their policies.

European monetary integration languished further in the mid 1970s, when discussions about the place of the United Kingdom dominated the European scene. Only at the end of the 1970s, with Roy Jenkins's speech in Florence and the initiative of Helmut Schmidt and Valéry Giscard d'Estaing, came monetary integration again to the forefront (Ludlow, 1982). However, the

---

2   Later, there were certain changes. Most important was the Council Decision of 18 February 1974 on the attainment of a high degree of convergence of the economic policies of the member states of the European Economic Community.

European Monetary System, started in March 1979, was a rather modest creation, when compared with the ambitions of the Werner plan.

Figure 5.1 - Evolution of the European economy

Real GDP and inflation[1]
(annual percentage changes)

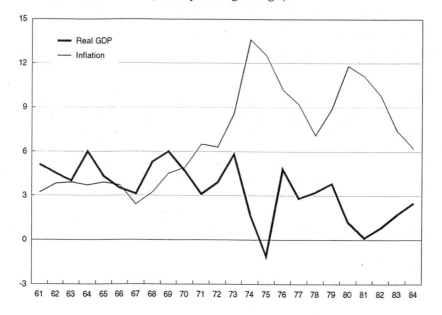

[1]   *1961-1980: EC9, 1981-1984: EC10.*

In the 1970s, the European Community's economic performance deteriorated markedly: economic growth slowed down and inflation shot up, leading to "stagflation".   This gave rise to important discussions among economic policy-makers, both at the world annual economic summits, which were initiated in 1975 (Dobson, 1991, 13), and at the European level. It would lead to the 1978 "concerted action", whereby Germany agreed to boost its economy with a budgetary package of 1% of GDP. So, the "golden sixties", with its strong economic growth performance, associated with Keynesian demand management policies (Hall, 1989), remained an implicit reference frame against which many policy-makers also approached the economic problems of the 1970s. The failure of the concerted action, led to serious reflections and discussions among policy-makers.

5.3 THE ELABORATION OF THE REPORT

The drafting of the Annual Economic Report at the European Commission went through several phases. The first draft was essentially prepared in Directorate-General II, Economic and Financial Affairs, which can be considered as the economic research department of the European Commission[3].

In order to better understand the philosophy behind the Reports, it is appropriate to consider the economic thought at the Commission. Originally, with the Community of the Six, the economic ideas at the Commission were to a large extent marked by French ideas of indicative planning and German ideas centred around the social market economy (Wegner, 1989, 285).

Table 5.1 - The Commission of the European Community

	President	Member responsible for DG II
1958	W. Hallstein (D)	R. Marjolin (F)
1968	J. Rey (B)	R. Barre (F)
1970	F.-M. Malfati (I)	R. Barre (F)
1973	F.-X. Ortoli (F)	W. Haferkampf (D)
1977	R. Jenkins (UK)	F.-X. Ortoli (F)
1981	G. Thorn (L)	F.-X. Ortoli (F)

French ideas were considered to be dominating at the Commission (Mortensen, 1990, 18). It is remarkable that, from the origin of the Commission until now, the commissioner responsible for DG II, has always been French, with the exception of the periods when the French held the presidency (Ortoli and Delors).

Robert Marjolin, the first commissioner from 1957 to 1967, had been the principal assistant to Monnet at the French Planning Office, famous for its five year plans (cf. Marjolin, 1986). The French planning office, while it was part of the French "Colbertist" tradition, was also a spearhead of Keynesianism in France, with the national accounts at its heart (Rosanvallon,

---

[3] For an overview of the functioning of the Commission and the development of its economic ideas, see Maes, 1996.

1987, 40)[4]. The central idea of French planning was that planning made it possible to avoid chance (cf. Massé, 1965). The issuing of guidelines for next year's budget, during the second quarter of the preceding year, which were moreover situated in a medium term perspective, certainly bore the imprint of the French planning tradition.

Among the German (social market) economists two tendencies can be distinguished: one more emphasising the market and "Ordnungspolitik" (policy of safeguarding the economic order, i.e. sound monetary and budgetary policy, competition policy, ...), while the other, more linked to the trade unions, emphasised the social dialogue.

There was also a quite important interaction between the Commission and the OECD (formerly OEEC): Marjolin had been the first secretary-general of the OEEC, from 1948 to 1955, and several other EC officials had worked at the OECD. Moreover, many officials, both of the Commission and the Member States, would assist at OECD meetings. The OECD was very important for the transmission of Anglo-Saxon economic ideas, especially before the accession of the United Kingdom in 1973.

Table 5.2 - A simplified presentation of Directorate-General II (Economic and Financial Affairs)[1]

Director-general	U. Mosca
Economic advisors	M. Wegner, P. Buffet, C.F. Cavanagh, M. Fratianni, A. E. Smith
Directorate A	"Economy of the Member States and Business Cycles", M. Emerson
Directorate B	"Economic Structures and Development", J. C. Morel
Directorate C	"Monetary Matters I", F. Boyer de la Giroday
Directorate D	"Monetary Matters II", ...[2]
Directorate E	"Budgetary Matters", P. Van den Bempt

[1] Situation as of January 1979. With the reform of March 1980 the monetary directorates would be merged, the budgetary directorate would be suppressed and a new directorate "Macro-economic Research and Policy", with M. Emerson as director, would be created.

[2] Open position.

---

[4]   In the 1960s (indicative) planning was very popular in several European countries. An example is also the Netherlands, where Tinbergen was the first director of the planning office.

The director-general of DG II has typically been an Italian. In 1979 Tommaso Padoa-Schioppa became director-general. He was not only a good administrator but also a brilliant economist. People describe him as combining a German rigor with Italian imagination and a profound economic culture, including mainstream Anglo-Saxon economics. He was then quite young (around 40), dynamic and rather ambitious[5]. One of his main aims, at DG II, was to reinforce the "analytical level" of the directorate general.

During Padoa-Schioppa's director-generalship, there was a profound reorganisation of DG II. Before this reform the directorates were "Economy of the Member States and Business Cycles" (the A Directorate), "Economic Structures and Development" (B), "Monetary Matters I and II" (C and D) and "Budgetary Matters" (E). The Annual Economic Report was mainly written in Directorate A "Economy of the Member States and Business Cycles", while the other directorates would supply contributions from their areas.

In March 1980 DG II was restructured. The main change was the creation of a new directorate called "Macroeconomic Research and Policy", with Michael Emerson as a director, and the abolition of the budgetary directorate. The creation of the new "Macro" directorate, which became responsible for the annual report, reflected a double aim. The "methodological" purpose was to pursue more academic-oriented research, as clearly reflected in the inclusion of the word "Research" in the name of the new directorate. Another indication was the creation of an econometric division in this new directorate[6]. The other purpose was to focus on macroeconomic policy for the European economy as a whole, instead of national economies. This reflected the idea that the Commission could have more influence on economic policies in the Member States if it could highlight the Community dimension of a certain national policy stance. This was mainly done in a newly created division, called "Concerted Action". Another motivation of the reform, of a completely different nature, was that DG II economists were tired of writing "tedious" national chapters and were looking for something intellectually more exciting. The abolition of the

---

5 Padoa-Schioppa had been for many years at the research department of the Banca d' Italia, one of the top policy-oriented research institutes in Europe, with strong connections with leading American and British universities (cf. Porta, 1996, 180). Padoa-Schioppa had been a student and, later, a visiting scholar at the Massachusetts Institute of Technology. He was close to Franco Modigliano: they published articles together (e.g. Modigliani and Padoa-Schioppa, 1978) and he contributed to Modigliani's Festschrift (Padoa-Schioppa, 1987).

6 This is also an indication of the tendency of internationalisation and Americanisation of economics in the post-1945 period, cf. Coats, 1996 or Backhouse, 1996.

budgetary directorate reflected also a change in the strategy of monetary integration at the Commission. It can be considered as the definitive burial of the Werner concept of economic and monetary union, with two centres of decision making: one for monetary policy and one for budgetary policy. With the creation of the European Monetary System, in March 1979, the emphasis was clearly on the monetary side. Michael Emerson, who had been in the Jenkins cabinet, had been involved in this.

An important role in the conception of the Reports was also played by the cabinets, especially the cabinet of the member of the Commission responsible for DG II[7]. They determined to a large extent the general orientation of the Reports. Sometimes, they have requested quite substantial revisions of a Report.

Before its acceptance by the Commission, the Report was also to be submitted to the Economic Policy Committee (EPC)[8], composed of senior officials of the Member States (ministries and central banks) and the Commission. In general, the discussions in the EPC did not lead to important changes in the Report.

5.4   THE STRUCTURE OF THE ANNUAL ECONOMIC REPORT

The Annual Economic Report consisted of two parts. The first presented an overview of the actual economic situation, the economic policy problems encountered, the implementation of economic policy and the outlook for the next year. The structure of this first part was designed to deal with the actual economic situation and the policy problems encountered. So, in 1973, there was a special section on the implementation of the Council Resolutions on the Actions against inflation (CEC, 1973, 9). In 1975 the first section was devoted to the very deep recession of that year (CEC, 1975a, 2).

The second part of the Report contained the guidelines for economic policy for the next year. The first section comprised general guidelines discussing the policy objectives and priorities for the Community, possible conflicts, and general guidelines for the coordination of economic policy. In the 1970s the policy conception was rather Keynesian and the discussion was, to a large extent, focused on the issue of whether policy should combat slow economic growth or high inflation. In the next section the policy

---

[7]   Every member of the Commission is assisted by a small group of personal collaborators, known as "the cabinet" (from its French name).

[8]   Established in 1974 and comprising the former Short-term Economic Policy Committee (1960), the Budgetary and the Medium-term Economic Policy Committee (1964).

guidelines were elaborated on a country by country basis. The Report contained orientations how individual Member States could use the different instruments (fiscal policy, monetary policy, incomes policy) in order to reach internal and external equilibrium.

Table 5.3 - *Typical structure of the Annual Economic Report*

Introduction
I. Actual situation and perspectives
    A. Actual situation
        1. The international context
        2. The economic situation in the Community
    B. The economic policies implemented
    C. The outlook for the next year
II. The guidelines for economic policy
    A. General guidelines
    B. The guidelines for Member States
III. Conclusions

Starting in 1978, the Commission's Annual Economic Report was published in *European Economy*, a new publication of the Directorate-General for Economic and Financial Affairs. From that date on, the Report was also supplemented by an Annual Economic Review, which presented a more detailed study of the economic situation in the Community. The review was organised around the major areas of macroeconomic analysis, discussing economic cycles, the balance of payments, prices and costs, monetary and exchange rate policies, budgetary policies and employment. Another innovation of the 1978 Report was the presentation of forecasts for the main macroeconomic aggregates for the coming years[9]. These changes were linked to the appointment of a new director for the A Directorate, namely Michael Emerson. He wanted to strengthen the analytical content of the Report and to focus more on the European Community as a whole, and not on the different countries. With the Review, which was a publication of DG II and not of the Commission, the economists of DG II had more freedom to elaborate their ideas. The tendency to focus on the macroeconomy of the European Community would be confirmed in 1980

---

[9] In some earlier reports forecasts and estimates for certain macroeconomic aggregates, especially real GDP growth, were sometimes mentioned in the text.

with the creation of the new Directorate "Macroeconomic Research and Policy".

5.5   A KEYNESIAN POLICY CONCEPTION IN THE FIRST REPORTS

According to the Council Decision on the Strengthening of the Coordination of Short-term Economic Policies, the Annual Report had an important role to play in the coordination of budgetary policies in the European Community (cf. infra). The main elements of this Council Decision were:

-   the Council will hold three meetings yearly to examine the economic situation, on the basis of documentation and proposals of the Commission (article 1);
-   during the second examination (during the second quarter), the Council will lay down appropriate guidelines for the main elements of the preliminary economic budgets (article 3);
-   the third examination is in the autumn. The Council will then, acting on a proposal from the Commission and after consulting the European Parliament and the Economic and Social Committee, adopt an Annual Report on the economic situation in the Community and shall establish the guidelines to be followed by each Member State in its economic policy for the following year[10] (article 4);
-   as soon as this Annual Report has been adopted by the Council, Governments shall bring it to the attention of their national parliaments so that it can be taken into account during the debate on the budget (article 5).

In the Council Decision, the main instrument mentioned was budgetary policy. The Decision specified that quantitative guidelines for the draft public budgets for the following year should be fixed before they were finally adopted (article 3). They should include the evolution of government expenditures, taxes and the budget deficit (or surplus) and its financing.

This emphasis on budgetary policy was in line with the Keynesian economic orthodoxy of the time. Very influential in policy circles was the "Heller Report", which defined the role of fiscal policy as, "not to balance the

---

[10] As in this paper, as a general rule, the Commission proposal of the Annual Economic Report is used, reference will be made to the Annual Economic Reports as documents of the Commission of the European Communities (CEC).

budget of the public sector, but to balance the economy as a whole" (OECD, 1968, 15). Monetary factors were not considered to be of great importance. Leijonhufvud (1969, 13) described this period, especially the mid 1940s and extending into the 1950s and 1960s, as the Keynesian Revolution's "Anti-Monetary Terror" (see also Maes, 1986).

In this context, with the focus on economic policy, Coddington's view, that the distinctive trait of Keynesianism is an "utilitarian view" of the public finances, seems the most appropriate. A prerequisite for taking such a utilitarian perspective of the public finances is that there must be a systematic, reliable connection between fiscal policy and effective demand in the economy, so typical for hydraulic Keynesianism (cf. Coddington, 1983). According to the OECD: "fiscal policy has become the most important instrument for managing the level and composition of demand" (OECD, 1968, 14). In line with these developments, Raymond Barre created a Directorate for "Budgetary Matters" at the Commission at the end of the 1960s.

Fiscal policy can, however, only determine nominal demand. In order that fiscal policy can influence the level of real activity a stable and reliable relationship between prices and output is necessary. This was found in the Phillips curve, showing a negative relationship between changes in prices and unemployment (cf. Phillips, 1958).

According to the (simplified) Keynesian framework, which permeated the Annual Economic Reports of the Commission in the 1970s, the main task of the policy-makers was to determine the preferred trade-off between unemployment and inflation. Demand management, especially budgetary policy, would then be used to reach the preferred trade-off.

The first Reports were also characterised by a business cycle perspective. Economic policy was explicitly described as "conjunctural policy" (e.g. CEC, 1973, 9). One of the main aims of macroeconomic policy was to stabilise the business cycle. This was in line with the general development of Keynesian economics, which, after the elaboration of the principle of effective demand had turned to the analysis of business cycles (cf. Hansen, 1951 or Hicks, 1950).

The first phase of economic policy-making is a diagnosis of the economic situation. So, the first part of the Report was dedicated to an analysis of the economic situation. In the Reports of 1972, 1973 and 1974, with prices more and more increasing, inflation was identified as the main economic problem to be tackled.

To combat inflation, different measures were proposed. However, one of the main messages of the Reports was that cutting inflation was not just a technical problem, but that a social consensus was necessary : "Inflation will not be controlled by technical measures without a collective effort to search for a greater economic and social coherence" (CEC, 1972, 8)[11].

On the technical side different policy options were proposed :

- regulation of demand (fine-tuning), by budgetary and monetary policy, so that bottlenecks can be avoided (CEC, 1972, 8);
- the strengthening of productive capacities. The objective here was to "remedy regional disequilibria" (CEC, 1972, 6)[12];
- a direct price policy. While admitting that this does not tackle the fundamental causes of inflation, direct action is considered useful (CEC, 1973, 12)[13].

One of the fundamental tasks of the Annual Economic Reports was also to contribute to a better coordination of economic policy among the Member States. The steering of the economy had then to be differentiated according to the economic situation in the Member States. One of the fundamental aims here was a greater convergence, in order to contribute to monetary integration in the Community.

In the first Reports no precise quantitative targets for economic policy were specified: the main problem was put in focus and proposals for policy were formulated. Guidelines for individual countries were adjusted according to the concrete situation of each country.

In 1973, W. Haferkampf, a German trade unionist, became the commissioner responsible for DGII. His main objective was to introduce, at the European level, the "social dialogue", which had worked so well in Germany. It led to the June 1976 "Tripartite Conference on Employment and Stability in the Community", with the participation of the Governments of the Member States, representatives of unions and employers' organisations and the Commission. The 1976 Report presented more concrete medium-term targets, reminiscent of the golden sixties, which were formulated at this conference (CEC, 1976, 9):

---

[11] See also CEC, 1972, 32, where also a just repartition of efforts and sacrifices is demanded, or CEC, 1973, 24, where the necessity of the active cooperation of all groups is emphasised.

[12] Regional policy became more prominent with the Paris summit of 1972, where it was decided to create the European Regional Development Fund. So it is not surprising to find references to regional matters in Community policy documents at this time.

[13] Also contributions of the Common Agricultural Policy in the actions against inflation are mentioned (CEC, 1973, 12).

- the simultaneous restoration of full employment and price stability as a matter of priority;
- an annual rate of real growth of the domestic product of the Community averaging around 5% in the period from 1976 to 1980;
- full employment by 1980;
- the gradual reduction in all member states of the annual rate of inflation to between 4% and 5% by 1980.

The Commission was also very well aware that member states could experience a conflict between the need to reduce inflation and the balance-of-payments deficit, and the objectives of economic recovery and employment. A differentiation of policy among countries was therefore necessary:

> The overall approach to the Community economy in 1977 must be to ensure that no obstacle is put in the way of the expansion in domestic demand, in those Member States where there are no external economic constraints and where a further slowdown in price increases is likely ... In those Member States faced with high underlying rates of inflation, sizeable trade deficits, and the threat of a vicious circle of monetary depreciation and rising prices, economic policy must be used to impose some constraints on consumer demand and to make the most of the stimuli provided by export demand (CEC, 1976, 10).

However, as compared with the ambitions of the Council Decision on the Strengthening of the Coordination, the influence of the Annual Economic Reports on the economic policies of the member states has been very limited. Countries gave priority to their own national economic objectives. This was especially clear after the 1973 oil crisis. This crisis was interpreted as mainly an inflationary shock in Germany, which then followed more restrictive policies, and as a deflationary shock in France, pursuing more expansionary policies. This led to an upsurge in the inflation differential between the two countries and obliged the French franc to leave the snake. The situation was aptly summarised in the Marjolin Report: "if there has been any movement it has been backward" (CEC, 1975b, 1).

In their work for the Delors Committee, Baer and Padoa-Schioppa (1989) argued that "insufficient constraints on national policies"was one of the main intrinsic weaknesses of the Werner Report: "These guidelines had the character of recommendations and there was no provision to ensure their observance. Such an approach could work only as long as there was a sufficiently strong policy consensus and willingness to cooperate. However, once that consensus began to weaken, more binding constraints on national policy would have become necessary" (Baer and Padoa-Schioppa, 1989, 57).

Figure 5.2 - Inflation in Germany and France in the 1960s and 1970s

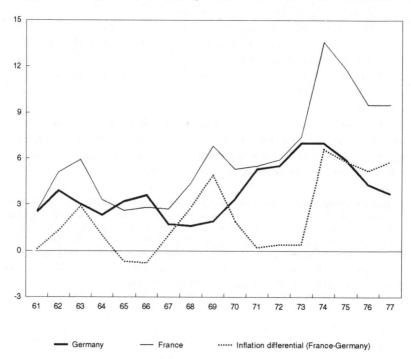

Germany   —— France   ····· Inflation differential (France-Germany)

Source: Eurostat databases - Newcronos.

5.6   CHANGES IN THE CONCEPTION OF MONETARY POLICY

The "Monetarist Counter-Revolution" questioned the Keynesian framework. One can distinguish three stages in the academic controversies. In the first stage discussions centred around the determination of nominal demand, monetarists emphasising the money supply, and not budgetary policy, as the main determinant of effective demand (Friedman, 1956). In a second stage the attention shifted towards the functioning of the labour market with the monetarists attacking the Phillips-curve (Friedman, 1968). In the third phase the formation of expectations became the focal point, when the monetarists advanced the "rational expectations hypothesis", implying that a change in policy can alter the behaviour of the economic agents (Lucas, 1976).

In Europe, the "Konstanz Seminars" played an important role in the spread of monetarism, also in the transmission of monetarist ideas to policy makers. The first one was organised by Karl Brunner in June 1970. Among the participants were: H. Schlesinger of the Bundesbank[14], R. Masera of the Banca d'Italia and M. Fratianni, an economic advisor at DG II in the second half of the 1970s[15] (cf. Neumann, 1972, 30).

In the early 1970s the conception of monetary policy in the Annual Economic Reports of the Commission was rather open-ended. Sometimes even the name "credit policy" was used (CEC, 1972, 7). Monetary policy concerned interest rates, the money supply and credit measures, but a coherent view was absent.

Gradually, however, a new policy conception emerged, quite close to the concept of the German Bundesbank, wherein monetary policy is geared principally against inflation and inflationary expectations. While, after the break-down of the Bretton-Woods system, smaller countries continued with exchange rate pegs, bigger countries started using the money supply as an intermediate target of monetary policy[16]. The Bundesbank set its first money supply target in December 1974, for the year 1975. The 1976 Report proposed the prior notification by the Member States of their money supply targets. It also proposed that the Member States should use common criteria for the expansion of the money supply in 1977: "a real rate of growth ... that would allow a more satisfactory utilization of capacity; a rate of price increase that would allow the rate of inflation to be gradually reduced to ... 4% to 5% by 1980" (CEC, 1976, 10).

So the Commission moved towards a framework in which monetary factors played a more important role. However, the Commission could be critical of the policy pursued in Germany. So contained the 1978 Report a quite specific recommendation for the money supply target of the German central bank:

> In the area of monetary policy, it would be desirable for the Bundesbank to bear in mind the need to support policy for growth and stability when fixing its monetary objective for 1979 (CEC, 1978a, 14).

---

[14] Schlesinger became a regular participant at the Konstanz seminar.

[15] Since the mid 1970s, DG II would employ a few "economic advisors", academics or senior officials from the Member States, e.g. M. Fratianni, A. Steinherr, F. Papadia, who would report directly to the Director-General. It would be another channel through which new ideas, from academia or the Member States, would be introduced in the Commission.

[16] For an analysis of the policy dilemma which the Bundesbank faced at the end of the Bretton-Woods system, cf. Emminger, 1977.

5.7   FROM CONCERTED ACTION TO SUPPLY SIDE ECONOMICS

The synthetical and compromise nature of the policy documents, came clearly to the foreground in the 1977 Report, which combined quite monetarist prescriptions for monetary policy with a very Keynesian approach towards budgetary policy. The Report added also to the pressures on German policy-makers to follow a more expansionary policy.

The 1977 Report noted a disappointing growth performance. It attributed this to the necessary restrictive monetary and budgetary policy in the countries with a deficit on the balance of payments and the absence of a more expansionary policy in the "strong currency" countries. Especially Germany was mentioned, where "public-sector deficits have been scaled down at a rate which can be regarded as very fast, given current needs" (CEC, 1977, 3). The Report argued for a "normative growth scenario" (CEC, 1977, 5). This, very Keynesian, idea was that the European economy required a demand injection of about 1% of GDP. The policy mix which the Report proposed emphasised a more expansionary budgetary policy, while monetary policy should be geared towards money growth and price targets, while wage claims should be properly related to productivity gains. Also certain structural measures were deemed necessary.

The 1978 Report conveyed a very different atmosphere. It saluted the improved economic perspectives for 1979, partly due to the "Concerted action", after the European Summit in Bremen and the G7 Summit in Bonn in July (CEC, 1978a, 11). It was, possibly, the first and last action of coordinated Keynesian demand expansion.

However, the euphoria did not last very long. The second oil shock, with its stagflationary effects, dominated the 1979 Annual Economic Report. A strategy in two successive phases was proposed to confront this shock:

> The first and immediate need, given that the oil price rise be fully communicated to the consumer, is to prevent a secondary increase in the rate of inflation. Thus should be created a certain room for manoeuvre for a second phase of policy. Control, over monetary aggregates should be kept steadily to present strict policies, but it may become possible and desirable, as inflation expectations are abated, to move in the course of 1980 to more supportive budgetary policy, if also investment and consumption were weaker than expected (CEC, 1979, 11).

The 1980 Report (CEC, 1980a) marked a break in comparison with the preceding studies. Most important was certainly the shift in economic policy orientation, away from active demand management policies and towards a more medium-term orientation, emphasising structural, supply-side oriented, policies. There was also an increase in the analytical level of the Report, reflecting the aims of Padoa-Schioppa and Emerson and the restructuring of DG II.

The new policy orientation was clearly set out in the Introduction of the Report: "While in the past economic policy was often perceived as a problem of demand management, in a world based on the assumption of unlimited supply of energy and raw materials, the importance and critical value of supply constraints and structural adjustment problems are now evident" (CEC, 1980a, 9). The break with the past, and the medium-term orientation of economic policy, was further illustrated and elaborated:

> The *concerted response* to the present general economic situation should be based on the right strategic mix of demand and supply policies and notably the right balance in their application to short- and medium-term problems. Short-term adjustments should be more moderate than at times in the last decade, and a heavier weight has to be given to reducing medium-term inflationary expectations and improving supply conditions in the economy. This in turn means a steadier management of monetary aggregates, exchange rates and budget balances than in earlier economic cycles, and giving a strong twist to the numerous policy variables within the overall structure of public expenditure, taxation and regulation in order to strengthen economic potential (CEC, 1980a, 13, original italics).

Behind the new policy orientation was a new view of the functioning of the economy, stressing the limits of demand management. This new view was in first instance based on an analysis of the failure of the concerted action of the Bonn summit. This failure was at the origin of an important discussion on the efficiency and possibilities of economic policy, especially budgetary policy[17].

The authors of the Report were also strongly influenced by two debates which were going on in the academic world. The first one concerned the Lucas critique and rational expectations. Commission economists became aware that economic agents were not responding in a mechanical or "Pavlovian" way to changes in economic policy. Policy-makers had to take into account that markets would anticipate policy measures. This further undermined the belief in the possibility of fine-tuning the economy and led to a greater emphasis on medium-term policies. The other influence reflected the McKinnon argument that monetary policy could only influence the nominal growth rate of GDP. Moreover, monetary policy was, in the long run, not independent of budgetary policy, via the financing of public deficits.

---

[17] This was not only a topic of discussion at the Commission, but also at other (international) institutions, especially the OECD.

The only way then to improve the trade-off between inflation and growth was to take measures on the supply side of the economy.

A reflection of these debates can be found in the last chapter of the Review (Perspectives and policy options), which offered a thorough analysis of the limits of demand management policy.   Two elements were emphasised: the external constraint and time lags.

The situation of the balance of payments, as also pointed out in McKinnon (1976), limits the possibilities of an expansionary policy response to combat the recession. This is so also when the recession has its origin in a restrictive fiscal and monetary policy stance in non EC countries, or a loss of market shares of the Community (CEC, 1980b, 135).

Other problems were related to the time profile of fiscal policy measures. It is only possible to have a clear view on the evolution of the economy with a time lag of some months or sometimes even quarters. Moreover, the preparation and implementation of measures takes time, leading to a risk of a pro-cyclical policy: "As perfect forecasts are impossible, will a discretionary budgetary policy only have an impact when the economy is out of the recession, and will so tend to reinforce rather than smooth the business cycle" (CEC, 1980b, 136).

Difficulties with forecasting were also a problem for the Commission itself. So were the forecasts of the Commission Services for 1980, made in the 1979 Report, rather off the mark. Real GDP grew with 0.1% in 1980 compared with a forecast of 0.6%. Inflation amounted to 11.8%, against a forecast of 9%, and the balance of payments deficit of the EC increased to 1.1%, whereas a deficit of 0.3% was foreseen.

Given the limits of a policy of fine-tuning, a medium-term orientation of budgetary and monetary policy was more appropriate.   Also, as the possibilities of macroeconomic policy were limited, the emphasis had to be on a more microeconomic oriented policy, with measures to improve the functioning of the different markets. Something which was in line with supply-side economics, which was gaining ground at that time (Feldstein, 1986).

On can also discern a more quantitative analysis of several issues. For example the detailed analysis of the influence of the two oil shocks on the terms of trade of the Community (CEC, 1980b, 38), the use of measures of capacity utilization in manufacturing in the analysis of the business cycle (CEC, 1980b, 45) and the introduction of government budget balances at constant activity (CEC, 1980b, 70). Compared to 1979, the number of pages of the Report increased from 13 to 24 and those of the Review from 80 to 108.

Table 5.4 - Main macroeconomic data

		Real GDP			Inflation			Current Account Balance of Payments			Government Deficit		
		Forecast	Estimation	Realisation	Forecast	Estimation	Realisation	Forecast	Estimation	Realisation	Forecast	Estimation	Realisation
EC9	1970			4.7			4.9			0.7			0.1
	1971			3.1			6.5			0.9			-0.6
	1972			3.9			6.3			1.0			-1.6
	1973		6.0	5.8			8.6			0.3			-1.1
	1974	4.5	2.7	1.7		12.4	13.6			-0.7			-2.0
	1975	3.5	-2.4	-1.1		12.5	12.5		0.1	0.3			-5.2
	1976	3.3	4.8	4.8	9.6	10.3	10.2	-0.1		-0.3			-3.7
	1977	4.0	2.5	2.8		9.5	9.2			0.3			-3.0
EC10	1978	3.5	2.6	3.2	8.3	6.9	7.1	0.5	0.5	1.0		-4.1	-3.7
	1979	3.5	3.1	3.8	7.0	8.9	8.9	0.5	-0.2	0.0	-4.5	-4.0	-3.5
	1980	2.0	1.3	1.2	9.0	12.0	11.8	-0.3	-1.5	-1.1	-3.9	-3.5	-3.6
	1981	0.6	-0.5	0.1	9.7	11.6	11.1	-1.2	-1.2	-0.4	-3.9	-4.4	-5.3
	1982	2.0	0.3	0.8	11.2	10.5	9.8	-0.9	-0.7	-0.4	-4.2	-5.0	-5.2
	1983	1.1	0.5	1.7	6.6	6.3	7.4	-0.4	-0.2	0.3	-4.9	-5.4	-5.0
	1984	1.5	2.2	2.5	5.6	5.1	6.2	0.0	0.0	0.3	-4.7	-5.3	-5.0
	1985	2.3			4.2			0.4			-4.8		
Average[1]		2.7	1.6	2.0	8.4	9.0	9.1	-0.4	-0.6	-0.2	-4.4	-4.6	-4.6

[1] Average of the years for which forecasts (made the preceding year) and estimations (made during the current year) are available

As for the reasons for these shifts in the Report, it is clear that the failure of the coordinated action of the Bonn summit had a traumatic effect on the Commission. It contributed to a re-examination of the limits and possibilities of economic policy.

In the 1981 Report (CEC, 1981a) and Review (CEC, 1981b) the supply-side approach to economic policy continued, even if the tone was less explicit than in 1980. Typical of this change in tone was the absence of an Introduction to the Report, where in 1980 so clearly the new approach was set out. However, the analysis of the supply side of the economy was elaborated with a new chapter in the Review: "Some structural properties of subsidies, investment incentives and energy taxation".

The Report also emphasised the interrelationship between budgetary and monetary policy, developing a "crowding-out" analysis. This further illustrated the difficulties of using budgetary policy for fine-tuning the economy:

> The first particularity of the outlook for 1982 is the acute interrelationship between budget and monetary policy. The sensitivity of interest rates to budget-policy variables is almost certainly much stronger now than at any time in the past. A budget policy allowing the deficit to rise is likely now to be relatively heavily offset in its stimulative effects on economic activity by increasing interest rates; conversely budget-policy action to reduce deficits is likely to be considerably offset in its contractionary effects by falling interest rates (CEC, 1981a, 12).

5.8   CONCLUSION

During the 1970s the economic paradigms behind the Annual Economic Reports of the European Commission changed quite dramatically. The changes reflected both the evolution of "academic" economics and factors which were more specific for policy institutions and for the European Commission itself.

One can observe an initial dominance of Keynesian economics, followed by a rise of monetarism and supply side economics. However, the Commission Reports, quite typical for an international policy institution, always presented a more synthetical view, combining elements of the different strands of thought, while the timing of the changes was related to concrete experiences in the policy world. From a methodological point of view, more sophisticated and econometric methods of analysis were increasingly used. Specific for the Commission is, moreover, the shift towards the analysis of the European economy as a whole, contrasting with the earlier focus on the national economies.

These shifts in paradigms were naturally complex processes. Policy formulation at the European Commission was certainly influenced by the general shift in paradigms, both the more ideological shifts from Keynesianism towards monetarism and supply side economics, as the more methodological shift towards more quantitative methods of analysis. The Commission stimulated these kind of interactions with the outside world, for instance through the presence of academic economic advisors and advisory councils. However, certain elements of the Reports are quite specific for the economic policy world and the Commission in particular. So is the greater emphasis on the European economy as a whole a reflection of both the greater degree of European integration and the aim of the Commission to push forward the integration process. The closeness to policy also plays a role in the timing of certain shifts in paradigms. So gained monetarism in importance with the breakdown of the Bretton-Woods system, when a new anchor for monetary policy was needed. The medium-term orientation of policy, with more emphasis on the supply side and structural adjustment, came to the forefront after the failure of the, very Keynesian, Concerted Action Plan of 1978. Changes in top personnel positions were also important, like the nomination of Padoa-Schioppa as director-general in 1979, who stimulated the use of more analytical methods of economic research.

REFERENCES

Backhouse, R. (1996), The Changing Character of British Economics, in Coats A.W. (ed.), The Post-1945 Internationalisation of Economics, *History of Political Economy*, Annual Supplement, 33-60.

Baer, G. and T. Padoa-Schioppa (1988), The Werner Report Revisited, in *Report on Economic and Monetary Union*, Office for Official Publications of the EC, April 1989, pp. 53-60.

CEC (1971), Rapport Annuel Sur la Situation Economique de la Communauté, *Journal Officiel*, no. L 253, 16 novembre 1971, 1-22.

CEC (1972), Rapport Annuel sur la Situation Economique de la Communauté, *Journal Officiel*, no C 133, 23 décembre 1972, 1-11.

CEC (1973), Rapport Annuel sur la Situation Economique de la Communauté, COM(73)1560final.

CEC (1974), Rapport Annuel sur la Situation Economique de la Communauté, SEC(74)3355final.

CEC (1975a), Annual Report on the Economic Situation in the Community, *Official Journal*, no. C 297, 29 December 1975, 1-20.

CEC (1975b), *Report of the Study Group "Economic and Monetary Union*, Marjolin Report, March.

CEC (1976), Annual Report on the Economic Situation in the Community, *Official Journal*, no. L 358, 29 December 1976, 2-27.

CEC (1977), Annual Report on the Economic Situation in the Community, *Official Journal*, no. L 323, 19 December 1977, 2-28.

CEC (1978a), Annual Report on the Economic Situation in the Community, *European Economy*, No 1, November 1978, 1-16.

CEC (1978b), Annual Economic Review, *European Economy*, No. 1, November 1978, 17-84.

CEC (1979a), Annual Economic Report, *European Economy*, No. 4, November 1979, 5-18.

CEC (1979b), Annual Economic Review, *European Economy*, No. 4, November 1979, 19-98.

CEC (1980a), Annual Economic Report, *European Economy*, No. 7, November 1980, 5-29.

CEC (1980b), Annual Economic Review, *European Economy*, No. 7, November 1980, 31-140.

CEC (1981a), Annual Economic Report, *European Economy*, No. 10, November 1981, 5-30.

CEC (1981b), Annual Economic Review, *European Economy*, No. 10, November 1981, 31-146

Coats, A.W. (1996), Conclusion, Coats A.W., (ed.), The Post-1945 Internationalisation of Economics, *History of Political Economy*, Annual Supplement, 395-400.

Coddington, A. (1983), *Keynesian Economics, The Search for First Principles*, London: Allen & Unwin.

Conseil (1971), Décision du Conseil du 22 mars 1971 relative au renforcement de la coordination des politiques économiques à court terme des Etats membres de la Communauté économique européenne, *Journal Officiel*, No. L 73, 27.3.71, 12-13.

Council-Commission of the European Communities (1970), *Report to the Council and the Commission on the Realisation by Stages of Economic and Monetary Union in the Community*, Werner Report, Luxemburg, October.

Dobson, W. (1991), *Economic Policy Coordination: Requiem or Prologue?*, Washington: Institute for International Economics.

Emminger, O. (1977), *The D-Mark in the Conflict Between Internal and External Equilibrium 1948-75*, Princeton Essay in International Finance, No. 122, June.

Feldstein, M. (1986), Supply Side Economics: Old Truths and New Claims, *American Economic Review*, Vol. 76, No. 2, 26-30.

Friedman, M. (1956), The Quantity Theory of Money: a Restatement, in Clower A.W., (ed.), *Monetary Theory*, Harmondsworth: Penguin, 1973, pp 94-111.

Friedman, M. (1968), The Role of Monetary Policy, *American Economic Review*, Vol. LVIII, March, 1-17.

Hall, P. (1989), Conclusion: The Politics of Keynesian Ideas, in Hall P., (ed.), *The Political Power of Economic Ideas: Keynesianism Across Nations*, Princeton: Princeton University Press, pp. 361-391.

Hansen, A. (1951), *Business Cycles and National Income*, New-York: W.W. Norton.

Hicks, J. R. (1950), *A Contribution of the Theory of the Trade Cycle*, Oxford: Clarendon Press.

Leijonhufvud, A. (1968), *On Keynesian Economic and Economics of Keynes*, Oxford: O.U.P.

Lucas, R. (1976), Economic Policy Evaluation: A Critique, *Journal of Monetary Economics*, 104-129.

Ludlow, P. (1982), *The Making of the European Monetary System*, London: Butterworth.

Maes, I. (1986), Did The Keynesian Revolution Retard the Development of Portfolio Theory?, *Banca Nazionale del Lavoro*, no. 159, Dec., 407-21.

Maes, I. (1996), The Development of Economic Thought at the European Community Institutions, in Coats A.W., (ed.), The Post-1945 Internationalisation of Economics, *History of Political Economy*, Annual Supplement, 245-276.

Maes, I. (2000), Macroeconomic Policymaking at the European Commission in the First Half of the 1980s,. in R. Backhouse and A. Salanti, (eds.), *Macroeconomics and the Real World. Volume 2: Keynesian Economics, Unemployment and Policy*, Oxford: O.U.P., pp. 251-269.

Marjolin, R. (1986), *Le Travail d'une Vie. Mémoires 1911-1986*, Paris: Robert Laffont.

Massé, P. (1965), *Le Plan ou l'Anti-hasard*, Paris: Gallimard.

McKinnon, R. (1976), The Limited Role of Fiscal Policy in an Open Economy, *Banca Nazionale del Lavoro*, no. 117, June, 95-117.

Modigliani, F. and T. Padoa-Schioppa (1978), *The Management of an Economy with "100% Plus" Wage Indexation*, Princeton Essays in International Finance, no. 130, Dec.

Mortensen, J. (1990), *Federalism vs Co-ordination*, Brussels: CEPS.

Neumann, M. (1972), Konstanzer Seminar on Monetary Theory and Monetary Policy, *Kredit und Kapital*, Beihefte, 10-30.

OECD (1968), *Fiscal Policy for a Balanced Economy*, Paris, December.

Padoa-Schioppa, T. (1987), Reshaping Monetary Policy, in Dornbusch R. et al., (eds.), *Macroeconomics and Finance. Essays in Honor of Franco Modigliani*, Cambridge: MIT Press, pp. 265-285.

Phillips, A.W. (1958), Unemployment and Wage Rates, in Ball R.J. and Doyle P. (eds.), *Inflation*, Harmondsworth: Penguin, 1970, pp. 277-297.

Porta, P. L. (1996), Italian Economics through the Postwar Years, Coats A.W., (ed.), The Post-1945 Internationalisation of Economics, *History of Political Economy*, Annual Supplement, 165-183.

Rosanvallon, P. (1987), Histoire des Idées Keynésiennes en France, *Revue Française de l'Economie*, Vol. 4, No. 2, 22-56.

Tsoukalis, L. (1977), *The Politics and Economics of European Monetary Integration*, London: Allen & Unwin.

Wegner, M. (1985), External Adjustment in a World of Floating: Different National Experiences in Europe, in Tsoukalis L., (ed.), *The Political Economy of International Money*, London: Royal Institute of International Affairs, pp. 103-135.

Wegner, M. (1989), The European Economic Community, in Pechman J., (ed.), *The Role of the Economist in Government*, New-York: N.Y.U. Press, pp. 279-299.

Annex 5.1 - Chronology

1969   December   Hague Summit: monetary union becomes an objective of the European Community

1970   October   Werner Report

1971   March   Council Decision on the Strengthening of Short-term Economic Policy Coordination
        August   Nixon announces the suspension of the dollar into gold
        December   Smithsonian agreement (new central rates and wider fluctuation margins)

1972   April   EEC narrows margins of fluctuation to 2.25% (EEC "Snake" in Smithsonian "tunnel")
        June   UK and Ireland leave EEC snake
        October   January 1974 is set as date for the second stage of EMU

1973   January   UK, Ireland and Denmark join the EC
        March   End of Bretton-Woods System (floating of EEC currencies against USD)
        Autumn   First oil price shock

1974   January   French franc drops out of EEC snake
        February   Council Decision on the attainment of a high degree of convergence of the economic policies of the Member States
        December   Bundesbank sets, for the first time, a money supply target (for 1975)

1975   July   French franc rejoins EEC snake

1976   March   French franc drops out of EEC snake

1978   June   G7 Bonn Summit (Concerted action plan)

1979   March   Creation of the European Monetary System
        October   Second oil price shock

6. Macroeconomic Thought at the European Commission in the First Half of the 1980s*

6.1 INTRODUCTION

In this paper an analysis is presented of macroeconomic thought at the European Commission, an institution which has become increasingly influential at shaping policy formulation at the European level.

A study of economic thought at a policy-making institution encounters certain specific problems, compared to the study of traditional academic economic texts. A crucial difference is that the economic theories and paradigms are less explicit, more hidden. Moreover, official documents involve many persons and, consequently, are more heterogeneous. So, any analysis of economic thought at a policy institution will involve a greater

* Reprinted from *Macroeconomics and the Real World. Volume 2: Keynesian Economics, Unemployment and Policy,* R. Backhouse and A. Salanti, (eds.), Oxford: Oxford University Press, pp. 251-268, with kind permission of Oxford University Press.

I would like to thank F. Abraham, R. Backhouse, A.P. Barten, A.W. Coats, S. Deroose, D. Dinan, M. Emerson, H. Famerée, M.M.G. Fase, M. Fratianni, H. Hagemann, D. Hausman, F. Ilzkovitz, J. Michielsen, T. Padoa-Schioppa, L. Pench, A. Salanti, A. Sapir, as well as the participants at the Bergamo conference on "Theory and Evidence in Macroeconomics", and at seminars at the University of Maastricht, the European Society for the History of Economic Thought (Valencia), the European Community Studies Association (Pittsburgh) and the Federal Reserve Bank of New York for useful comments and suggestions. The usual restrictions apply.

degree of "rational reconstruction" than more traditional analyses of economic thought.

This study concentrates on macroeconomic thought at the European Commission in the early 1980s, when unemployment became more and more the dominating economic issue in Europe. The paper starts with background sketches of the European Community in the early 1980s and policy-making instances at the European Commission. This is followed by an overview of the monitoring and forecasting of economic developments at the Commission, a crucial feature of life at a policy-making institution. Thereafter, the focus is on economic thought at the Commission, focusing on the Annual Economic Reports, the main macroeconomic policy document of the Commission. Particular attention will also be given to the debate on macroeconomic policy with the "Dornbusch Group", an academic advisory group of the Commission. A last section compares academic economics with economics at policy-making institutions, drawing on the experiences at the European Commission in the early 1980s.

6.2   THE EUROPEAN COMMUNITY IN THE EARLY 1980s

The early 1980s were a period of morosity at the European Commission: the European economy was in the doldrums and the integration progress was stalling.

Europe's economic performance in the early 1980s was rather disappointing: economic growth was low and unemployment was increasing strongly, while inflation was high and declined only stubbornly. Part of the reason for it was certainly the second oil shock of the autumn of 1979, which gave a stagflationary shock to Europe's economy. Moreover, the European performance contrasted markedly with the situation in the United States, where the recovery, from 1983 onwards, was very strong and unemployment started declining, something which several observers associated with Reagan's supply side economics. "Eurosclerosis" was the term used to characterise the economic situation in the Community (Giersch, 1987).

The European integration process was also in the doldrums. The issue which dominated the European debate in the first half of the 1980s was the British contribution to the European budget, famous with Mrs Thatcher's phrase "I want my money back". A solution would only be reached at the Fontainebleau summit of June 1984, clearing the way for the European Community to concentrate on integration furthering projects (Annex 6.1).

Figure 6.1 - Main economic indicators for the European Community and the United States

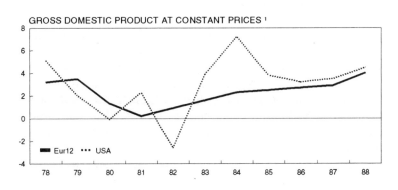

GROSS DOMESTIC PRODUCT AT CONSTANT PRICES [1]

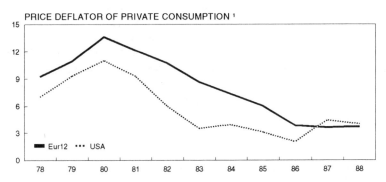

PRICE DEFLATOR OF PRIVATE CONSUMPTION [1]

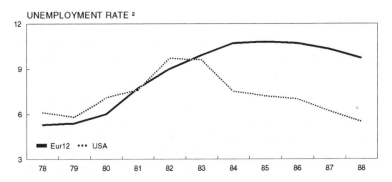

UNEMPLOYMENT RATE [2]

Source: *European Commission.*
   [1] *Annual percentage change.*
   [2] *Percentage of civilian labour force.*

The main impetus to the integration process came from the European Monetary System (EMS), which was founded in March 1979 (Ludlow, 1982). However, the first years of the EMS were very difficult: there was a lack of convergence of economic policies and performances, especially inflation, and there were several realignments. The development of the EMS was one of the main preoccupations of economic policymakers at the European Commission. Tensions in the EMS were exacerbated from May 1981 onwards, when Mitterrand was elected as French President and followed an isolated Keynesian policy strategy. This led to a loss of competitiveness of the French economy, capital outflows and speculative pressures against the French franc, leading to several realignments. With the change of policy orientation in France, towards more orthodox economic policies after the March 1983 realignment, the EMS became into more stable waters.

The sphere of morosity in the European Community was further reinforced by the rather lacklustre performance of the Thorn Commission (1981-1984), which did not take noticeable initiatives to further the European integration process. This would change dramatically in January 1985, with the Delors Commission, which developed several projects to reinvigorate the European economy and the integration process. Of special importance were the internal market project and the Cooperative Growth Strategy for more Employment.

6.3   POLICY-MAKING INSTANCES AT THE EUROPEAN COMMISSION

It can be useful to note that the term "commission" is used both for the College of the Commission, the body of commissioners, and for the services of the commission, the administration. Also, every member of the Commission disposes of a small group of collaborators, his so-called "cabinet", typical of the French administrative system.

It is the College of the Commission which is ultimately responsible for policy-making at the European Commission. However, macroeconomic policy-making was mainly at the level of the Member States and so the responsibilities of the Commission were rather limited. They concerned mainly the orientation and coordination of the national macroeconomic policies (Mortensen, 1990 and Wegner, 1989)[1] (see Annex 6.2).

Inside the Commission, it is mainly the president and the member with the responsibility for DG II (Economic and Financial Affairs, which can be considered as the macroeconomic research department of the Commission) who are most involved in macroeconomic policy-making. From 1981 to 1984, Gaston Thorn, a Luxemburger, was president and François-Xavier Ortoli, a Frenchman, was responsible for DG II. According to witnesses, they were both relatively easy-going people, who left the administration a lot of freedom. Ortoli was mostly interested in monetary matters. With the new commission in 1985, Jacques Delors, a Frenchman, took, besides the presidency, also the responsibility for monetary matters. Alois Pfeiffer, a German trade unionist, became responsible for DG II. The economic man in his cabinet, Ludwig Schubert, would play an important role in macroeconomic policy-making[2].

The director-generals of DG II have typically been Italians. From June 1979 to March 1983, Tommaso Padoa-Schioppa was Director-General of DG II. He was succeeded by Massimo Russo.

Padoa-Schioppa had a profound impact on DG II: according to witnesses, he was not only a skilful administrator, but also a brilliant economist and very well connected. People describe him as combining a German rigor with Italian imagination and a profound economic culture, including mainstream Anglo-Saxon economics. He was then quite young (around 40), dynamic and rather ambitious[3].

His main focus of attention was the reinforcement of the European Monetary System, which he considered as the "priority of the priorities". Another of his main preoccupations was the strengthening of the analytical level of DG II. An important element hereby was a reorganisation of DG II, in March 1980.

---

[1]　Over time, this coordination function of the Commission has increased in importance. So, with EMU, which started in January 1999, sovereignty in the field of monetary policy was transferred to the European Central Bank and the Commission's role in the coordination of macroeconomic policies was reinforced, especially with the Broad Economic Guidelines.

[2]　Schubert was influenced by Karl Schiller, the father of the *"Konzertierte Aktion"* (concerted action) in Germany.

[3]　Padoa-Schioppa had been at the research department of the Banca d'Italia, one of the leading policy oriented research institutes in Europe, with strong connections with prominent American and British universities, for many years (Porta, 1996, 180). Padoa-Schioppa had been a student and, later, a visiting scholar at the Massachusetts Institute of Technology. He was close to Franco Modigliani: they published together (e.g. Modigliani and Padoa-Schioppa, 1978) and he contributed to Modigliani's Festschrift (Padoa-Schioppa, 1987).

After this reorganisation, DG II consisted of four directorates:

- the A Directorate: National Economies, with P. Van Den Bempt (B) as director. The A Directorate was responsible for monitoring and analysing the economic situation on a "vertical" basis, country by country. It consisted of four divisions, three of them followed the different countries of the Community, the fourth the rest of the world;
- the B Directorate: Economic Structures and Community Policies, can be considered as a kind of "economic service", where the various policies of the Community (sectoral, industrial, competition ...) were followed and analysed;
- the C Directorate: Macroeconomic Research and Policy, with M. Emerson (UK) as director. This was a newly founded directorate, which reflected a double aim. The "methodological" purpose was to pursue more academic oriented research, as clearly indicated in the word "Research" in the name of the new directorate. The other purpose was to focus on macroeconomic policy for the European economy as a whole. This also reflected the idea that the Commission could have more influence on economic policies in the member states if it could highlight the Community dimension of a certain national policy stance. The director of the C directorate was usually the main author of the Annual Economic Report, the most important macroeconomic policy document of the Commission (*supra*).
  The directorate consisted of five units: concerted action (a newly created division, responsible for a "horizontal" analysis of the Community economy and for policy actions at the Community level); short-term forecasts (responsible for the coordination and consistency of the twice yearly forecasting exercises); business cycle surveys (responsible for the coordination and aggregation of business and consumer surveys, which were executed by different institutes in the Member States); medium-term forecasts; econometric models (a newly created division, the purpose was to give DG II more autonomy in econometric modelling, this group would later be merged with the unit for medium-term forecasts);
- the D directorate: Monetary Matters, with J.-P. Mingasson (F) as director. It consisted of four divisions, focusing on the EMS, the balance of payments situations, monetary policy in the different countries, and capital markets.

Also other reforms contributed to the strengthening of the intellectual and analytical capacities of DG II, like the organisation of seminars (both by

DG II economists and outsiders) and the reinvigoration of the group of advisers (economists, both academics and national policy-makers, who were on a temporary basis at the Commission). Padoa-Schioppa also launched a new series of publications, the "Economic Papers" (which were the sole responsibility of the author). This caused quite a stir in the Commission, as officials publishing in their own name in an official publication of the European Commission was a completely new phenomenon for the Commission.

Of particular importance was certainly the collaboration with the Centre for European Policy Studies (CEPS), located in Brussels, especially with the foundation (and funding by DG II, cf. Ludlow, 1983, 2) of the CEPS Macroeconomic Policy Group. This Group was also known as the Dornbusch Group, after its first Chairman.

DG II economists would have meetings with the members of the CEPS group, in which the macroeconomic situation and the policy challenges for the European Community would be discussed. The CEPS economists would offer their comments on policy documents of the Commission, especially the Annual Economic Report, and they would also, every year, write their own paper. Initially, the Dornbusch Group was set up as an internal advice group. Later, under the pushing of the academics, it was decided to publish the papers of the Dornbusch Group, both as a CEPS paper and as an "Economic Paper" of the Commission.

This triangular collaboration (Dornbusch Group, Commission, CEPS) offered DG II several advantages: it strengthened the analytical and intellectual level of the economic policy debate, it allowed the Commission to penetrate into the world of the "economic intelligentsia", and it exposed the services of DG II to emulation and contradiction. Moreover, it was also a way to let top American academics get to know the European Community and to analyse Europe's economic problems.

The "Economic Papers" of the Dornbusch Group would cause quite some turmoil, especially in the cabinets but also among the Commissioners. Several people asked the question why the Commission should pay people "who make our life difficult". Senior DG II officials, like Padoa-Schioppa and Emerson, defended the principle of publishing the work of the Dornbusch Group. They argued that the cooperation with the Dornbusch Group was very important for DG II, both for improving its analytical capacity and for increasing its influence in the academic world. Consequently, one had to "accept the rules of the game" and let the Dornbusch Group publish the results of its research. They were herein supported by Ortoli, the Member of the Commission responsible for DG II.

6.4   THE MONITORING AND FORECASTING OF ECONOMIC ACTIVITY AT THE COMMISSION

Policy decisions need to be based on a solid understanding, not only of how the economy works and its present state, but also of its future course. In practice, policy-makers are confronted with many time lags: good data about the economic situation become only available with delay, the decision-making process itself can take time, just like the implementation of policy, and it also takes time before policy measures have an effect on the economy. Thus policy-makers have no choice but to take decisions on the basis of estimates and forecasts of economic activity (Llewellyn et al., 1985, 73).

At the European Commission then, as at other policy-making institution, a lot of time was and is spent with monitoring and forecasting the economic situation. This was undoubtedly, as regards time and resources, a core activity of the A and C directorates, which were the main directorates involved in macroeconomic policy-making at the Commission.

At the core of this monitoring and forecasting activity were the forecasting rounds. These forecasting rounds were organised twice a year, in the spring (April-May) and the autumn (September-October) (CEC, 1984c, 191). They concerned the main macroeconomic data: growth, inflation, unemployment, the government deficit, etc., with the national accounts at the centre of the forecasts. They covered the current and the following year.

These forecasts performed a basic role in macroeconomic policy-making at the Commission, as they delivered the data material on which the analysis of the economic situation and the policy recommendations of the Commission would be based[4]. For instance, the data in the Annual Economic Report, which was published in November, would be the estimates and forecasts of the autumn round.

Given this crucial importance of the forecasting activities, it seems appropriate to elaborate somewhat on its organisation, which was coordinated by the Short-term forecast unit in the C directorate:

- the forecasting round would start with a "position paper". This described the main events since the last forecasting round and the evolution of the economic situation. It also contained the basic assumptions regarding interest rates and exchange rates, oil and commodity prices, world trade and the evolution of economic activity

---

[4] One can contrast this with "academic" analysis, which is mostly based on existing data, and is so a kind of "historical" analysis, even if often of the recent past.

in the rest of the world. This position paper would be discussed in a general meeting by all the persons who were involved in the forecasts;
-   typical for the Commission, as an international institution, was a trade-consistency exercise, involving both trade-volume consistency (changes in countries' export volumes must have their counterpart in changes in partner countries' import volumes) and trade-price consistency (each country's import price has to have its counterpart in the export prices of the countries from whom it imports);
-   the country desks of the A Directorate would, on the basis of the assumptions in the position paper and all possible information about their economy, elaborate their forecasts. The national desks had a quite large degree of freedom about their methods of forecasting. In many cases a "judgmental" approach was followed;
-   there were also consultations with national experts (ministries, central banks and national research institutes). In a first round this would happen on a bilateral basis, with the desk officers visiting their nation's capitals. Towards the end of the round, there would be a general meeting, where DG II would present its forecasts to officials from the Member States.

This would all take place in several rounds, a long iterative process, wherein forecasts were continually revised and revised, until a final storage. One should also mention the general assumption of no changes in economic policy, which is typical for forecasting at the Commission, and for policy institutions in general.

These short-term forecasts would form a kind of benchmark against which the economic situation would be monitored in the periods between two forecasting rounds. In the monitoring (and forecasting) process, the Commission relied also on surveys, for which a special unit in the C Directorate was responsible. In fact, since 1961, the Commission coordinated business surveys in industry in the Community. Later, in 1970, consumer surveys were integrated in this programme (CEC, 1997, 203).

DG II would also make medium-term forecasts. Here, more use would be made of econometric models. In the early 1980s DG II invested heavily in an econometric model unit so as to be less dependent on outside experts and to acquire a greater degree of autonomy.

DG II had already some experience with econometric modelling. In the early 1980s DG II used two models: Eurolink and Comet. Eurolink was a system of econometric models, based on four existing national models: Sysifo for Germany, Metric for France, Prometeia for Italy and the Oxford model for the United Kingdom. There were quite some differences between these models. Sysifo was disaggregated into fifteen branches, Metric into eight and Prometeia and the Oxford model into three. They were linked together by DG II officials, with the assistance of external advisors. Simulations with the Eurolink model were presented in the 1984 Annual Economic Review (CEC, 1984b, Ch. 9).

The Comet model was primarily a medium-term model. It was set up to improve the quality of the medium-term forecasts of the Commission. The project was started in 1969 and assigned to a team at the Centre for Operations Research and Econometrics at the Catholic University of Leuven under the responsibility of Professor A.P. Barten. At times, there were tensions between the model team and DG II, partly due to the fact that the model team was at the University of Leuven and not at the Commission.

Comet consisted basically of a set of country models, one for each member country, of similar structure. The models were then connected by a model describing the bilateral trade flows between the countries (Barten and d'Alcantara, 1984). Senior DG II officials reproached the model to be too Keynesian, and not to pay sufficient attention to the monetary sector and the supply side[5]. It was probably an element which induced DG II officials to set up their own model unit.

The new model unit of DG II set out to build two econometric models: the Compact model, an aggregated macromodel for the Community as a whole, and Quest, a multicountry model[6]. Simulations with the Compact model were presented in the 1985 Annual Economic review (CEC, 1985 b, Ch. 6).

6.5   MAIN LINES OF MACROECONOMIC THOUGHT AT THE COMMISSION

The following analysis of the economic thought at the European Commission is to a large extent based on the Annual Economic Reports of the Commission, the main macroeconomic policy document of the Commission.

The drafting of the Annual Economic Report at the European Commission went through several phases. The first draft was essentially prepared in Directorate-General II, Economic and Financial Affairs, and

---

5   Something which was contested by the model builders.
6   Also the European Central Bank has constructed two models: an aggregate model for the European economy as a whole and a multicountry model, composed of similar models for the economies of the Euro area.

more specifically in the C Directorate "Macroeconomic Research and Policy".

An important role in the conception of the Reports was also played by the cabinets, especially the cabinet of the member of the Commission responsible for DG II. They determined to a large extent the general orientation of the Reports. Sometimes, they requested quite substantial revisions of a Report.

Before its acceptance by the Commission, the Report was also submitted to the Economic Policy Committee (EPC), composed of senior officials of the member states (ministries and central banks) and the Commission. In general, the discussions in the EPC did not lead to important changes in the Report.

Macroeconomic thought at the Commission was, to a large extent, a synthesis and compromise of the main schools of macroeconomic thought in the European countries, especially the three big ones: Germany, France and the United Kingdom[7].

German economic thought was centred around the social market economy. Two tendencies can be distinguished. The more free market oriented German economists would emphasise that economic policy was, in essence, *"Ordnungspolitik"*, i.e. a policy to create a sound and secure framework within which markets can operate. The main tasks of economic policy are then: (a) monetary policy: assure price stability; (b) fiscal policy: rather limited task for the government; and (c) structural policy: a more passive role, competition policy is emphasised. The other tendency, more Keynesian, with Karl Schiller as an important representative, emphasised the social dimension of the "social market economy". It was linked to the social democrats and the trade unions and considered a dialogue between the social partners (trade unions and employers) as a crucial element of its strategy to stimulate growth and employment.

In general, German economists mostly emphasised that economic policy consisted in the application of certain basic economic principles (especially the respect of market mechanisms and wage moderation) to the actual economic situation. It has many similarities with Roy Harrod's characterisation of Keynes's view: "Following Marshall, he (= Keynes) believed ... that progress in economics would be in the application of theory to practical problems. His recipe for the young economist was to know his Marshall thoroughly and read his Times every day carefully, without

---

[7] For an overview of post-1945 economic thought in Europe, see the contributions in Coats, 2000. An interesting overview of the German ideas can also be found in Schefold, 1998, who focuses on the debates in the *"Verein für Socialpolitik"*.

bothering too much about the large mass of contemporary publication in book form" (Harrod, 1951, 381).

Initially, French economic ideas were very influential at the Commission. Robert Marjolin, the first commissioner for DG II, had been the principal assistant to Monnet at the French Planning Office, famous for its five-year plans (Marjolin, 1986). The French Planning Office, while being part of the French "Colbertist" tradition, was also a spearhead of Keynesianism in France, with the national accounts at its heart (Rosanvallon, 1987, 40). Later, Malinvaud was influential, especially with his distinction between "Keynesian" and "classical" unemployment (Malinvaud, 1977).

Anglo-Saxon ideas in the post-war period followed different fads: Keynesianism, monetarism and supply-side economics. This was also so at the Commission, even if monetarism was never very popular. From a methodological point of view, the Anglo-Saxons favoured generally a more analytical approach, whereby economic policy recommendations would be based on more refined economic research. They especially favoured the developing of DG II's model building capacity.

Initially, an important transmission channel for Anglo-Saxon ideas was the OECD. Many Commission officials, including Marjolin, had worked at the OECD and there were many interactions between the OECD and the Commission.

Anglo-Saxon ideas received a big boost with the nomination of Padoa-Schioppa as director-general of DG II (see *infra*). Also, younger economists had a more Anglo-Saxon education, more of them having studied in the United States and having a Ph.D.

At the beginning of the 1980s, the Commission's analytical framework was medium-term oriented, with an important role for supply-side and structural elements (Maes, 1998, 14). The general view was probably best presented in the 1980 Annual Economic Report:

> The concerted response to the present general economic situation should be based on the right strategic mix of demand and supply policies and notably the right balance in their application to short- and medium-term problems. Short-term adjustments should be more moderate than at times in the last decade, and a heavier weight has to be given to reducing medium-term inflationary expectations and improving supply conditions in the economy (CEC, 1980, 13).

In the early 1980s, the European economy was coping with a serious stagflation, after the second oil shock of 1979 and high US interest rates. In its analysis, the Commission strongly emphasised the structural aspects of the crisis: "the accumulated back-log of adjustments and on our growing incapacity to respond quickly to the recent changes in the economic environment. The increased structural rigidities in our economies and social behaviour have changed profoundly the long-term dynamics of the business cycle" (CEC, 1982, 11).

6.6   THE EMPLOYMENT DEBATE WITH THE CEPS GROUP

In the 1980s, unemployment more and more dominated the economic scene. This was reflected in the 1984 Annual Economic Report of the Commission, where the title of the introduction was: "The dominant problem of unemployment" (CEC, 1984a, 9). This rise of unemployment happened against a background of a hesitant recovery, but important progress in stabilisation policies and monetary convergence.

Unemployment would become the main theme of the debate between the Commission and the CEPS Macroeconomic Policy group. The CEPS group, consisting mostly of "sophisticated Keynesians", many with an American background, argued for a more reflationary fiscal policy. Their position was elaborated in two reports:

- "Macroeconomic Prospects and Policies for the European Community", in April 1983, by G. Basevi, O. Blanchard, W. Buiter, R. Dornbusch and R. Layard. The Group argued that there was no evidence that "unemployment is all and without exception, or even predominantly, a real wage problem" (Basevi et al., 1983, 3). They favoured a coordinated expansionary policy, accompanied by incomes policy;
- "Report of the CEPS Macroeconomic Policy Group. Europe: the Case for Unsustainable Growth", in April 1984, by R. Layard, G. Basevi, O. Blanchard, W. Buiter and R. Dornbusch. They argued that the European economy should, for some years, grow faster than its sustainable long-term growth rate, in order to reduce the margin of unused resources. A temporary fiscal expansion and an accommodating monetary policy was necessary.

The major disagreement between the Commission and the CEPS group, in 1983 and 1984, was about the nature of the European unemployment problem, whether it was "Keynesian" or classical. The CEPS Group estimated that the NAIRU was maximum 7.5%, while actual unemployment was more than 10% (Layard et al., 1984, 4). The Commission, in its analysis, put more emphasis on the importance of "classical" unemployment:

Estimates of the present level of NAIRU (non-accelerating-inflation rate of unemployment) vary widely, with the most extreme views holding that the present unemployment rate is very close to the NAIRU. Although the debate about the relative extent of Keynesian, classical and structural unemployment is still far from closed, it may at all events be concluded from the above remarks that classical and structural unemployment has increased over the past 10 years (CEC, 1984b, 100).

In its analysis of the unemployment problem, the Commission strongly emphasised that economic growth had become less labour-intensive. According to Commission estimates the stock of capital per employed person had risen at an average annual rate of 2.5% in the preceding decade (CEC, 1984a, 24). The rise in relative labour costs, which was at the origin of this capital deepening, was not only the consequence of increases in nominal wages but also of the rise of non-wage labour costs. Substitution was further stimulated as the cost of capital was kept low, partly due to fiscal advantages. For the Commission, the increase of public expenditure, as well as the structure of expenditures and taxes, was one of the causes of the increase in unemployment.

Another reason for the increase in classical unemployment, according to the Commission, were the growing rigidities in the labour markets in Europe. They were the result both of legislation and of collective agreements. These were generally introduced in the golden sixties, in order to protect weaker groups. However, the Commission noted that: "Some of these regulations have proved to be ill-adapted to new circumstances and may ... have hindered employment creation" (CEC, 1984a, 33)[8].

The employment strategies, proposed in the Annual Economic Reports of 1982, 1983 and 1984, were very broadly based and comprised: (a) a stable macroeconomic framework; (b) an improvement of the competitiveness of the enterprise sector, especially the strengthening of the internal market; and (c) measures concerning the labour market, including wage moderation, more differentiated wage settlements and a "systematic reappraisal of labour market regulations and conventions" (CEC, 1984a, 34).

In a certain sense this debate can seem somewhat paradoxical: it was the policy-makers at the European Commission who were defending the "new" paradigm of supply-side economics, while the academics were in favour of the "old" Keynesian paradigm. It certainly shows that policy-makers can be open to new economic theories. It is also a clear indication that DG II in the

---

[8]   Michael Emerson, in a study published in his own name, argued that: "in Western Europe today there is a need for some correction of excesses of labour market regulation and social security programs" (Emerson, 1988, 3).

early 1980s was very alert to what was happening in the academic world and integrating this into its analysis of the economic situation in Europe. Moreover, the Commission had just had a very bad, if not traumatic, experience with a coordinated Keynesian demand expansion. The "concerted action", after the European Summit in Bremen and the G7 Summit in Bonn in 1979, led to an increase in inflation and balance-of-payments deficits in the early 1980s (Maes, 1998, 404). It led European Commission officials to focus on the supply side, especially the increased rigidities in Europe's labour markets. These rigidities made Europe certainly different from the United States, with its flexible markets, where many of the members of CEPS Group lived.

In 1985, both the Commission and the CEPS Group refocused their analysis and policy prescriptions. The CEPS Report "Employment and Growth in Europe: A Two-Handed Approach" of June 1985 was written by O. Blanchard, R. Dornbusch, J. Drèze, H. Giersch, R. Layard and M. Monti. It argued that the European unemployment problem did not have a single cause. Consequently, a "two-handed" approach was necessary, combining structural measures on the supply side and a "boost" to start the process. This boost had to come from timely supply measures, sustained and validated by demand (Blanchard et al., 1985, 30). One can note here that the new accents of the CEPS Report go together with certain changes in the composition of the Group, like the inclusion of Herbert Giersch, who had been emphasising the structural aspects of Europe's economic problems.

The 1985 Annual Economic Report of the Commission proposed a more focused economic strategy: the Cooperative Growth Strategy for more Employment. This cooperative strategy called for "balanced contributions" of different parties: the Community, the governments of the member states and the social partners. The aim was to strengthen growth in Europe and to make it more employment-creating. The strategy was based on a combination of moderate real wage increases, in order to improve profitability, and support for demand: "Only if wage moderation is accompanied by a sufficient level of aggregate demand can one have confidence that the process of improving profitability and restructuring demand (relatively more investment and relatively less consumption) will be rapid enough and not involve drastic deflation that would place social consensus under considerable strain. Only in this way can wage moderation fulfil its employment function." (CEC, 1985a, 10).

The change in emphasis in 1985, with the Cooperative Growth Strategy, is linked to the arrival of a new European Commission, under the presidency of Jacques Delors, which revitalised the European integration process, especially with the internal market project.

The Cooperative Growth Strategy for more Employment was elaborated under A. Pfeiffer, a German trade unionist, who was the Commissioner responsible for DG II, and L. Schubert, the economic man in his cabinet. Compared to earlier Reports, the Cooperative Growth Strategy was more macroeconomic in nature, with less emphasis on differentiated patterns of wage cost levels and labour market flexibility. The strategy was also more based on a social dialogue between the employers and the trade unions[9].

6.7   ACADEMIC ECONOMICS AND ECONOMICS AT POLICY-MAKING INSTITUTIONS

It is interesting to make an analysis of the differences between academic economics and economics at a policy-making institution, like the European Commission. In practice the borderline between academic economics and economics at policy-making institutions is non-existent. Many economists have been part of both worlds, not only in the course of their life, but also simultaneously, combining jobs. The European Commission, in the early half of the 1980s, has very strongly favoured this interaction. Part of the reason for this was certainly that senior policy-makers, like Padoa-Schioppa and Emerson, had strong academic contacts and were well at home in the academic world.

However, there are some interesting and important differences. So is the inspiration for analysis and research at policy-making institutions mostly very different from academic research. At policy-making institutions, concrete and actual issues, with which senior policy-makers are confronted, will mostly be at the basis of research projects. Policy-relevant research is at a premium. This contrasts with basic academic research, "blue sky research", which is driven by theoretical problems or by possibilities of new econometric techniques (Portes, 1997, 56). At policy-making institutions, theory and technique have a more ancillary function. Moreover, economists at policy-making institutions mostly need a quick judgement, as there is less time for in-depth analysis of problems.

So, for policy institutions, it is important that economic theory can select and highlight the relevant features for policy-making. One can think here of Schumpeter's characterisation of the economics of J.M. Keynes:

---

9   It is also remarkable that, in 1984, the Annual Economic Report comprised fifty pages, compared to one hundred and thirty six pages for the Annual Economic Review (the analytical economic studies of the Commission services). In 1985 the Report counted seventy six pages but the Review only sixty eight pages.

What I admire most in these and other conceptual arrangements of his is their *adequacy*: they fit his purpose as a well-tailored coat fits the customer's body. Of course, precisely because of this, they possess but limited usefulness irrespective of Keynes's particular aims. A fruit knife is an excellent instrument for peeling a pear. He who uses it in order to attack a steak has only himself to blame for unsatisfactory results (Schumpeter, 1946, 287, original italics).

There are also differences in the empirical material between economics at policy-making institutions and academic institutions. Policy-makers are strongly concerned about the actual economic situation and the future perspectives. Economists at policy-making institutions, like the European Commission, put a lot of time and effort at the monitoring and forecasting of the economic situation. This also implies that a lot of attention is given to the methodology of statistics, as a good comprehension of the coverage and quality of statistics is necessary. This rather contrasts with academic economists, who mostly work on the basis of existing economic data, leading to a more "historical" kind of analysis, even if of the recent past. Academic economists, in general, will pay relatively less attention to the methodology of the data, as they are more concerned with theoretical refinements and econometric techniques.

Moreover, economics at policy-making institutions, like the Commission, is a compromise, a search for consensus between different tendencies and persons. This contributes naturally to the eclectic and synthetical nature of economics at policy-making institutions. This can sometimes lead to rather paradoxical situations. So was the 1983 Report of the Commission very positive on nominal income targeting, which was advocated by the CEPS Group, but it praised also the strategy of monetary targeting in several Member States. This searching for a consensus implies also that economists at policy-making institution should be good team members, also with non-economists. There are limits to "independent originality" in policy-making institutions. As remarked by one observer, "Economists working in government service have a vested interest in promoting consensus on basic issues of economic analysis. Academics, on the other hand, while they must ride with the tide, have a vested interest in differentiating their product" (Marris, 1986, 109).

Work at international policy institutions, like the European Commission, is even more about consensus building, as the aim is to get the preferred economic policies accepted and implemented by the member states. Hereby, one can remark that "skills in communication and the art of persuasion are generally at a premium in international agencies, given their limited powers" (Coats, 1986, 167). However, also to have an impact inside a multinational (and multilingual) organisation, communication and negotiation skills are more important than in national organisations. Writing clear and accessible papers and achieving consensus in meetings can be more important than "academic brilliance". Marris's remarks about the OECD apply equally well to the European Commission: "'good economics', merges almost imperceptibly into the art of persuasion" (1986, 113).

One also has to distinguish, at policy institutions, between background studies and direct policy work. The, more academic, background studies have certainly become more important during the last decades. Policy-makers need to know how the economy functions, so thorough analysis is needed.

For analytical studies policy-making institutions will often cooperate with academics. This interaction with the academic world was strengthened in the Commission in the early 1980s, especially under the influence of Padoa-Schioppa. The main elements were the cooperation with the CEPS Macroeconomic Policy Group and the launching of a new series of publications, the Economic Papers. Naturally, as there are "cultural" differences between the worlds of academics and policy-makers, there can be clashes, often about the publication of research work, which also happened at the Commission. However, the tendency at policy-making institutions is for more analytical, academic research, even if the attitude towards the academic world of senior policy-makers plays a very important role herein. This also implies that policy-making institutions themselves will do certain types of research, which earlier were done by outside academic experts. A clear example is the setting up of a modelling division at DG II in the early 1980s.

6.8   CONCLUSION

During the early 1980s the European economy was in the doldrums, with unemployment more and more dominating the scene, and the European integration process was languishing. In its Annual Economic Reports the European Commission presented its analysis of the situation and proposed its macroeconomic policy strategy.

In its analysis of the economic situation and discussion of policy proposals, the services of the Commission were clearly influenced by developments in the academic world. During the 1980s, these interactions between the academic world increased strongly, especially under the impulse of Tommaso Padoa-Schioppa, the director general of DG II (Economic and Financial Affairs). His main aim was to improve the analytical capacity of the Commission services. Strengthening contacts with the academic world was a crucial element of his strategy to reform DG II. The interaction with the academic world was even institutionalised with the foundation of the CEPS Macroeconomic Policy Group, which comprised several distinguished academics, and which held joint seminars with the economists of the Commission.

However, economics at a policy-making institution like the European Commission has several characteristics which distinguish it from academic economics. So is the inspiration for analysis and research at policy-making institutions mostly very different from academic research. At policy-making institutions, concrete and actual issues, with which senior policy-makers are confronted, will mostly be at the basis of research projects. This contrasts with basic academic research which is more driven by theoretical problems or possibilities of new techniques. There are also differences in the empirical material between economics at policy-making institutions and the academic world. Policy-makers are strongly concerned about the actual economic situation and the future perspectives. Consequently, economists at policy-making institutions, like the European Commission, put a lot of time and effort at the monitoring and forecasting of the economic situation. This rather contrasts with academic economists, which mostly work on the basis of existing economic data, leading to more "historical" kind of analysis, even if of the recent past. Moreover, at policy institutions, consensus building is very important. There are limits to "independent originality", so valued in the academic world. Economics at policy institutions, like the Commission, is a compromise between different tendencies and persons, whereby an economic strategy has to be shaped which is also politically feasible. It all contributes to the eclectic and synthetical nature of economics at the Commission.

REFERENCES

Barten, A.P. and G. d'Alcantara (1984), COMET III: Econometric Model Building for the European Community, mimeo, Leuven: Katholieke Universiteit Leuven.

Basevi, G. et al. (1983), *Macroeconomic Prospects and Policies for the European Community*. Brussels: CEC, Economic Papers, 12, April.

Bean, C. (1994), European Unemployment: A survey. *Journal of Economic Literature*, 32, 573-619.

Blanchard, O. et al. (1985), *Report of the CEPS Macroeconomic Policy Group. Employment and Growth in Europe: A Two-handed Approach.* Brussels: CEC, Economic Papers, 36, June.

CEC (1980), Annual Economic Report. *European Economy*, 7, November, 5-29.

CEC (1982), Annual Economic Report. *European Economy*, 14, November, 5-32.

CEC (1983), Annual Economic Report. *European Economy*, 18, November, 5-44.

CEC (1984a), Annual Economic Report. *European Economy*, 22, November, 5-54.

CEC (1984b), Annual Economic Review. *European Economy*, 22, November, 55-190.

CEC (1984c), Technical Annex. *European Economy*, 22, November, 191-200.

CEC (1985a), Annual Economic Report. *European Economy*, 26, November, 5-80.

CEC (1985b), Annual Economic Review. *European Economy*, 26, November, 81-156.

CEC (1997), The Joint Harmonised EU Programme of Business and Consumer Surveys. *European Economy,* 6, 1-231.

Coats, A.W. (ed.), (1986), *Economists in International Agencies*. New York: Praeger.

Coats, A.W. (ed.), (2000), *The Post-1945 Development of Economics in Western Europe*. London: Routledge.

Emerson, M. (1988), *What Model for Europe ?* Cambridge, MIT: MIT Press.

Giersch, H. (1987), Eurosclerosis. What is the Cure ? *European Affairs*, 4, Winter, 33-43.

Harrod, R.F. (1951), *The Life of John Maynard Keynes*. Harmondsworth: Penguin.

Jacquemin, A. and L. Pench (1997), What Competitiveness for Europe ? in Jacquemin A. and L. Pench (eds.), *Europe Competing in the Global Economy*. Cheltenham UK and Lyme, US: Edward Elgar, pp. 1-43.

Layard, R. et al. (1984), *Report of the CEPS Macroeconomic Policy Group. Europe: The Case for Unsustainable Growth*. Brussels: CEC, Economic Papers, 31, April.

Llewellyn, J., S. Potter and L. Samuelson (1985), *Economic Forecasting and Policy - the International Dimension*. London: Routledge.

Ludlow, P. (1982), *The Making of the European Monetary System*. London: Butterworth.

Ludlow, P. (1983), Introduction, in Dornbusch R. et al., *Macroeconomic Prospects and Policies for the European Community*. Brussels: CEPS, April.

Maes, I. (1996), The Development of Economic Thought at the European Community Institutions, in Coats A.W. (ed.), The Post-1945 Internationalisation of Economics, *History of Political Economy*, Annual Supplement, 245-276.

Maes, I. (1998), Macroeconomic Thought at the European Commission in the 1970s: the First Decade of the Annual Economic Reports of the EEC. *Banca Nazionale del Lavoro Quarterly Review*, 207, 387-412.

Malinvaud, E. (1977), *The Theory of Unemployment Reconsidered*. Oxford: Blackwell.

Marjolin, R. (1986), *Le Travail d'une Vie. Mémoires 1911-1986*. Paris: Robert Laffont.

Marris, S. (1986), The Role of Economists in the OECD, in Coats A.W., (ed.), *Economists in International Agencies*. N.Y.: Praeger, pp. 98-114.

Modigliani, F. and T. Padoa-Schioppa (1978), *The Management of an Economy with "100% Plus" Wage Indexation*. Princeton: Essays in International Finance, 130, Dec.

Mortensen, J. (1990), *Federalism vs Co-ordination*. Brussels: CEPS.

Nickell, S. (1997), Unemployment and Labor Market Rigidities: Europe versus North America. *Journal of Economic Prespectives*, 11, 3, 55-77.

Padoa-Schioppa, T. (1987), Reshaping Monetary Policy, in Dornbusch, R. et al., (eds.), *Macroeconomics and Finance. Essays in Honor of Franco Modigliani*. Cambridge, MIT: MIT Press, pp. 265-285.

Porta, P. L. (1996), Italian Economic through in the Postwar Years, in Coats A.W., (ed.), The Post-1945 Internationalisation of Economics, *History of Political Economy*, Annual Supplement, 165-183.

Portes, R. (1997), Users and Abusers of Economic Research, in Van Bergeijk, P. et al., (eds.), *Economic Science and Practice.* Cheltenham UK and Lyme, US: Edward Elgar, pp. 49-59.

Rosanvallon, P. (1987), Histoire des Idées Keynésiennes en France. *Revue Française de l'Economie*, 4, 2, 22-56.

Schefold, B. (1998), Die Wirtschafts - and Sozialordnung der Bundesrepublik Deutschland im Spiegel der Jahrestagungen des Vereins für Socialpolitik 1948 bis 1989, mimeo.

Schumpeter, J. (1946), John Maynard Keynes, *Ten Great Economists.* London: Allen and Unwin, 1962, pp. 260-291.

Wegner, M. (1989), The European Economic Community, in Pechman, J. (ed.), *The Role of the Economist in Government.* New York: N.Y.U. Press, pp. 279-299.

Annex 6.1 - Main events

1979   March   Creation of the EMS
         Autumn   Second oil shock

1981   January   Beginning of Thorn Commission
                   Reagan inaugurated as US president
         May   Mitterrand elected in France
         October   General realignment in the EMS

1982   June   General realignment in the EMS
         October   Kohl becomes chancellor in Germany

1983   March   General realignment in the EMS

1984   June   Fontainebleau Summit, agreement on the European
                   budget

1985   January   Beginning of Delors Commission
         March   European Council agrees on single market project
         July   General realignment in the EMS
         November Cooperative Growth Strategy presented in the Annual
                   Economic Report

Annex 6.2 - Main macroeconomic policymakers at the European Commission[1]

President: G. Thorn (L)[2]

Commissioner responsible for DG II: F.-X. Ortoli (F)[3]

DG II   Director-General: T. Padoa-Schioppa (I)[4]
Deputy Director-General: M. Wegner (D)
Directorate A (National Economies): P. Van den Bempt (B)
Directorate B (Economic Structures and Community Policies): ...[5]
Directorate C (Macro-economic Research and Policy):
M. Emerson (UK)

1. Concerted action
2. Short-term forecasts
3. Business cycle surveys
4. Medium-term forecasts
5. Econometric models

Directorate D (Monetary Matters):   J.-P. Mingassson (F)

---

[1]   In January 1983.
[2]   From January 1985:   J. Delors (F).
[3]   From January 1985:   A. Pfeiffer (D).
[4]   From March 1983:   M. Russo (I).
[5]   Open position.

PART 3:

The Making of European Monetary Union

L'Europe ne se fera pas d'un coup ni dans une construction d'ensemble: elle se fera par des réalisations concrètes créant d'abord une solidarité de fait.

Plan Schuman, May 1950

La construction européenne, comme toutes les révolutions pacifiques, a besoin de temps - le temps de convaincre, le temps d'adapter les esprits et d'ajuster les choses à de grandes transformations. Il y a aussi, toutefois, les circonstances qui bousculent le cours du temps et il y a l'occasion qui se présente à son heure.

Monnet, Mémoires, Tome 2, 647

7. EMU from a Historical Perspective*

7.1 INTRODUCTION

In this paper three topics are investigated: the genesis of the European Economic and Monetary Union, the reasons why the efforts to create a single European currency were finally successful and also Belgium's role in the preparation for monetary union.

Although the start of the European integration process dates back to a few years after the Second World War, the first formalised attempt to create an economic and monetary union was not made until 1970, when the so-called Werner Report (commissioned by the European Council) outlined the main features of EMU and the road to its achievement. However, due to strong turmoil in the international economy (the collapse of the Bretton-Woods system and the oil crisis) and the absence of policy coordination and political will, this first attempt at monetary union proved not to be successful. Not

* Co-authors: Smets J. and J. Michielsen. Published, in Dutch, as "De EMU: De Uitdaging", Ooghe H., et al. (eds.), ced Samson, pp. 37-99. An abridged draft was published as "EMU from an Historical Perspective" in Ooghe H., F. Heylen, R. Vander Vennet and J. Vermaut (eds.), *The Economic and Business Consequences of the EMU. A Challenge for Governments, Financial Institutions and Firms,* Boston: Kluwer Academic Publishers, pp. 53-92, reprinted with kind permission from Kluwer Academic Publishers.

Paper prepared for the 24th Flemish Scientific Economic Congress, Ghent, 17-18 March 2000. The authors would like to thank all the people who provided helpful assistance for this project. A special word of thanks goes to the members of the commission of the congress as well as to J. Delors, M. Emerson, H. Köhler, A. Lamfalussy, T. Padoa-Schioppa, T. Peeters, K.-O. Pöhl, J.-J. Rey, W. Schönfelder, B. Snoy, J. van Ypersele and P. Werner for interesting discussions and insights. The usual restrictions apply.

until the end of the 1970s was the monetary integration process resumed, more specifically with the establishment of the European Monetary System. Despite considerable difficulties, especially during the first years, the EMS contributed to a broadening of the *"acquis communautaire"*, on the basis of which a genuine project for monetary union could be set in motion. This took place on the basis of the "Delors Report", which, commissioned by the European Council, produced a blueprint for an economic and monetary union and specified the successive stages which would have to be completed. Further negotiations resulted in the Treaty of Maastricht, which, despite the serious difficulties within the EMS during the years 1992-1993, finally led to the creation of EMU in 1999.

The successful achievement of EMU was attributable both to structural long-term developments and to the specific momentum of the integration process. The first-mentioned factors include the strengthening of the economic and financial integration in the European Union, the emergence of a broad consensus on economic policy objectives (with the emphasis on a medium-term stability-oriented policy), the increasing political willingness to transfer sovereignty to the European level and the desire to build up Europe's international role. Against this background economic and political developments in the second half of the 1980s created a window of opportunity: the marked rapprochement between France and Germany and the internal market project generated a powerful momentum in the European integration process. Europe's political leaders resolutely seized this opportunity. The flexibility in the Treaty of Maastricht (mainly the opt-out clauses), the technical quality of the preparations and the continuous political support from prominent European decision-makers brought the project to a successful conclusion.

As a small member state, Belgium has consistently made a positive contribution to the monetary integration process. It has taken various initiatives which have promoted that process (for instance as regards the operation of the EMS, the definition of an ambitious scenario for the changeover to the euro, economic-policy coordination, etc.).

The examination of EMU from a historical perspective brings out the following main lines of force:

- the history of monetary unification shows that EMU is the result of a long process of gradual building on prior achievements. Although that process was repeatedly interrupted owing to a diversity of economic and political difficulties, it nevertheless appears to be the culmination of a trend which was contributed to by all the (including negative) experience gained. It is undoubtedly greatly to the credit of

Europe's political leaders that they were able to appreciate these developments correctly and to respond to them with a visionary and forward-looking project, sometimes in the face of strong opposition;

- a striking aspect of EMU's success is that the project succeeded in overcoming great resistance because it was flexible enough to address specific concerns despite the high degree of consistency as regards its aims and conditions of access. Examples of this are the provisions that enabled EMU to be launched without the participation of all the EU Member States, the avoidance of a fundamental debate on the finality of political union, etc. The success of this pragmatic approach is perhaps instructive regarding the way in which further steps will have to be taken, at a time when the European Union is embarking on a phase of both deepening and widening;

- the monetary aspect of EMU is indisputably more firmly elaborated than the economic aspect and EMU is not coupled with a genuine political union, unlike other monetary unions. One is admittedly entering uncharted territory in this respect. Economic and monetary history does not offer ready-made examples or models here. However, monetary union does in turn appear to be strengthening integration and coordination in other fields (both economic fields, e.g. employment policy, and political ones, such as security and foreign relations). With regard to what else the European adventure has in store, one must rely on the inherent specific momentum of the process of European integration.

7.2   HISTORICAL OVERVIEW

7.2.1   On the Origins of the European Monetary Integration Process[1]

In order to understand the process of European monetary integration it would be useful to look at three traumatic events which haunted policy-makers in the post-war world: the Second World War, the Great Depression and hyperinflation in Germany.

The Second World War marked a turning point in European history. It was a catastrophe that led to the almost total collapse of Europe, and which saw the central position which Europe had occupied in the world surrendered to the United States and to the Soviet Union. It also discredited the previous

---

[1]   See also Annex 7.1.

international order, based on the nation-state[2]. People became increasingly persuaded that a united Europe was the only solution to avoiding a new war on the continent and to regaining international influence. Several initiatives for European integration were taken, further stimulated by the beginning of the Cold War. Of great importance was the congress of European federalists at The Hague, in May 1948 (Delors, 1996, 7). The congress was attended by a host of influential politicians, such as Churchill, Adenauer, Blum, Mitterrand, Spaak and de Gasperi, and was at the origins of the European Movement.

A process of Franco-German reconciliation lay at the heart of developments towards European integration. These developments often promoted a Franco-German alliance that would become the motor of the integration process. For the French, this Franco-German relationship would also be a means of containing German power, as evidenced by the Schuman plan for a European Coal and Steel Community, and also later in monetary matters. For the Germans the memory of the Second World War was particularly traumatic, since it was they who had started it. The war profoundly marked post-war German politics. As a result avoidance of German dominance in Europe became a fundamental line in German foreign policy in the post-war period.

The Great Depression of the 1930s, which was characterised by mass unemployment, trade wars and competitive devaluations, was another trauma. It was influential in shaping the post-war international economic order: fixed but adjustable exchange rates with the Bretton-Woods system and free trade with the GATT. These international institutions formed the framework inside which attempts at European economic integration in the post-war period would take place (Van der Wee, 1986). The Great Depression also furthered the dominance of activist Keynesian theories, justifying government intervention to steer the economy. The irony is, of course, that these activist policies, which encouraged every country to focus on its own internal objectives, contributed to the demise of the fixed exchange rate regime in the early 1970s.

In Germany, a third trauma haunted (economic) policymakers: the hyperinflation of the 1920s, which completely destroyed the economy and impoverished large classes of the German population. Price stability would become a fundamental aim of economic policy in Germany, the prime responsibility of a strong and independent central bank. Price stability and a strong German mark would be one of the few things Germans were proud of

---

[2]   An exception is the United Kingdom. Churchill called the Second World War "Britain's finest hour".

in the post-war period. This certainly helps to explain a certain German reticence towards European monetary integration as well as the emphasis on price stability in the Maastricht Treaty.

7.2.2 A First Attempt at Monetary Union

The start of the integration process

The real start of the process of European integration can be traced back to the Schuman Declaration of May 1950, which provided the basis for the European Coal and Steel Community. The Declaration stated clearly that: "The solidarity in production will make it plain that any war between France and Germany becomes not merely unthinkable, but materially impossible ... this proposal will build the first concrete foundation of a European federation which is indispensable to the preservation of peace".

In October 1950 a new French plan followed, the Pleven Plan, which aimed to establish a European Defence Community. However, it was defeated in the French Assembly in August 1954 by a coalition of Gaullists and Communists. It showed that defence was too close to national sovereignty to be transferred to the European level. European integration could only make progress along less sensitive economic lines. New negotiations followed, leading to the Rome Treaty and the creation of the European Economic Community in January 1958. The Treaty would, de facto, be of a constitutional order, as it was to transform economic and legal rules in the countries of the Community (Padoa-Schioppa, 1998, 9).

From an economic point of view, the Treaty of Rome emphasised the creation of a common market and the elaboration of certain common policies. The chapters on macroeconomic policy were rather sketchy and monetary union was not one of the original objectives of the Community. Two factors can, to a large extent, explain this orientation. First, the international monetary system established at Bretton Woods already provided a stable monetary framework for the Community. Second, the creation of a customs union was already considered to be a very far-reaching objective.

At the Hague Summit of December 1969 an ambitious programme to relaunch European integration was established, comprising both a widening (enlargement) and a deepening (economic and monetary union) of the Community.

Several factors contributed to the change in atmosphere that placed economic and monetary union in the spotlight and made it one of the Community's official objectives:

- the successful completion of the customs union and, somewhat less satisfactorily, of the common agricultural policy before the end of 1969. A new forward thrust seemed necessary to maintain the momentum and even to avoid retrogression;
- disenchantment with the central position of the American dollar in the Bretton-Woods system and with the benefits the United States derived from the international role of the dollar. There was a sentiment, especially nourished by the French, that the Community needed its own "monetary individuality"(Bloomfield, 1973, 11);
- fear about the future of the fixed exchange rate system, also in the European Community. Economic developments following the May 1968 events in France contributed to severe exchange crises, leading to a devaluation of the French franc and a revaluation of the German mark in 1969. The countries of the Community feared that further exchange rate instability could lead to the disintegration of the customs union and the demise of the common agricultural policy;
- the coming to power of new political leaders both in France and Germany. In 1969 General de Gaulle resigned and Pompidou was elected as president in France. He and his finance minister, Giscard d'Estaing, followed a more pro-European policy. The other major event was the formation of a new government in Germany by the Social Democrats and the Free Democrats with Willy Brandt as chancellor. The Brandt government supported the EMU project, one of the reasons being the need to counterbalance its Ostpolitik (recognition of the German Democratic Republic).

The Werner plan

At the Hague Summit the Heads of State and Government requested the Council to draw up a plan with a view to creating an economic and monetary union. A committee, chaired by the Luxembourg prime minister Pierre Werner, produced a report in October 1970 (Council-Commission of the European Communities, 1970, commonly known as the Werner Report). It contained a programme for the establishment in stages of an economic and monetary union by 1980.

The Report first presented a general picture of monetary union:

> A monetary union implies inside its boundaries the total and irreversible convertibility of currencies, the elimination of margins of fluctuation in exchange rates, the irrevocable fixing of parity rates and the complete liberation of movements of capital. It may be accompanied by the

maintenance of national monetary symbols or the establishment of a sole Community currency. From the technical point of view the choice between these two solutions may seem immaterial, but considerations of psychological and political nature militate in favour of the adoption of a sole currency which would confirm the irreversibility of the venture (Werner Report, 10).

Monetary union therefore implied a considerable change from the situation that prevailed. At that time only the convertibility of currencies was established, while, according to the Treaty of Rome, countries were only obliged to liberalise those capital movements which were necessary to ensure that the common market functioned correctly.

On an institutional level, the Report proposed that two Community organs should be created: a centre of decision for economic policy and a Community system for the central banks. This also implied a revision of the Treaty of Rome.

The Report considered that economic and monetary union could be achieved in the next ten years, "provided the political will of the Member States to realise this objective, solemnly declared at the Conference at The Hague, is present" (Werner Report, 14). It proposed a plan to attain EMU in three stages. However, it did not lay down a precise timetable for the different stages. Rather it wanted to maintain a measure of flexibility, while concentrating on the first phase.

It proposed that the first stage should commence on 1 January 1971 and cover a period of three years. The main elements were: (a) reinforcement of procedures for consultation and policy coordination; (b) further liberalisation of intra-Community capital movements and steps towards an integrated European capital market; (c) narrowing of exchange rate fluctuations between Community currencies.

In the Werner Committee, there was a heated debate between the "economists", led by Germany, and the "monetarists", among them France, about what should have priority: policy coordination or narrowing of exchange rate fluctuations (Werner, 1991). The compromise solution was that there had to be "parallel progress" in both areas.

A basic ambiguity lurked in the background of the Report regarding the crumbling Bretton-Woods system. On the one hand, unease with the Bretton-Woods system was one of the driving forces behind European monetary integration. On the other, the European attempt to narrow exchange rate fluctuations took the framework of the Bretton-Woods fixed exchange rate system for granted.

The failure of Europe's first attempt at monetary union

Immediately after its publication, the Werner Report was heavily criticised by the orthodox Gaullists in France (Tsoukalis, 1977, 104). Their criticism centred on the supranational elements of the Report. It induced a change in the policy of the French government, leading to a dilution of the proposals of the Report. In particular, the creation of new Community institutions was dropped.

Amid the international monetary crisis, which reached a first climax with Nixon's "temporary" suspension of the gold convertibility of the dollar in August 1971, progress on European monetary integration was difficult. In March 1973 it was decided to limit intra-EEC fluctuation margins to 2.25%, instead of the 4.5% of the Bretton-Woods system, after the Smithsonian Agreement of December 1971. It would lead to the birth of the "European snake" in the "Bretton-Woods tunnel". The Paris Summit of October 1972 further confirmed the aim of economic and monetary union and set January 1974 as the date for the transition to the second stage.

Figure 7.1 - The proposal for a European snake in the Bretton-Woods tunnel[1]

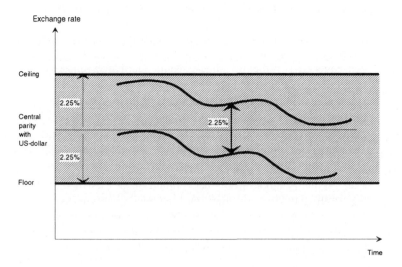

[1] Situation after the Smithsonian Agreement of December 1971 to widen the margins of fluctuation of each currency with respect to the US-dollar from 0.75%. to 2.25%.

The final breakdown of the Bretton-Woods system was very differently perceived in the European Community. For the Bundesbank, floating was "the only way out" of the conflict between internal and external equilibrium and made it possible for monetary policy to be focused on its domestic objective of price stability (Emminger, 1977, 53). For the French, the disappearance of the tunnel reinforced German monetary dominance in the European Community, as it turned the snake into a de facto German mark zone. Moreover, without being shielded by the Bretton-Woods tunnel, it was much more difficult for the French franc to respect the fluctuation margins with the mark, contributing to the eventual departure of the French franc.

This first attempt at EMU was certainly not successful. The Marjolin Report spoke of a "failure" and further described the developments between 1969 and 1975 thus: "if there has been any movement it has been backward" (Commission of the European Communities, 1975, 1). In early 1974, at the end of the first stage of EMU, the situation can be summarised as follows:

- policy coordination: common guidelines had been adopted by the Council of Ministers. Their impact was, however, rather limited. Even the Commission, in its assessment of the first stage, admitted that policy coordination had not gone very far "beyond recommendations of a very general nature" (Commission of the European Communities, 1973, 6). This became even more obvious after the oil price shock of October 1973, when France and Germany followed radically different policy objectives. France gave priority to expansionary policies in order to combat the deflationary consequences of the oil shock, while Germany followed a more restrictive policy to counter its inflationary effects. This led to substantial differences in inflation between the two countries;
- the narrowing of exchange rate fluctuations: after the departure of the French franc in January 1974, the snake only comprised Germany, Denmark and the Benelux countries. Moreover, several currency realignments took place. Giscard d'Estaing the French Finance Minister at the time, described the snake as "un animal de la préhistoire monétaire européenne" (Tsoukalis, 1977, 130);
- financial market integration: to combat exchange rate fluctuations, the countries of the Community progressively extended the use of exchange controls. Even the German authorities who, after the Second World War, had established a regime of freedom of capital movements, introduced capital controls.

The enlargement of the Community in 1973 further complicated matters. With the election victory of the Labour party in February 1974, the European scene became dominated by the renegotiations of the British entry terms. Economic and monetary union faded from the agenda.

Figure 7.2 - Inflation in Germany and France in the 1960s and 1970s

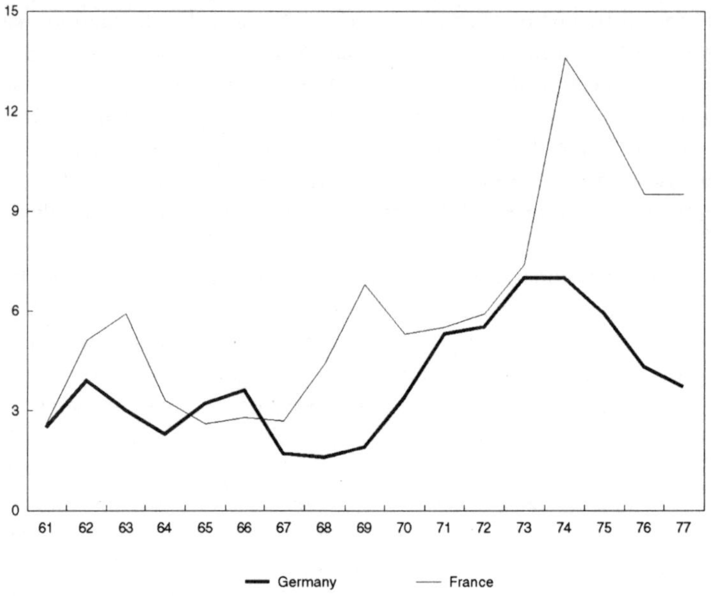

Source: Eurostat databases - Newcronos.

Fundamentally, this first attempt at monetary unification was unsuccessful not only due to the unstable international environment (the collapse of the Bretton-Woods system and the oil crisis), but also because the process of European integration was not sufficiently far advanced to make monetary union a realistic objective. National governments were still strongly attached to their national monetary sovereignty and the pursuit of national economic objectives. In Germany, priority was given in the first instance to the fight against inflation, while in France economic growth was considered a more important objective. This view was supported by the then influential theory of the Phillips curve, according to which there was a stable relationship between inflation and unemployment. Policy-makers could then select their preferred trade-off between inflation and unemployment[3].

7.2.3   The European Monetary System (1979-1987)

Background

The events of the 1970s stimulated debates about European monetary integration both in the academic world and among policy-makers. Most academics were rather sceptical about the feasibility of a monetary union, emphasising that in a Phillips-curve world, inflation between countries would only be equal by accident (cf. Magnifico, 1971). However, bold and innovative proposals were also launched to create a (parallel) common European currency. One of the most daring initiatives was certainly the so-called "All Saint's Day Manifesto" (Basevi et al., 1975), favouring a market-led approach to monetary union. The basic idea was that with one reform two objectives could be attained: a single European currency and the eradication of inflation. The Manifesto recommended that the central banks of the European Community should issue a parallel European currency with a constant purchasing power, called the "Europa". Initially, the central banks would only issue Europas against their national currencies, on the demand of the economic agents. This new currency would compete with national currencies in all monetary functions. However, proposals of this kind failed to win over policy-makers, who were extremely doubtful about the feasibility of these schemes.

In the second half of the 1970s, European leaders became increasingly worried about the stagnation of the European integration process and the ensuing risk that the achievements of the past could fall apart. Roy Jenkins, the president of the European Commission, tried to revive the monetary union project, especially in his famous Florence speech (Jenkins, 1977). The following year, the French president Giscard d'Estaing and the German chancellor Helmut Schmidt played a crucial role in the relaunching of the monetary integration process with the creation of the European Monetary System (cf. Ludlow, 1982). The European Monetary System was agreed upon by the Heads of State in a Resolution at the Brussels summit of

---

3   Moreover, "The Case for flexible Exchange Rates" (Friedman, 1953) became particularly influential in the 1970s. It stated very forcefully that flexible exchange rates were the appropriate instrument for attaining external balance and that they would give each country more freedom to pursue its own internal objectives.

December 1978. Formally, the EMS started in March 1979. The legal basis was an agreement between the central banks of the European Community.

The European Monetary System was launched against considerable scepticism, especially from academic economists but also from monetary experts who still had vivid memories of the snake unravelling. However, eminent political leaders strongly pushed for the EMS and succeeded in getting it off the ground. It can therefore be argued that the creation of the EMS was a "victory of political intuition over expert opinion" (Mortensen, 1990, 28).

Objectives

Whether the setting-up of the European Monetary System can be considered a second attempt at monetary union, still remains an issue for discussion. The main argument that supports this is that the EMS agreement specified the creation of a European Monetary Fund within two years of the start of the EMS. However, the functions of this Fund were never really agreed upon, and the plans were shelved in December 1980. In any case, the conclusions of the Bremen Council (July 1978) did not mention economic and monetary union but a "scheme for the creation of closer monetary cooperation leading to a zone of monetary stability in Europe", a clearly less ambitious project. The more limited objectives of the European Monetary System were also reflected in the legal form which it assumed: an agreement between the central banks of the Community, whereas the Werner Report was aiming at a change in the Treaties, with the creation of a European System of Central Banks.

Monetary stability, the objective of the EMS, had a double dimension: internal and external. This was a compromise and synthesis between the ideas of the "monetarists", led by France, emphasising the importance of external stability (exchange rate stability) and of the "economists", led by Germany, advocating internal stability (price stability) and the coordination of economic policy.

Characteristics of the European Monetary System

The European Monetary System was composed of three main elements: the exchange rate mechanism (ERM), credit mechanisms and the European Currency Unit (or ECU).

At the core of the European Monetary System was the exchange rate mechanism. This may seem somewhat paradoxical, since not all currencies in the European Community participated. The original members were: the

German mark, the Dutch guilder, the French franc, the Danish krone, the Belgian/Luxembourg franc, the Irish pound and the Italian lira.

Characteristics of the exchange rate mechanism were:

-   the fixing of central rates between the participating currencies[4];
-   initially, a normal fluctuation margin of 2.25% above and below the bilateral, central rate, (with the exception of a 6% fluctuation margin for Italy). This fluctuation margin defined a ceiling and a floor at which the central banks had an obligation to intervene. Intramarginal interventions were voluntary and subject to mutual agreement;
-   realignments of the central rates were only possible by common agreement of all the participating countries. This implied that unilateral decisions on devaluations or revaluations, as in the Bretton-Woods system, were not allowed. It stressed the Community character of the exchange rates between the participating currencies.

Several credit mechanisms were foreseen: very short-term, short-term and medium-term, as well as the mechanism of Community loans. While the first two were central bank financing for currency support, the latter two offered balance of payment assistance linked to policy adjustment programmes.

The ECU was created. It was a basket currency comprising the currencies of the European Community, including those currencies that did not participate in the exchange rate mechanism. The original aim was for the ECU to play an important role in the functioning of the ERM, both as an indicator of the source of tensions in the foreign exchange markets and as a means of settling central bank debts arising from currency support operations. However, this first aspect never took shape and the second was subject to restrictions. Instead, the ECU took on a significant role in the international financial markets.

The EMS was the result of very difficult negotiations, especially inside Germany, between the Chancellor and the Bundesbank (Pöhl, 1996, 201). The original Giscard-Schmidt plan, in which the Bundesbank had not been involved, foresaw a much more symmetrical system, one of the fundamental aims of the French. It comprised, amongst other things, the partial pooling of official reserves and an expanded use of the ECU, both as a means of settlement between central banks and, in due course, as a new reserve asset (Ludlow, 1982, 82). The Bundesbank, still haunted by the trauma of

---

4   While the EMS formally provided for central rates in ECU of the participating currencies, de facto, these served mainly for the determination of the bilateral central rates.

unlimited interventions in the Bretton-Woods system, was determined to avoid a system with unlimited intervention obligations (Ungerer, 1997, 154). It managed to ensure the imposition of limits on credit facilities in the EMS and also of the repayment of credits in hard currencies and not only in ECUs. Moreover, it was given assurances that in an emergency it could temporarily suspend interventions. With its intervention obligations thus limited, the Bundesbank could safeguard its ability to focus German monetary policy on the domestic objective of price stability, which would further the role of the German mark as the anchor currency of the EMS.

Functioning of the EMS[5]

The first years of the European Monetary System were very difficult, characterised by several realignments, a lack of convergence of economic performance and the weak co-ordination of economic policy. Even the European Commission was rather pessimistic. It noted that the two realignments of 1982 "give serious cause for concern, since the frequency and the size of the adjustments threaten a gradual erosion of the system's credibility" (CEC, 1982, 35). An explanation for this was sought in the impact of policy divergences and the absence of sufficient mechanisms in the system that could exert discipline.

It was also decided, "provisionally", to delay the institutional development of the system, in particular the transformation of the European Fund for Monetary Cooperation into a fully-fledged European Monetary Fund[6].

The year 1983 can be considered a turning point in the European Monetary System, especially in the relationship between the French franc and the German mark.

In May 1981 François Mitterrand became the first socialist president of the Fifth Republic in France. He started with a strong activist economic program, including an expansionary budgetary policy and nationalisations (cf. Sachs and Wyplosz, 1986). This reinforced the divergences in policy preferences between France and Germany. The ensuing loss of competitiveness of the French economy and capital outflows repeatedly put

---

5   For an analysis and evaluation of the European Monetary System, see, e.g., De Grauwe, 1992, Fratianni, M. and J. von Hagen, 1992, Giavazzi and Giovannini, 1989, Giavazzi, Micossi and Miller (eds.), 1988, Maes, 1991 and van Ypersele and Koeune, 1989.
6   The European Fund for Monetary Cooperation would remain in function until the foundation of the European Monetary Institute in January 1994.

strong pressures on the French franc, leading to increases in interest rates and several devaluations.

Figure 7.3 - Exchange rates of some European currencies vis-à-vis the German mark in the 1980s
(indices 1987=100)

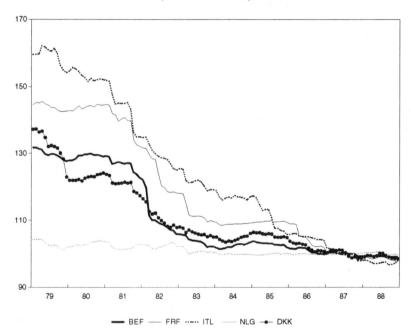

Source: NBB.

Faced with renewed heavy pressure on the French franc in March 1983, Mitterrand realised that he could not continue with his activist policies. Instead he opted for reinforcing the integration of France into the European Community. This implied that in order to avoid further devaluations of the French franc, he would have to pursue a more orthodox economic policy, which was christened a *"politique de rigueur"*.

This represented a very fundamental change in the French policy towards European monetary integration. Since the end of the 1960s, France had officially favoured European monetary integration, but it had wanted, at the same time, to preserve its sovereignty in economic policy-making. With the devaluation of 1983, French policy-makers realised that the two were incompatible and accepted the discipline of the European Monetary System, without giving up their complaints about the asymmetric functioning of the EMS.

A similar kind of shift towards more orthodox policies can be discerned in several other European countries in the early 1980s, such as Belgium, Ireland and Denmark. This convergence of economic policy contributed to a greater convergence of inflation, which in turn led to more exchange rate stability in the EMS, whereby realignments were less frequent and less important (see Table 7.1).

However, realignments remained awkward events. The realignment of January 1987 did indeed engender some bitter feelings among the participants. During the negotiations, a consensus was quickly reached on the necessary adjustment between the French franc and the German mark. However, discussions about the percentage of the "devaluations" and "revaluations" of the different currencies were acrimonious and long-running. The realignment of January 1987 was therefore a rather traumatic experience for policy-makers. It was a factor that contributed to the shelving of the realignment issue.

With the realignment of January 1987, the finance ministers requested the Committee of Central Bank Governors to work out proposals to strengthen the EMS. This would give rise to the so-called "Basle-Nyborg" agreement of September 1987. The agreement comprised certain changes in the operational provisions of the EMS, facilitating interventions. However, the communiqué also emphasised that these measures were part of a comprehensive strategy to foster cohesion within the EMS. Important elements were policies directed at sufficient convergence towards internal stability and the use of instruments other than foreign exchange interventions, such as the use of the fluctuation bands and, in particular changes in interest rates. For the central bank governors this probably marked the end of institutional monetary reform in Europe for many years to come (Gros and Thygesen, 1998, 93).

Table 7.1 - An overview of the functioning of the exchange rate mechanism of the EMS
(normal fluctuation margin of 2.25%)

Date	DEM	NLG	FRF	DKK	BEF/LUF	IEP	ITL	ESP	GBP	PTE	ATS	FIM	GRD
13.03.79	Start	Start	Start	Start	Start	Start	Start[1]						
24.09.79	+2.0			-2.9									
30.11.79				-4.8									
23.03.81							-6.0						
05.10.81	+5.5	+5.5	-3.0				-3.0						
22.02.82				-3.0	-8.5								
14.06.82	+4.25	+4.25	-5.75				-2.75						
21.03.83	+5.5	+3.5	-2.5	+2.5	+1.5	-3.5	-2.5						
22.07.85	+2.0	+2.0	+2.0	+2.0	+2.0	+2.0	-6.0						
06.04.86	+3.0	+3.0	-3.0	+1.0	+1.0								
04.08.86						-8.0							
12.01.87	+3.0	+3.0			+2.0								
19.06.89								Entrance[1]					
08.01.90							-3.7[2]						
08.10.90									Entrance				
06.04.92										Entrance[1]			
14.09.92	+3.5	+3.5	+3.5	+3.5	+3.5	+3.5	-3.5	+3.5	+3.5	+3.5			
16.09.92									Exit				
17.09.92							Exit	-5.0					
23.11.92								-6.0		-6.0			
01.02.93						-10.0							
14.05.93								-8.0		-6.5			
02.08.93	Enlargement of the fluctuation margins to 15% (DEM and NLG keep 2.25% fluctuation margin)												
09.01.95											Entrance		
06.03.95								-7.0		-3.5			
14.10.96												Entrance	
25.11.96							Entrance						
16.03.98						+3.0							Entrance

[1] Fluctuation margin of 6%.   [2] Reduction of fluctuation margin from 6% to 2.25%.

147

7.2.4   The Maastricht Process[7]

The relaunching of the monetary union project

Meanwhile, in 1985, the European Community was given a fresh and strong impetus by the adoption of the internal market program. Its aim was to achieve the fully free circulation of goods, services, people and capital by 1992. One of the cornerstones was the creation of a European financial market (cf. Servais, 1991). It also led to the "Single European Act", the first important modification of the Treaty of Rome. The Act also contained the first reference in the Treaties to Economic and Monetary Union[8].

This relaunching of the European Community was, to a large extent, made possible by the strong pro-European orientation of France and Germany, headed by François Mitterrand and Helmut Kohl. The strong leadership of Jacques Delors at the European Commission also played an important role.

For the exchange rate mechanism of the EMS the years from 1987 to 1992 were a kind of "golden period": exchange rates were stable and pressures in the financial markets for realignments were weak or absent. After the realignment of January 1987, there would be no further realignments until September 1992. Furthermore the fluctuation margin of the Italian lira was reduced from 6% to 2.25% and other currencies (the Spanish peseta, the British pound and the Portuguese escudo), became members of the exchange rate mechanism.

The completion of the internal market, with the liberalisation of capital movements, was also having consequences for monetary policy. A popular theme among central bankers and finance ministry officials in the second half of the 1980s was the so-called "impossible triangle", indicating that it is impossible to have free capital movement, fixed exchange rates and an autonomous monetary policy at the same time[9]. During the 1980s and early 1990s capital mobility had increased enormously in the European Union. With stable exchange rates in the ERM, there was no longer much room for an autonomous monetary policy, except in the anchor country. The European Community therefore had to live with the disadvantages of monetary union, while enjoying few of its advantages.

---

[7]   For an overview of the main steps in this process, see Annex 7.2.

[8]   In effect, the short chapter on EMU fell short of Delors' initial project (Grant, 1994, 73).

[9]   This is a typical example of the Mundell-Fleming analysis, cf. Padoa-Schioppa, 1987. For some estimates of capital mobility, cf. Commission of the European Communities, 1990, 160.

Table 7.2 - Cross-border transactions in bonds and equities[1]

	1975	1980	1985	1990	1991	1992	1993	1994	1995	1996	1997	1998
Germany	5	7	33	57	55	85	170	158	172	200	257	334
France	-	5	21	54	79	122	187	197	187	258	314	415
Italy	1	1	4	27	60	92	192	207	253	470	677	640

Source: BIS.

[1] *Gross purchases and sales of securities between residents and non-residents, as a percentage of GDP.*

Only a few months after the Basle-Nyborg agreement, debates about Europe's monetary future were opened again. In a memorandum of January 1988, the French finance minister, Edouard Balladur, argued that the exchange rate mechanism still had some important defects, notably its asymmetry. In February, Giuliano Amato, the Italian treasury minister, also submitted a memorandum, criticising the lack of an "engine of growth" in the EMS.

In his memorandum, Balladur argued that it was not necessarily the currency that was at the lower fluctuation margin which was "responsible" for the tensions. In the case of an unduly restrictive monetary policy in the anchor country, all currencies would appreciate against the US-dollar, something which could create tensions in the system and run counter to the interests of the European economies. Balladur criticised the German dominance of the system: "Il faut éviter qu'un seul pays ait, de fait, la responsabilité de fixer les objectifs de politique économique et monétaire de l'ensemble du système" (Balladur, 1988, 19).

Although, the Balladur Memorandum focused on adapting the way in which the EMS functioned, it also argued that it was necessary to reflect on further institutional steps in the monetary construction of Europe. With the liberalisation of capital movements and the internal market, an integrated economic area would be created: "La logique voudrait qu'une zone à monnaie unique soit alors créée" (Balladur, 1988, 20).

Balladur's Memorandum found a perceptive ear in Germany, not at the Bundesbank or the Finance Ministry (see Stoltenberg, 1988), but at the Foreign Ministry. Genscher had already emphasised, in a speech to the EU ambassadors on 24 March 1987, that the question of the institutional development of the EMS should be "*enttabuisiert*" and taken up again. Several factors converged in making economic and monetary union and a

European Central Bank a key theme for Genscher: (a) it was an attractive theme among the business community in Germany, a natural constituency of Genscher's liberal democratic party; (b) it fitted in perfectly with Genscher's pro-European convictions. It was important for Genscher to strengthen the process of European integration, which he considered as still fragile after the Euro-sclerosis of the first half of the 1980s; (c) Genscher was also strongly influenced by French complaints about the German dominance of the EMS and wanted to do something about this. The German Presidency of the Council of Ministers, in the first half of 1988, offered just such an opportunity (Schönfelder and Thiel, 1996, 29). In February 1988, Genscher, in his personal capacity, published a Memorandum wherein he argued strongly for a European Monetary Union and a European Central Bank.

Genscher's point of departure was that, from an economic point of view, an European Monetary Union with a European Central Bank was a necessary step in completing the European internal market (Genscher, 1988, 6). He then set out the conditions for the creation of a monetary union, emphasising the new economic order that had to be created. This comprised an independent central bank, with price stability as a fundamental objective of monetary policy and a prohibition of monetary financing of government budget deficits. Genscher explicitly recommended the German model, inspired not only by the Bundesbank Act but also by the Stability Act, in which economic policy had to be focused on broad macroeconomic objectives, including not only price stability, but also growth and employment[10]. He further recommended that a committee of wise men be set up at the Hanover Summit in June.

At that time, early in 1987, Helmut Kohl was still quite open to the issue of monetary union. On the one hand, he was sensitive to the arguments of Stoltenberg that EMU was only possible if a sufficient degree of convergence was achieved (coronation theory). On the other, he was under pressure from the advocates of EMU, like Genscher, but also from Mitterrand, for whom he had a high esteem and who often complained about the asymmetric functioning of the EMS. Moreover, Kohl gradually realised that EMU was unavoidable if he wanted to realise his vision of a "United States of Europe", a recurrent theme in his speeches at that time. Of crucial importance was the Franco-German bilateral summit at Evian, early in June 1988, when Kohl and Mitterrand decided to push ahead with EMU (Howarth, 1999b).

---

[10] The "Stability Act" was the product of Karl Schiller, one of Germany's most prominent Keynesians and Finance Minister of the Social Democrats (Hagemann, 2000).

Important progress was further made at the Hanover meeting of the European Council on 27 and 28 June 1988. It confirmed the objective of economic and monetary union and decided to entrust to a Committee the task of studying and proposing concrete stages leading towards this union. The Committee was chaired by Jacques Delors, who had the confidence of Kohl and Mitterand, and, as a former finance minister, the technical expertise. The governors of the central banks - in a personal capacity - were also on the Committee. Delors wanted them to be members, both because of their technical expertise and because this would bind them to the monetary union project. In a first reaction, Karl-Otto Pöhl, the president of the Bundesbank, even considered refusing to serve on the Committee (Pöhl, 1996, 196). The Committee produced its report for the June 1989 meeting of the European Council (Committee for the Study of Economic and Monetary Union, 1989, hereafter referred to as the Delors Report).

The Delors Report

The Delors Report would assume a crucial role as a reference and anchor point in further discussions, just as the Werner Report nearly two decades earlier.

The Delors Report basically revolved around two issues: first, which economic arrangements are necessary for a monetary union to be successful? Second, which gradualist path should be designed to reach economic and monetary union?

In defining the necessary conditions for a monetary union, the Delors Report referred back to the Werner Report (Delors Report, 18): (a) the assurance of total and irreversible convertibility of currencies; (b) the complete liberalisation of capital transactions and full integration of banking and other markets; (c) the elimination of margins of fluctuation and the irrevocable locking of exchange rate parities.

The Delors Report also provided a characterisation of economic union (Delors Report, 20): (a) the single market within which persons, goods, services and capital can move freely; (b) competition policy and other measures aimed at strengthening market mechanisms; (c) common policies aimed at structural change and regional development; (d) macroeconomic policy coordination, including binding rules for budgetary policies.

In the Delors Committee, the design and structure of a monetary union gave rise to a debate between the French and the Germans. Jacques de Larosière, the governor of the Banque de France, argued for "a pragmatic approach, centred around the gradual fulfilment of the final objective ultimately chosen" (de Larosière, 1988, 177). He proposed the creation of a

European Reserve Fund, which would be built up progressively. One of its functions could be intervention in the foreign exchange markets. The position taken by de Larosière was therefore in line with the classic French ideas of strengthening support mechanisms for weak currency countries.

Karl-Otto Pöhl, the president of the Bundesbank took a "fundamentalist" approach, emphasising the new monetary order which had to be created: "Above all agreement must exist that stability of the value of money is the indispensable prerequisite for the achievement of other goals. Particular importance will therefore attach to the principles on which a European monetary order should be based" (Pöhl, 1988, 132). He argued for price stability as the prime objective of monetary policy, which had to be conducted by an independent central bank.

The fundamentalist approach would be deeply influential in the Delors Report and inspire a number of principles that would figure prominently in the Maastricht Treaty (Padoa-Schioppa, 1994, 9). The Delors Report proposed, on an institutional level, the creation of an independent "European System of Central Banks", which would be responsible for the single monetary policy. A modification of the Treaty of Rome was therefore necessary.

To attain economic and monetary union the Delors Committee proposed three stages. However, the Committee underlined the indivisibility of the whole process: "the decision to enter upon the first stage should be a decision to embark on the entire process " (Delors Report, 31).

The three stages were, in contrast to the emphasis by the Werner Report on the first stage, all worked out in considerable detail. These stages implied, from an institutional and legal point of view: the preparation of a new Treaty (first stage), the creation of a new monetary institution (European System of Central Banks, second stage), and the transfer of responsibilities to this new institution (third stage). From an economic and monetary point of view, these stages implied an increased convergence and a closer coordination of economic policy.

The European Community followed the path indicated in the Delors Report. The first stage started in July 1990 and the intergovernmental conference on economic and monetary union, along with another one on political union, opened in Rome in December 1990.

Meanwhile, the broader European scene was changing dramatically with the breakdown of the iron curtain and German unification, contributing to speeding up of the process of European monetary integration. The German government's policy line could almost be summarised in Thomas Mann's dictum: "Wir wollen ein europäisches Deutschland und kein deutsches Europa" (Schönfelder and Thiel, 1996, 12).

The Maastricht Treaty

The intergovernmental conferences reached their climax at the Maastricht Summit of Heads of State and Government in December 1991. The Maastricht Treaty marked a step forward for the European community in the same way that the Treaty of Rome had done. It created a so-called European Union, based on three pillars.

The first pillar has at its core the old Community, but carrying greatly extended responsibilities with it. The main element here is economic and monetary union. The second pillar is for foreign and security policy. The third one concerns cooperation on such topics as immigration, asylum and police. These last two pillars are intergovernmental bodies in which the Commission, Parliament and Court have a more restricted say. The new Treaty also extended the powers of the European Parliament.

Economic and monetary union has a kind of asymmetrical structure. Monetary policy is centralised. It is the responsibility of the European System of Central Banks, composed of the European Central Bank and the national central banks, which are all independent. The primary objective of monetary policy is price stability. Without prejudice to the objective of price stability, the ESCB will support the general economic policies in the Community. This part of the Treaty went quite smoothly through the intergovernmental conference. The preparations in the Delors Committee and the Committee of Governors certainly contributed to this.

The responsibility for other instruments of economic policy, like budgetary policy and incomes policy, remains basically decentralised, resting with the national authorities. However, member states have to regard their economic policies as a matter of common concern and coordinate them accordingly. Important elements in this coordination process are the Broad Economic Guidelines, the multilateral surveillance process and the excessive deficit procedure[11].

The coordination process of budgetary policy had been the topic of some of the most tense discussions during the intergovernmental conference. The French had proposed a *"gouvernement économique"*, whereby the European Council would provide for broad orientations for economic policy, including monetary policy. This provoked a strong clash with the Germans, for whom the independence of the European Central Bank was *"a conditio sine qua non"*. However, the Germans were also convinced of the necessity of a coordination of other economic policies, especially budgetary policy, as they

---

[11] Later they were supplemented with the Growth and Stability Pact and the Euro Group.

determined the environment in which monetary policy had to function. The agreement was only reached after intense negotiations, including secret bilateral discussions between the French and the Germans.

The Maastricht Treaty also specified the path to EMU, another very difficult issue during the intergovernmental conference. The second stage started in January 1994. The main elements of this second phase were the creation of the European Monetary Institute, the precursor to the European Central Bank, and the abolition of the monetary financing of public authorities.

Stage Three, economic and monetary union itself, started on 1 January 1999[12]. In order to participate, the Member States had to fulfil certain conditions, especially central bank independence and the achievement of a high degree of sustainable convergence. Of special importance in these assessments were four "convergence" criteria:

- price stability - the member state should have an inflation rate no more than 1.5% above the average of the three EC countries with the lowest inflation rates;
- sustainability of public finance - national budget deficits must be less than 3% of GDP. The public debt ratio must not exceed 60% of GDP, or be declining at a sufficient rate;
- currency stability - a national currency must not have been devalued in the previous two years and must have remained within the normal fluctuation margins of the exchange-rate mechanism;
- interest rates - long-term interest rates should be within two percentage points of the average of the three countries with the lowest inflation rates.

The conditions for the start of monetary union, namely a fixed date and the satisfaction of the convergence criteria, were again the outcome of a debate between the monetarists and the economists. The monetarists, especially France and Italy, insisted on a fixed date to ensure the start of monetary union, while the economists, in particular Germany, insisted on economic criteria so that only countries which were "fit" could participate in the monetary union.

---

[12] In the Treaty, two dates are mentioned: 1997, if a majority of countries could fulfil the criteria, and 1999 as an ultimate date.

The ERM crisis[13]

The completion of the internal market and the relaunching of the monetary union project created a general atmosphere of "Europhoria", which reached a climax with the agreement on the Maastricht Treaty. This further contributed to a belief in the stability of the exchange rates in the EMS, inducing investors to buy "high yield" currencies like the Italian lira, the Spanish peseta or the British pound. This led to a decline in the interest rate differentials of these "high yield currencies" compared to the German mark.

Figure 7.4 - Interest rate differentials of some European currencies vis-à-vis the German mark in the 1990s[1]

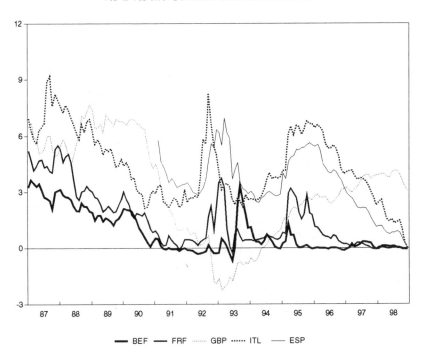

Source: NBB.
   [1] *Three month euro-deposits.*

---

13 See Buiter, Corsetti and Pesenti, 1998 and Eichengreen and Wyplosz, 1993.

In this climate of "Europhoria" of the late 1980s and early 1990s
investors believed that exchange rate risk was negligible. However,
notwithstanding a remarkable convergence in inflation rates in the European
Union, the economic fundamentals of several currencies began moving away
from their central rates: with stable exchange rates and with still higher
inflation (compared to Germany), countries like Italy, the United Kingdom,
Spain and Portugal, were becoming increasingly less competitive. This was
also reflected in growing deficits on the current account of their balance of
payments.

Figure 7.5 - The ERM crisis: economic fundamentals

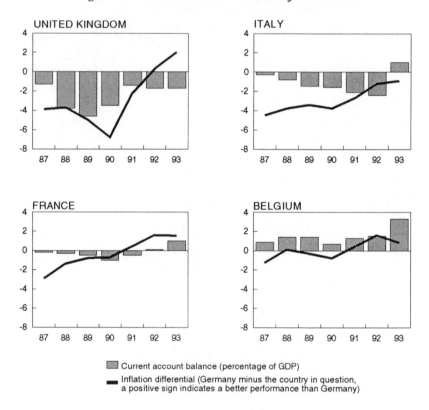

Sources: EC, NBB.

Meanwhile, German unification led to an increase in the budget deficit and to inflationary pressures in Germany. Consequently, the Bundesbank pursued a more restrictive monetary policy, contributing to an increase in German interest rates and making the German mark more attractive.

Beneath the apparent quietness of the foreign exchange markets, pressures were thus building-up which could unleash a storm. The trigger for the crisis turned out to be the no vote in the Danish referendum of May 1992, which brought about a drastic change in the psychological climate. Doubts about the achievement of monetary union resurfaced and increased further when opinion polls showed that there was a possibility that the French could also reject the Maastricht Treaty in their referendum in September.

Figure 7.6 - Exchange rates of some European currencies vis-à-vis the German mark in the 1990s
(indices 1987=100)

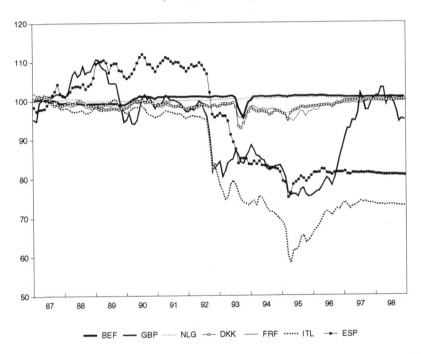

Source: NBB.

In this climate of uncertainty about monetary union, the financial markets rediscovered exchange rate risk and started looking once more at the economic fundamentals behind the central rates. In the summer, financial investors turned en masse against the Italian lira and the British pound, two currencies with weak fundamentals. The result was that both were forced out of the exchange rate mechanism in September 1992.

Having made big profits on the lira and the pound, the markets turned against the Spanish peseta and Portuguese escudo, also currencies with weak fundamentals. They had to be devalued several times but they managed to stay in the exchange rate mechanism.

Domino effects were widespread and the financial markets also attacked the French franc, Danish krone and Belgian franc, core currencies of the ERM with sound fundamentals, especially in terms of inflation and balance of payments. However, the monetary authorities strongly defended these currencies. After discussions at the highest level, the Bundesbank supported the French franc for substantial amounts. In the first half of 1993 the financial markets became quieter.

However, tensions flared up again in the summer of 1993. Since central banks were limited in their ability to contain these speculative capital movements, it was decided in August 1993 that the fluctuation margins of the ERM should be widened from 2.25% to 15%. The objective was to confront speculators with the possibility that a currency could fall and rise again inside the new bands. However, the central rates were maintained, since, in the opinion of policy-makers, they were based on sound economic fundamentals. They could therefore act as an anchor for the financial markets.

After the decision of August 1993 to widen the fluctuation margins to 15%, several currencies such as the French franc, the Danish krone and the Belgian franc depreciated against the German mark. These were certainly dark hours for the EMU project, and doubts became widespread.

However, at the end of 1993, the financial markets started to realise that the depreciation of these currencies was not appropriate and a process of correction began. The governments in the European Union also took measures to improve the competitiveness of their economies and to reduce budget deficits. An example is certainly Belgium's Global Plan for Employment, Competitiveness and Social Security, adopted in November 1993.

Budgetary consolidation in the European Union was important both in defending directly the exchange rate and also in meeting the convergence criteria, indispensable for maintaining the credibility of the monetary union project, and also thereby contributing to the calming of the foreign exchange markets. Thanks also to these budgetary measures, the budget deficit for the

European Union as a whole diminished from 6.2% of GDP in 1993 to 2.4% in 1997.

Figure 7.7 - Government deficit in the European Union[1]
(as percentage of GDP)

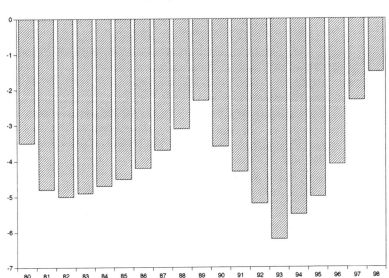

[1] *EU14 (EU15 with the exclusion of Luxembourg, 1980-91: West Germany).*

Thus bolstered by budgetary consolidation and institutional progress towards monetary union (cf. *infra*), exchange rates returned to their central rates and became more stable again. At the end of 1996 the Italian lira reentered the exchange rate mechanism.

Stage Two

Notwithstanding the ERM crisis and resistance in certain countries (especially Denmark and the United Kingdom, but also France and Germany), the Maastricht ratification process was concluded and the Treaty became effective on 1 November 1993, ten months later than initially planned.

The second stage of economic and monetary union started on 1 January 1994 and the European Monetary Institute (EMI) was set up on schedule. The EMI played an important role in the coordination of monetary policies in Stage Two and, in particular, in the preparation of Stage Three, especially the single monetary policy and the scenario for the introduction of the euro (cf. Lamfalussy, 1996).

Table 7.3 - *Main features of the changeover scenario*

	Delineation of periods	Main action points within each period
	early 1998	
1st period	Decision by the Heads of State or of Government on the Member States participating in the euro	- Establish the ECB and the ESCB and make them operational
	1st January 1999	
2nd period	Start of Stage Three of EMU: - Irrevocable fixing of conversion rates among the currencies of participating Member States and the euro - Entry into force of legislation relating to the introduction of the euro - Euro introduced in non-cash form Euro banknotes *1st January 2002* and coins introduced *at the latest*	- Conduct of the single monetary and foreign exchange policy in euro by the ESCB as from day one - New tradable public debt issued in euro
3rd period	National banknotes and coins lose legal *1st July 2002* tender status *at the latest*	- Implement the complete change-over of the public administration - Withdraw national banknotes and coins - Monitor the complete changeover of the private sector

Source: EMI, 1993, 48.

One of the main issues unresolved at the time concerned the concrete scenario for the changeover to the single currency. This was a very complex and delicate issue, as it affected the banking system, financial markets, enterprises and the public at large. The European Commission issued a "Green Paper on the Practical Arrangements for the Single Currency" (CEC, 1995) in May 1995 and in so doing brought the issue to the fore. The

EMI published its scenario for the changeover in November 1995 (EMI, 1995). The documents of the Commission and the EMI formed the basis for the scenario that was finally adopted by the European Council in December 1995.

The European Council of Madrid in December 1995 took some very important decisions: it affirmed the date of 1 January 1999 as the starting date of the third stage; it decided on the name "euro" for the future single currency; and it adopted the scenario for the changeover to the single currency.

The proposed scenario outlines three separate periods: the first period starts when the European Council decides on which countries satisfy the convergence criteria. Crucial in this phase is the creation of the European Central Bank. The second period starts on 1 January 1999 when the euro becomes the official currency, while national currencies become non-decimal subdivisions of the euro. It ends when euro notes and coins are introduced. From the start of this period onwards, exchange rates between the participating countries are irrevocably fixed and the ESCB conducts the single monetary policy in euros. Furthermore, the participating countries will issue their new debt issues in euros. The aim of these decisions was to create a "critical mass" so that the financial markets would shift towards the euro. The third period starts on the day that euro notes and coins are introduced and should have a maximum duration of six months.

The decisions made at the Madrid Summit strengthened confidence in the EMU process, as evident in the decline of interest rate spreads with the German mark. They also marked the moment from which the international financial community started to take the EMU process seriously.

An important topic in the EMU negotiations in this period was also the "Stability and Growth Pact". Discussions were launched with the proposal by Theo Waigel, the German finance minister, in November 1995, that a "Stability Pact for Europe" should be concluded. This would tighten the rules on budgetary behaviour for the EMU participants and include automatic sanctions. After long and extended negotiations, a political agreement was reached at the Dublin Summit in December 1996. The Stability and Growth Pact requires that, under normal circumstances, the budget deficit should not exceed the 3% limit. Moreover, to prevent budgetary excesses, countries have to present "Stability" programmes. Furthermore, where the 3% ceiling is not respected, sanctions are possible[14]. The legal texts were agreed upon at the June 1997 Amsterdam summit.

---

[14] For a further analysis of the Growth and Stability Pact, see Buti and Sapir, 1998 and OECD, 1999.

New procedures have also been developed to reinforce the surveillance and coordination of economic policies among the countries participating in the euro-zone. Of special importance is the so-called Euro Group, where finance ministers of the eleven countries which participate in the euro area can meet informally to discuss issues which are related to the specific responsibilities which they share as members of the euro area (Maystadt, 1998, 22).

The monetary and exchange rate policy of the future monetary union was also an important topic of discussion. The drafting of the provisions on the international exchange rate policy of the Union was a laborious balancing act in order to define the responsibilities of the political and monetary authorities, and to ensure the compatibility of exchange rate policies and the ECB's primary aim of price stability. Another problem was related to the asymmetrical structure of EMU, with a centralised monetary policy and a decentralised budgetary policy, for which national governments remained responsible. There was therefore no "natural" representative of the budgetary pole in international negotiations. Furthermore as not all countries were expected to take part in EMU on 1 January 1999, it was important to develop a new exchange rate mechanism for the "pre-ins". Agreement on this ERM II mechanism, with the euro at the centre, was reached at the December 1996 Dublin Summit.

Meanwhile, the EMI also worked on the preparation of the single monetary policy in phase three, and published several reports on this issue (see, especially, EMI, 1997). However, as according to the Maastricht Treaty, the single monetary policy was a responsibility of the ECB, official decisions could only be taken in the second half of 1998.

The final decisions

At a special summit of the Heads of State and Government in May 1998 in Brussels it was confirmed that economic and monetary union would start with 11 countries: Belgium, the Netherlands, Luxembourg, Germany, France, Italy, Spain, Portugal, Ireland, Austria and Finland.

The EU Council followed the Commission Recommendation that 11 of the 15 countries of the European Union fulfilled the conditions for adopting the single currency (CEC, 1998a): Denmark had notified that it would not participate in the third stage of economic and monetary union; Greece had fulfilled its legal obligations regarding central bank independence, but did not fulfil any of the convergence criteria; Sweden had made insufficient progress in the fulfilment of these legal obligations and did not fulfil the convergence criterion regarding the exchange rate; the United Kingdom had notified that it did not intend moving on to the third stage of economic and monetary union on 1 January 1999.

Essential elements in the procedure had been the "convergence reports" of the Commission and the EMI which had to examine the compatibility of national legislation with the Treaty and the Statute of the ESCB and the achievement of a high degree of sustainable convergence.

The compatibility of national legislation with the Treaty and the Statute of the ESCB involved three elements (EMI, 1998, 12):

- independence of national central banks. This comprised three features: institutional, personal and financial independence;
- the legal integration of the national central banks in the ESCB, which necessitated measures in addition to those designed to ensure independence;
- legislation other than the statutes of the national central banks.

Sustainable convergence was focused on the four "convergence criteria": price stability, the government budgetary position, exchange rates and long-term interest rates.

Both reports observed a broad progress in the field of price stability. Moreover, it was noted that several underlying factors indicated that the inflation performance was sustainable, and not the effect of cyclical or temporary factors (CEC, 1998b, 66):

- price stability has become the primary objective of monetary policy;
- the disinflation process is supported by adequate wage behaviour. Several factors seem to explain the moderation in wages: both trade unions and employers appear to have attached greater credibility to the resolve and ability of monetary authorities to achieve price stability; there have been profound changes in wage-setting procedures, e.g. the removal or modification of formulae for automatic wage indexation in several countries; wage negotiations seem increasingly to have taken into account developments on the real side of the economy, like the development of productivity; countries have stepped up their efforts to improve the employability and adaptability of labour;
- more appropriate domestic reactions to changes in import prices, reducing the pass-through ratio from import prices to final prices.

Figure 7.8 - Key convergence indicators

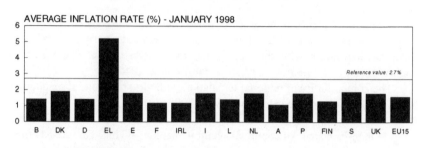

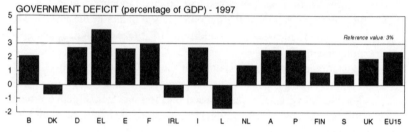

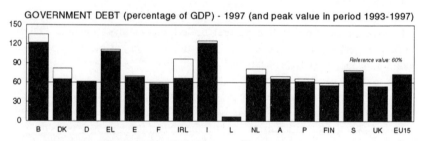

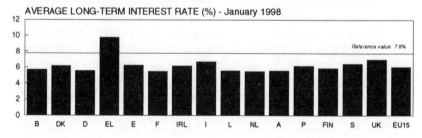

Source: CEC, 1998b.

Figure 7.9 - Inflation convergence in the European Union

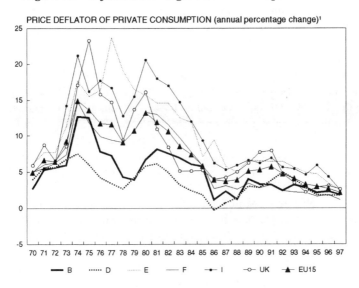

PRICE DEFLATOR OF PRIVATE CONSUMPTION (annual percentage change)[1]

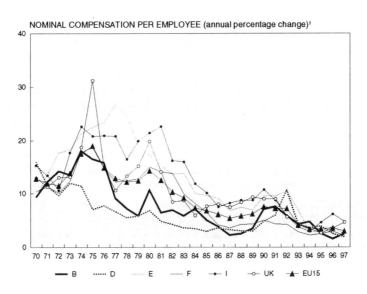

NOMINAL COMPENSATION PER EMPLOYEE (annual percentage change)[1]

Source: CEC.
       [1] 1970-1991: WD.

Important progress was also made concerning the government budgetary situation. In all countries of the Union, with the exception of Greece, the 3% criterion was respected. The overall budget deficit for the European Union amounted to 2.4% of GDP in 1997, a remarkable improvement compared to the 6.2% of GDP in 1993. This budgetary consolidation was to a large extent the result of cuts in current expenditures, an indication of the sustainable character of the improvement. The government debt criterion was respected, since the debt to GDP ratio was below 60% or declining[15]. Only Greece still remained the subject of a decision on the existence of an excessive deficit.

Exchange rates of the European Union currencies were quite stable in the period from March 1996 to February 1998. These smooth and quiet conditions on the exchange markets can principally be explained by growing market expectations of a timely launch of EMU with a large number of countries, itself a reflection of the growing convergence, the steady progress in preparations and the strength of the political commitment to EMU. The Italian lira and the Finish markka had not participated for the full two-year period in the exchange rate system of the EMS. However, as they had not experienced severe tensions during the review period, they were judged to have displayed sufficient stability. There were no realignments during the review period. However, in March 1998, after the review period, the Irish pound was revalued by 3% against the other ERM currencies.

Substantial progress was also made regarding the interest rate criterion. From the end of 1994 long-term interest rates in the European Union have converged downwards. Several factors can account for this development: the decline of inflationary pressures, budgetary consolidation and stable exchange rates in the European Union, as well as the decline of yields in the United States.

The convergence reports also examined certain additional factors, as required by the Treaty: the development of the ECU, the results of the integration of markets, the situation and the development of the balances of payments on the current account and the development of unit labour costs and other price indices.

While both reports noted major improvements in terms of convergence, they also argued that further efforts were necessary. The EMI stated that:

---

[15] A special case was Germany where the public debt ratio was 61.3% in 1997 and was going up. However, the debt ratio was close to 60% and expected to decline in 1998. Moreover the German debt ratio was affected by the costs of German unification.

Within the context of a single monetary policy, the adjustments seen over the recent past need to be carried substantively further. Indeed, decisive and sustained corrective policies of a structural nature are warranted in most countries. These requirements for lasting policy adjustments result from the combined burden from (i) high and persistent unemployment, which according to the analysis conducted by the EMI and other international organisations is largely of a structural nature; (ii) demographic trends, which are expected to place a heavy burden on future public expenditure; and (iii) the high level of public debt, which will weigh on current budgets of many Member States until debt levels are reduced. (EMI, 1998, 4).

7.3 WHY WAS EUROPE'S ATTEMPT AT EMU SUCCESSFUL?

On 1 January 1999, EMU effectively started with eleven countries. The question investigated in this section is why this attempt was successful, in contrast to the fate of the Werner plan in the 1970s. Two types of factors can be distinguished: first, long-term structural developments which created a favourable background and, second, the dynamics of the process of European integration in the 1980s and 1990s. It was the period when "history accelerated" (Delors, 1992, Ch. 3), creating a "window of opportunity", which has been skilfully exploited with the help of appropriate policy-decisions and meticulous preparations. However, on numerous occasions the project could easily have become derailed or at least been postponed for a considerable period. It could therefore be argued that the achievement of EMU should not be taken for granted.

7.3.1 Long-term structural factors

Four long-term structural factors can be identified which prepared the way for the key decisions on EMU: an increasing degree of economic integration, a growing consensus on macroeconomic policy objectives, an increasing underlying political will and Europe's international aspirations.

A greater degree of economic integration

Economic integration in Europe has advanced substantially during the last decades. Trade interdependence, as measured by the level of intra-EU area trade as a percentage of GDP between 1970 and 1995, has increased. Euro area intra-industry trade flows for manufactured goods have also risen over the same period, especially for countries that were not founding members of the European Community. Income from wealth has become more internationally diversified, due to growing financial integration in Europe and foreign direct investment flows. Economic linkages between the European countries have therefore increased significantly. This interdependence has reduced the effectiveness of changes in exchange rates as an instrument of economic policy, and this strengthened the logic of monetary integration.

Table 7.4 - Foreign direct investment flows in euro area economies
(as a percentage of GDP)

Country	Inward investment from other euro area countries		Outward investment to other euro area countries	
	1986-1990	1991-1995	1986-1990	1991-1995
Austria	0.26	0.28	0.17	0.24
Belgium-Luxembourg	1.86	2.93	1.32	3.01
Finland	0.07	0.13	0.45	0.28
France	0.29	0.45	0.63	0.58
Germany	0.12	0.10	0.46	0.56
Ireland	0.15	0.07	0.00	0.00
Italy	0.16	0.17	0.28	0.28
Netherlands	0.62	0.98	0.65	1.44
Portugal	0.88	0.93	0.05	0.37
Spain	1.12	1.03	0.22	0.18

Source: OECD, 1999, 101.

Figure 7.10 - Openness of the European economies in 1970 and 1995
(exports of goods as percentage of GDP)

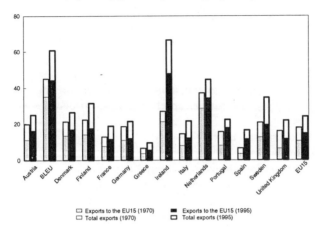

☐ Exports to the EU15 (1970)   ■ Exports to the EU15 (1995)
☐ Total exports (1970)   ☐ Total exports (1995)

Source: IMF.

Figure 7.11 - Intensity of intra-euro intra-industry trade
(manufactured goods)

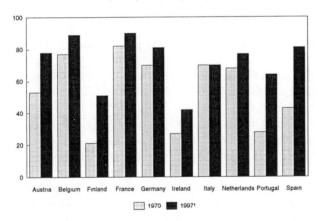

▦ 1970   ■ 1997¹

Source: OECD, 1999, 99.
        ¹ 1996 for Netherlands, Portugal and Spain.

More consensus on policy objectives

There have been profound changes in economic thought and society between the 1970s and 1990s. At the beginning of the 1970s Keynesianism was still very influential among economic policy-makers in the European Community (Maes, 1998). It was characterised by an emphasis on activist budgetary policy and a belief in a stable Phillips curve, i.e. a reliable relationship between prices and unemployment, which made it possible for policy-makers to steer the economy towards their preferred trade-off between inflation and unemployment.

The "Monetarist counter-revolution" questioned the Keynesian framework, leading to thrilling debates, initially mainly in the academic world. In a first stage, discussions centred on the determination of nominal demand, monetarists emphasising the money supply and not budgetary policy, as the main determinant of effective demand. In a second stage, the attention shifted towards the functioning of the labour market, with the monetarists attacking the Phillips curve (Friedman, 1968). The stagflation of the 1970s further indicated the limits of activist policies and was an important factor in the decline of Keynesianism among policy-makers (McNamara, 1999, 129).

Gradually a new consensus developed which moved away from active demand management policies towards a more medium-term orientation, emphasising structural, supply-side oriented policies. A core ingredient of the new strategy was that monetary policy should be conducted by an independent central bank and geared to price stability. This was further supported by academic studies, both theoretical and empirical, which indicated that central bank independence went together with greater stability and a better economic performance (see Grilli, Masciandaro and Tabellini, 1991 and Fischer, 1994).

The movement towards medium-term, stability-oriented policies reflected not only changes in economic theory but also deeper changes in society. In the early 1970s the legacy of May 1968 was still keenly felt. Distribution conflicts were quite common in most European countries, as was apparent from recurrent strikes in most countries and the strong position of the communist parties in France and Italy. In the 1980s and 1990s distribution conflicts receded, leading to profound changes in the wage-setting procedures, such as the removal or modification of formulae for automatic wage indexation. This contributed to more appropriate wage movements.

An increasing underlying political will to achieve European integration

The Second World War constituted a trauma for European policy-makers. Avoiding a new war became the fundamental aim of the post-war politicians and European integration appeared to be an obvious instrument.

France and Germany have been the main movers in EMU. In this respect one can refer to the crucial role of Brandt-Pompidou, Schmidt-Giscard and Kohl-Mitterrand (with the supportive role of Delors, first as French finance minister, then as President of the European Commission).

The French-German axis has been a driving force despite (or in a certain sense due to) significant differences in interests and priorities. In Germany there was an historically motivated, deep-seated fear of inflation among most of its population. European monetary arrangements were only acceptable if price stability could be safeguarded. Consequently the Bundesbank could always count on popular support if it felt that stability was at risk. Kohl did not follow the Bundesbank where he did not agree with its advice concerning vital political issues (like the monetary conditions of German unification) but nevertheless fully supported it in its efforts to ensure that the future ECB was committed to price stability and independent of political instructions. In effect, he made this a German condition for EMU. While political Bonn was the EMU driving-force, it did not overlook monetary Frankfurt.

France traditionally regarded monetary policy as an integrated part of the policies of the Government. Besides establishing Europe as a counterweight to the United States, French monetary policy has been increasingly dictated by the steady increase of German economic power and the dominance of the German mark. A strict German monetary policy not only tended to force an appreciation of the European currencies against the dollar, thereby deteriorating Europe's competitive position, but they also confronted France in particular with a difficult choice. As long as devaluation was a means to restore its competitive position (and was as such incorporated in French industrial strategy), the recurrent pressure on the French franc and the difficult negotiations around parity realignments threatened French political and monetary prestige and credibility. The history of the snake and the first years of the EMS give ample evidence of this situation. Against this background two major developments help to explain the French move to EMU: first, the waning of orthodox Gaullist influence which allowed initiatives which implied that European integration had become a fact of life and that attachment to national sovereignty had receded; second, the recognition that only a European pooling of national monetary policies could put an end to German dominance.

It would be erroneous to attribute the political support of European integration exclusively to the Franco-German alliance. The role of the Benelux countries and Italy, for example, should not be overlooked. Especially so when relations between France and Germany were strained, and the necessary political support had to be drummed up to safeguard the continuity of the integration process.

The dominant role of France and Germany has also been facilitated by the "wait and see" attitude of the United Kingdom towards EMU. Britain's sceptical attitude was well summarised by John Major (1993), who spoke of the "mantra of full economic and monetary union", which has "all the quaintness of a rain dance and about the same potency".

Europe's international role

The strengthening of Europe's international role has always been recognised as a forceful argument in favour of more economic and monetary integration. It would reduce Europe's exposure to international economic disturbances and its dependence on US policies. A genuine international reserve currency would permit Europe to share in what de Gaulle called "the exorbitant privilege of the dollar" and strengthen Europe's voice in international economic and monetary policy-making.

However, the practical implementation of a common external policy in the economic and monetary field has been complicated and delayed by policy divergences and vested national interests. The relationship of the big three (France, Germany and the United Kingdom) with the United States was dictated by different motivations. While the United Kingdom remained attached to an historically privileged relationship with the US, France wanted to challenge US monetary policy and insisted on common dollar policies to that end. Germany was less interested in confrontational policies, taking into account the US military presence on its territory as a protection against the East and its growing importance as the principal representative of Europe in the international community. Moreover, the Bundesbank feared that excessive interventions in the foreign exchange markets would undermine its monetary stability goals, although it could not ignore the worries of German industry during bouts of severe weakness of the American dollar. The German authorities argued that convergence towards stability was the most efficient way of protecting Europe against external monetary disturbances. They also took the realistic view that a common dollar policy remained an empty box so long as the US was opposed to external constraints on their monetary policy. With the benefit of hindsight the German approach seems to have prevailed. The progress achieved in the field of stability convergence in Europe mitigated the asymmetrical effects of dollar instability on European exchange rates, while US willingness to take part in active monetary cooperation has remained exceptional, primarily designed to serve US commercial interests (for example the Plaza Accord of 1985).

7.3.2 A Strong Dynamics

While the long-term structural factors created a favourable background, a combination of events, initiatives and policy decisions in the mid-80s generated a dynamic process, a "window of opportunity", which has proved decisive. A distinction can be made between initiatives leading to the decisions taken at the 1988 Hanover European Summit, the negotiations leading to the signing of the Maastricht Treaty and the management of the subsequent transition period until 1 January 1999.

The Single Market dynamics

Besides constituting the primary building block of an economic union, the agreement on the European single market has also stimulated the debate on the linkage between the single market and monetary integration (Emerson, 1991, 59). Was the adoption of a single currency necessary to perfect the free trade in goods and services that were called for in the Act? In other words, does a single market require a single currency (or another form of monetary integration)? Contrary to the views expressed by a number of mainly Anglo-Saxon economists, the European Commission argued in "One Market, One Money" (CEC, 1990) that the implications of the Single Market Act largely exceeded the scope of a free trade zone and held the view that the EMS did not warrant a degree of monetary stability required to reap the benefits from a single market. Indeed, although there was considerable evidence that the effectiveness of capital controls had already been greatly eroded, it was felt that the implementation of full capital liberalisation, as part of the single market programme, would mean that the EC was faced with the prospect either of renewed exchange rate instability or the need to heighten the degree of monetary policy coordination to the point that national monetary sovereignty had little substance left.

The single market/currency arguments also benefited from the changing economic environment in Europe at that time. As a reaction to the period of europessimism in the early 80s, politicians and business leaders believed that a truly frontier-free market of more than 300 million consumers would result in a dynamic impetus, boosting investment and efficiency. The 1992 program quickly began to gain credibility, in part because of new treaty powers that enabled majority voting to expedite the passing of legislation required on many such matters. This did indeed have a dynamic effect on the strategic plans of many enterprises that scrambled to position themselves in expectation of this new environment. The creation of the Association for Monetary Union in Europe (AMUE) under the aegis of Helmut Schmidt and Valéry Giscard d'Estaing promoted business support for EMU as a completion of Europe's single market.

Franco-German rapprochement on European monetary issues

Even after the French decision of March 1983 to opt for the EMS, different views on the proper functioning of the System continued to dominate the monetary relationship between France and Germany. France did not like to be placed in a position where reserve losses, due to the support of a weak franc, would force it either to adopt the German priorities or to leave the system. German dominance in the EMS was then a very sensitive issue for French policy-makers. During Franco-German negotiations, Jacques Attali even called the German mark the "*force de frappe allemande*". This did not mean that French policy-makers rejected external discipline but it reflected a desire to ensure that the policy stance in the EMS would not be exclusively determined by the Bundesbank.

France first tried to achieve this objective by putting forward limited technical proposals for EMS reform. The ECU played a prominent role in these reform packages. Creating ECUs on behalf of deficit countries would mitigate the pressure of reserve losses, provided surplus countries were obliged to accept ECUs without limits or other acceptability restrictions. In addition, urging the promotion of the ECU seemed to be a good strategy. For its proponents (mainly the financial community) the ECU was associated with further European integration, even though no official statement or scenario had been published regarding its development into a single European currency. However, according to Szász (a former director of the Nederlandsche Bank), instead of facilitating a consensus on the proper functioning of the EMS, the French tactics of small, technical steps stiffened the defensive attitude of the Bundesbank which considered more generous EMS-financing as a threat to monetary stability. Although the Bundesbank could count on a hands-off approach by the German government, it became increasingly irritated by the awkward position it was in. It was publicly presented as the main obstacle to further European integration, always saying no to everything that was proposed, in particular concerning the ECU. However, instead of giving in on its stability aim, the Bundesbank took a more offensive stance by raising the issue of the remaining limits to capital liberalisation and was supported in this by Bonn.

Szàsz (1999, 82) views this development as a crucial stage preceding the political decisions on EMU in the late eighties. Noting Germany's firm views on stability and convergence and confronted with the German claim of capital liberalisation (supported by Delors as President of the Commission), France came to the conclusion that the only way to influence German monetary decision-making was by completely transferring it to the European level.

Securing the agreement on the Maastricht Treaty[16]

The negotiations leading to the Maastricht Treaty have undoubtedly benefited from the outstanding work performed by the Delors group, the substantive contributions from the various institutions involved in the preparatory process and the underlying political drive.

The failure of the earlier attempt at monetary union in the 1970s had been thoroughly analysed by the Delors Committee which identified four intrinsic weaknesses in the Werner Report: insufficient constraints on national policies, institutional ambiguities, excessive confidence in the ability of policy instruments to affect policy goals in a predictable way and a lack of internal momentum (Baer and Padoa-Schioppa, 1988, 57). Without underestimating the value of the Werner Report, the Delors Committee as well as the negotiators of the Maastricht Treaty learnt from these weaknesses when launching the new scheme. Three elements played a crucial role in the preparations for EMU (Rey, 1999, 5): (a) from the outset, in the Delors Report and in the Maastricht Treaty, the final outlook of the third phase has been well defined; (b) the negotiation and approval of the Maastricht Treaty, implied, at an early stage, a major political engagement. This gave this attempt at monetary union a greater transparency and a democratic legitimacy; (c) the technical involvement of the central banks was very intense. It gave the project, especially in the monetary sphere, a robust and professional character.

The agreement on the Maastricht Treaty has also been facilitated by the insertion of a certain degree of flexibility in the Treaty provisions, such as the derogation procedures and the absence of a clear description of the aims and precise content of EPU. Indeed, the negotiators of the Maastricht Treaty, including Helmut Kohl, have themselves removed from the draft treaty the

---

[16] For an analysis of the negotiations on the Maastricht Treaty, see Dyson and Featherstone, 1999 and Italianer, 1993.

proposal to assign to the Union "a federal vocation", without specifying another ultimate objective of the EPU. While this omission was decided on UK insistence, something in line with their traditional attitude, it has occurred without much discussion. This rather indicates the general feeling at the Summit that a discussion would have been futile. According to de Schoutheete (1997), the EC countries have constantly avoided a fundamental debate on the final aims of European integration. They have opted instead for a pragmatic approach based on (often flexible) deadlines and procedures applied by the Community institutions (Commission, European Parliament, Court of Justice) with increasing constraints on national policies.

The agreement on the Treaty was also secured by the creation of the "Cohesion Fund". Countries in the "periphery" of the Union, especially Spain, feared that the economic policies necessary to qualify for EMU would have negative effects on the lesser-developed countries. To remedy this the Cohesion fund was created, a new kind of structural fund which provided financing for projects in countries with a low GDP per capita.

While German unification probably accelerated the monetary integration process, especially the intergovernmental conferences (Köhler and Kees, 1996, 150), diverging views are held on its precise role in the political agreement leading to the Maastricht Treaty. On the one hand, not being in a position to delay or stop German unification, Mitterrand insisted on accelerating the process of European integration. This linkage is also apparent in the assurance which German officials gave to their European partners at that time ("We do not pursue a German Europe but a European Germany") and demonstrated Kohl's statesmanship. On the other hand, the momentum towards EMU had been building-up before German unification, with the Genscher Memorandum, the Hanover summit and the Delors Report as important milestones. References by French politicians, during the campaign on the Maastricht referendum, to EMU as a price paid by Germany for its reunification caused irritation in Germany.

As the transfer of monetary sovereignty was a major German concession, the German authorities attached to it conditions, which in turn implied other significant concessions, in particular for France. The most delicate one was the granting of central bank independence. Opposition to central bank independence was deeply rooted in the French tradition: the perception of the link between monetary and economic policy with the requirement of an appropriate institutional balance between monetary and political authorities (insistence on a "*gouvernement économique*"); the belief that low inflation does not require central bank independence and resistance to it by the French Treasury (Howarth, 1999a). The acceptance of central bank independence by the French political leaders has followed a rather obscure road. The Bank of

France Governor at the time, Jacques de Larosière, who subscribed to the Delors Report, including the principle of central bank independence, claims that he was understood and supported by President Mitterrand. The latter, however, continued to allow the Treasury to push for more political control of central banks throughout the IGCs of 1991 and himself made misleading statements on the issue during the campaign prior to the September 1992 French referendum on the Maastricht Treaty. However, it became clear that Mitterrand was not prepared to allow demands on the maintenance of a political control of the ECB to derail the negotiations but preferred to use them for bargaining purposes.

The acceptance of Frankfurt as the seat of the ECB was a departure from a claim that the ECB would not be located in an important financial centre in Europe. Apparently it had been recognised that Kohl needed this concession as an additional argument to boost his attempts to reassure the hesitant German population as well as the small savings banks, a significant part of the German financial community.

Reaching the point of no return

During the first half of the 1990s the credibility of the EMU-project was seriously affected. This raised the question as to whether, despite its stronger underpinning, the Maastricht Treaty would not undergo the same fate as the Werner plan.

A combination of developments and policies have avoided this outcome:

- a strong political determination by most of Europe's leaders to move ahead. Helmut Kohl in particular stood firm, despite signs of low public support in Germany. Jacques Chirac, as the newly elected French president, also quickly became a staunch supporter of the monetary union project;
- the positive impact of the exchange rate decisions and adjustment policies adopted in response to the 1992-1993 EMS-crisis;
- the approval of the changeover scenario by the Madrid Summit in December 1995, which was followed by the adoption of national changeover plans involving the various sectors of the economy in the preparatory stage;
- the quality of the technical preparation, in particular the smooth EMI discussions on a framework for the single monetary policy and the wholesale payments system;
- stronger economic growth in 1997 which not only made it easier to attain the budgetary convergence criteria but also improved the

general sentiment vis-à-vis the EMU project as it weakened the criticism of EMU as having a deflationary impact;

- the desirability of achieving EMU before concentrating on the difficult issue of a significant widening of the EU.

This sequence of events strengthened the credibility of the project in the eyes of the financial markets. Once a postponement was discarded as a valid option, the attention became focused on the list of participants.   This contributed to stable exchange rates and the disappearance of interest rate differentials, making it easier for countries to meet the convergence criteria and thereby further reinforcing the credibility of the project. It made for a strong dynamics with a positive interaction of policy actions and market forces.

7.4   THE IMPACT OF EMU ON THE PROCESS OF EUROPEAN INTEGRATION

Progress in the field of European monetary integration has further contributed to a deepening of the European integration process.   This was already discernible from very early on. The Werner Report emphasised the political importance of EMU thus:

> Economic and monetary union means that the principal decisions of economic policy will be taken at Community level and therefore that the necessary powers will be transferred from the national plane to the Community plane. These transfers of responsibility and the creation of the corresponding Community institutions represent a process of fundamental political significance that entails the progressive development of political co-operation. The economic and monetary union thus appears as a leaven for the development of political union which in the long run it will be unable to do without." (Werner Report, 1970, 26)[17].

Progress in monetary integration has typically occurred in parallel with measures taken in the field of regional cohesion. The fear, whether or not it was justified, that monetary integration would lead to a concentration of activity in the centre of the Community, was a recurring theme in the discussions.   The Werner Report recognised that in an economic and monetary union, structural and regional policies would have a role to play. The decision to go ahead with EMU at the Paris Summit of 1972 was linked

---

[17] English and French draft of the Werner Report. In the Dutch draft "the creation of the corresponding Community Institutions" is not mentioned.

to an agreement on the creation of the European Regional Development Fund. The fear of potential adverse regional effects as a result of EMU, together with British pressures, played an important role in this (Swann, 1995, 303). In the late 1970s during the EMS negotiations, actions were discussed: "to strengthen the economies of the less prosperous member countries ... essential if the zone of monetary stability is to succeed" (Conclusions, Bremen Summit, July 1978). The final EMS agreement therefore contained measures for some limited transfers of resources. A decade later, the Maastricht Treaty provided for the creation of a new kind of structural fund, namely the Cohesion Fund.

With the relaunching of the monetary integration project in the second half of the 1980s, discussions quickly turned to the political implications of EMU. It was then decided to have two intergovernmental conferences: one on economic and monetary union and another one, however much less well prepared, on political union. The Maastricht Treaty provided for a strengthening of the political dimension of the European Union, especially with the provisions on a common foreign and security policy and cooperation in the fields of justice and home affairs, be it on an intergovernmental basis. Moreover, the Maastricht Treaty also contained a protocol on social policy, concluded between the member states, with the exception of the United Kingdom.

In the 1990s the process of deepening of European integration has certainly continued. The Amsterdam Treaty of June 1997 reinforced the provisions on a common foreign and security policy and cooperation in the fields of justice and home affairs. It also added an important chapter on employment policies. Furthermore at the Cardiff summit of June 1998 it was decided that the surveillance and coordination of structural policies should be reinforced. Moreover, the coordination of tax policies has become an important theme.

It would certainly not be correct to attribute the further deepening of the European Union in the 1990s exclusively to EMU. Other factors, like Europe's structural unemployment problems and the desirability to deepen the Union before a further enlargement, have also played a role. However, it would also be wrong to underestimate the momentum which the monetary union project has generated and the impulses it has given for stimulating the integration process.

7.5   BELGIUM'S ROLE IN THE CREATION OF EMU

The role of a small country in the EMU process which has become increasingly dominated by France and Germany is not an obvious one. What counts is not only the country's own views on the integration strategy, but also the use of opportunities for securing a position and having a say in the European process of deliberation and negotiation.

7.5.1   General Positive Attitude

EMU has always been an objective of Belgium's European policy, but as an intermediate stage on the road to political integration. Once the direct route was blocked by the French Parliament's rejection of a European Defence Community in 1954, the Benelux countries proposed working to achieve economic integration which might culminate in political integration. This approach was approved by the ECSC Ministers for Foreign Affairs at the Conference of Messina in June 1955 and the Benelux countries would have preferred the insertion of this option in the Treaty. Although the Treaty went beyond the narrow concept of a common market (provisions on common policies, common institutions, majority voting were also included), the emphasis was clearly on the creation of a common market rather than more far-reaching forms of integration.

There has always been a high degree of consensus in Belgium regarding the EMU objective. This is also true in relations between the political and monetary authorities, and consequently the delicate subject of the central bank's independence has not been an issue. This consensus has certainly made it easier for Belgium's representatives to play a constructive role in the EMU debate.

One should also mention that the academic community in Belgium has always been very much interested in European matters and that European integration has been an important topic of research for the Belgian academic community (Maes, Buyst and Bouchet, 2000). This research was well appreciated in Community circles, as many Belgian academics have participated in important working groups of the European Commission like the Marjolin Report, (Peeters, 1973) and One Market, One Money (Van Rompuy, Abraham and Heremans, 1991).

7.5.2   Key Concepts of the Belgian EMU Strategy

This section only contains a brief description of the selected headlines of the integration strategy that the Belgian authorities have followed and supported during the whole genesis of EMU as well as during the latest transitional stage. It is obvious that a full catalogue of the positions that have been taken by the Belgian delegation during the Treaty negotiations, for example, falls outside the scope of this exercise.

Parallelism with a monetarist emphasis

The monetarist emphasis in the integration strategy cannot be denied if this implies that monetary cooperation and integration can act as a catalyst for economic convergence, and that there is therefore no need to wait for complete convergence as "economists" would prefer.

Exchange rate stability has always been central to Belgium's moves to promote European monetary cooperation; there are several reasons for this. The first is the very open Belgian economy and the geographical composition of Belgium's foreign trade. Proposals aimed at keeping the French franc in the snake and the EMS exchange rate mechanism or securing its return therefore attracted special attention. A second consideration was that a common market could not operate efficiently without exchange rate stability, and a single market without a single currency would remain incomplete and vulnerable. Finally, there was also the conviction that exchange rate stability was essential for economic and monetary convergence as a policy constraint, which was therefore linked to other policy measures.

A second area in which Belgium has been active, and one that is indeed related to exchange rate co-operation, concerns the mechanisms of monetary solidarity (official credit and settlement facilities). The basic idea here was that such mechanisms not only promoted mutual monetary cooperation but, by demonstrating a collective stance, were also a more efficient way of averting currency speculation than isolated national measures.

Belgian monetary experts such as Robert Triffin were already taking their inspiration from this type of idea in their contributions to the study concerning reform of the Bretton-Woods system in the 1960s. It was therefore no surprise that, in part, the same experts and ideas resurfaced in the preparation of the Hague Summit and in the subsequent work carried out by the Werner group. Triffin contributed to Jean Monnet's Action Committee for the United States of Europe, which was consulted by Willy Brandt in order to prepare the Hague Summit (Monnet, 1976, 610). As chairman of the expert committee acting in the framework of the Werner group, the then governor of the National Bank of Belgium, Hubert Ansiaux, left his mark on the proposals designed to elaborate mutual support mechanisms. Later too, at the time of the snake and the EMS, the Belgian representatives continued to focus particularly on developing and streamlining the EC credit mechanisms for balance of payments purposes. This was so, for instance, during the preparations for the EMS. Resistance came, however, from the Germans, who wanted to impose limits on this type of credit facility because of the possible threat to price stability, while the Belgians placed greater emphasis on the solidarity aspect.

Although it took this monetarist view, Belgium still agreed, from the start, like in the Werner Report, with the consensus on the need for parallel progress in the economic and monetary spheres. This concept of parallelism provided a bridge between "economists" and "monetarists", ensuring that the EMU project would not be halted by dogmatic differences of opinion. Apart from parallelism as a compromise solution, the Belgian government also realised that monetary cooperation was not sustainable without sound economic fundamentals and economic convergence. Coordination of economic policy had to make a contribution here, not only by recommending suitable policy measures to Member States but also by enhancing their effectiveness by mutual coordination of national measures. However, it was found that the EC mechanisms specifically intended for coordinating economic policy were inadequate because they mostly involved cumbersome consultation procedures without any real commitment on policy, and were therefore too informal. In practice, it was therefore the EMS stability convergence that determined the process.

To secure the transition to the EMU, the Belgian government pressed for the inclusion of deadlines in the Treaty, not only to ensure definite action in the process of deciding on the launch of EMU, but also to provide a catalyst for attainment of the convergence criteria, which is what actually happened in practice.

Finally, it should be mentioned that given the importance they attached to an EMU with a social policy dimension, the Belgian authorities found it regrettable, that, in this respect, the content of the Maastricht Treaty was rather weak. Only towards the end of the transition period did the situation became ripe for more concrete initiatives. After the change of government in the UK a social chapter could be included in the Treaty of Amsterdam and in 1997 the European Council made progress with regard to a coordinated employment policy.

Scope for different speeds

The Tindemans report to the European Council in December 1975, produced at a time when, owing to increasing economic and monetary divergence within the EC, the atmosphere was not appropriate for the relaunch of EMU, determined for the first time the elements of a multi-speed integration. Member States which were in a position to make progress had to be able to do so without waiting for the ones which lagged behind. The latter would receive the necessary assistance and be judged on their performance by the competent EC institutions with a view to catching up. The snake was to provide the primary framework here, becoming the pivot of the new strategy subject to greater coordination of economic and monetary policy (Rey, 1994, 32).

Such a strategy of two or more speeds must not be confused with an "à la carte" Europe in which different countries would aim at different objectives. The objectives would remain the same for everyone but be achieved at varying rates. To safeguard unified objectives, the process would have to continue within the Community legal system. This meant, among other things, that the Community institutions must not be kept out of it (as happened to the Commission in the snake) but must remain involved in the whole set-up and exercise their powers.

Although this topic in the Tindemans report was initially treated with quite widespread scepticism because of fears that the Community would disintegrate, the idea of a multi-speed strategy gradually gained more acceptance. It proved to be a useful instrument for organising the accession of new Member States and was applied efficiently in the EMS. The Maastricht Treaty itself is an example of how participation can be staggered.

Rejection of the parallel currency strategy

The Delors group rejected the "parallel currency strategy", which corresponded to the official Belgian standpoint. According to that strategy, a parallel currency, if it was sufficiently attractive, could drive the national currencies out of circulation via the private market and thus survive as a single currency. In the latter half of the 1970s in particular, study groups, in which Belgian academics played a leading role, put forward such ideas and proposals in order to revitalise the EMU objective via an alternative route (cf. De Grauwe, Heremans and Van Rompuy, 1975). Although several variants of the parallel currency were devised, they all came up against the same problem, namely the impossibility of neutralising a lack of political will by using technical formulae and financial market forces.

The Delors group naturally set its sights mainly on the ECU, which at that time had already gained a significant position in the financial markets. In view of the leading role which Belgian banks had secured on the ECU market, the Belgian government could not deny its importance for the financial sector. Moreover, the creation of the official ECU as a payment and credit instrument between central banks was particularly welcome in the first phase of the EMS as a way of financing interventions in support of the Belgian franc. At the same time, however, the government faced the risk that the attractions of the ECU for Belgian investors would lead to the diversification of portfolios which the public traditionally held in Belgian francs, and hence to an unwanted outflow of capital (Michielsen, 1986, 33).

In this situation the Belgian government did recognise the ECU as a fully-fledged foreign currency and created the conditions for the smooth operation and expansion of the private ECU market. On the other hand, it rejected the request by Belgian banks to give the ECU preferential status, and place it on an equal footing with the Belgian franc. Such a move, which none of the EC partners was considering, would undoubtedly have impaired the Belgian franc's image and hampered the recovery policy.

A credible and coherent scenario for the launch of the single currency

Already in 1993 a Treasury - National Bank - Belgian Bankers' Association working party was set up to devise a "changeover plan" for the introduction of the single currency in Belgium. This early initiative allowed Belgium to play a creative role in both the preparations for the euro scenario approved at the Madrid Summit in December 1995 and its subsequent implementation in the national changeover plans. The essential principles of the Belgian approach may be summarised as follows:

- the introduction of the single currency had to coincide with the launch of EMU in order to underpin the credibility of the project. Since technical constraints prevented a Big Bang on 1 January 1999, the single currency did at least have to put into circulation in cashless form;
- the "critical mass" or volume of transactions needed at the start of the single currency had to be sufficiently large to form a basis for further penetration. Apart from money market operations, government issues were mainly relied on as the lever that would create a capital market in the new currency. At the Madrid Summit the German government consented to the use of the single currency for new government issues

in exchange for agreement that the new currency would be called the euro rather than the ECU;

- public administrative authorities had to be made ready for operating in euro with the outside world from the start, in accordance with the principle of "no compulsion, no prohibition". This was considered to be an essential, logical extension of the application of the same principle in the private sector. After initial hesitation in a number of countries, this part of the Belgian changeover plan was eventually adopted almost universally.

A European economic government

When the idea of a "European economic government" was launched, the Belgian government gave its wholehearted support to the concept, as greater decision-making power for the ECOFIN Council was regarded as essential both to strengthen the economic side and to counterbalance the monetary side which could be based on a unified monetary policy. However, the concept was not adopted in the Treaty for two reasons: first, since economic policy was still a national matter, people objected to the creation of a new institution, and second, the terminology in itself was sufficient to give the impression of a threat to the independence of the ECB.

Belgium certainly had no intention of tampering with the independence of the ECB. On the contrary, that independence would be made more secure if the political authorities were to give the monetary authorities the most accurate information possible on the direction of economic policy and conduct a well-coordinated economic policy. However, the debate that the Belgian government had helped to initiate concerning the economic aspect of EMU did lead to Article 103 of the Treaty. This article provides for annual broad economic policy guidelines of the Member States and the Community, which then form the basis for the multilateral supervision of the ECOFIN Council, empowered to make recommendations to any Member State whose policy is inconsistent with the guidelines or which could jeopardise the proper functioning of EMU.

In December 1993, under the Belgian presidency of the Council, the procedure was initiated so as to make an immediate break with the disappointing experience of economic policy coordination during the pre-EMU period, in order to bolster faith in EMU (Maystadt, 1998, 11). Although the importance of the enhanced procedure in the successful transition to EMU is not obvious, the Belgian government remained convinced that, once EMU had been launched, the ECOFIN Council would have to become a kind of economic government regardless of what it was called.

7.5.3   Actual Contribution

The actual contribution of individual countries to the creation of EMU is hard to assess. Subject to a more detailed study, the following factors can be put forward for Belgium:

- through Benelux, Belgium was among the leading players in relaunching the concept of Europe after the failure of the Pleven plan in 1954 and in bringing about the Treaty of Rome. The Benelux countries were also very much involved in working out the Werner plan, but strategically the Netherlands belonged to the "economists" camp while Belgium supported the "monetarists". Although afterwards the Benelux countries regularly made their presence felt as a positive pressure group, especially in regard to political co-operation, there were serious reservations about the usefulness of the Benelux agreement itself as a forerunner or integration model. A common economic and monetary policy was unattainable or even undesirable in view of the differences between Belgium and the Netherlands, and both countries therefore in fact opted to gear the aims of Benelux to those of Europe. A well-known exception was the monetary agreement (the "worm") which on 21 August 1971 limited the bilateral fluctuation margins to 1.5%, thus forming the only fixed but adjustable parity mechanism in Europe until the start of the snake in April 1972. However, the smooth operation of the "worm" was hampered by the divergent policies adopted by the Benelux countries, so that in 1976 it was decided to abolish the agreement;

- experience with the BLEU agreement was also irrelevant to EMU at European level. Apart from the fact that it lacked essential characteristics of EMU, the BLEU was on far too small a scale to provide a testing ground for European integration;

- Belgium's contribution to the EMU strategy adopted (cf. *supra*) was not negligible. In addition, there were the efforts to bring about consensus. Since Germany and France were jointly making their mark on the decisions, this was a specific opportunity for moves to promote Franco-German agreement. A typical example was the

Belgian contribution to the preparations for the EMS when Belgium was chairing both the Monetary Committee and the Committee of Central Bank Governors. Although the instrument was subsequently hardly ever used in exchange rate policy, the Belgian idea of the divergence indicator opened the way for an agreement on the provisions of the EMS resolution of December 1978. Another example was the proposal Belgium made during the intergovernmental conference on the Maastricht Treaty to call the new institution of the second stage, the "European Monetary Institute" (Schönfelder and Thiel, 1996, 132). It was instrumental in bridging the differences between the French, proposing the creation of the European Central Bank and the Germans who were in favour of a "Council of Presidents of Central Banks";

- for a small country like Belgium, chairing permanent policy groups (Monetary Committee, Committee of Central Bank Governors, Economic Policy Committee) as well as taking a turn in the rotating presidency of the Council was indeed a good opportunity to stimulate action or to table compromise proposals. The Belgian representatives used the opportunities offered to the best of their ability;

- every EMU country made a definite contribution by qualifying for membership. For Belgium, this meant a sustained recovery policy which at the monetary level permitted a gradual alignment with the hard EMS currencies, culminating in the strict pegging to the German mark. Modernisation of the range of financial and money market instruments ensured that, in technical terms, entry to the euro area was virtually trouble-free. However, the impact of the earlier fiscal deficits forced the Belgian government onto the defensive with regard to the budgetary convergence criteria, and in particular the debt ratio. On the one hand, the Belgian government, despite its doubts about the economic relevance of the stipulations of the debt criterion, did not want to give the impression that it was against budgetary discipline and so risk to be excluded from EMU membership right from the start; on the other hand, the 60% maximum debt ratio was out of reach according to any realistic assumptions. The Belgian representatives therefore successfully steered towards flexibility in the definition of the rule.

REFERENCES

Baer, G. and T. Padoa-Schioppa (1988), The Werner Report Revisited, *Collection of Papers. Committttee for the Study of Economic and Monetary Union,* Luxembourg, April 1989, pp. 53-60.

Balladur, E. (1988), Mémorandum sur la Construction Monétaire Européenne, *ECU,* no. 3, 17-20.

Basevi, G. et al., (1975), A Manifesto for European Monetary Union and Monetary Reform, *The Economist,* November 1.

Bloomfield, A. (1973), The Historical Setting, in B. Krause and W. Salant, (eds.), *European Monetary Unification and its Meaning for the United States,* Washington: Brookings, pp. 1-30.

Buiter, W., G. Corsetti and P. Pesenti (1998), Interpreting the ERM Crisis: Country-specific and Systemic Issues, *Princeton Studies in International Finance,* no. 84, March.

Buti, M. and A. Sapir (1998), *Economic Policy in EMU,* Oxford: Oxford University Press.

Commission of the European Communities (1973), Attainment of Economic and Monetary Union, *Bulletin of the EC,* Supplement 5/73.

Commission of the European Communities (1975), *Report of the Study Group 'Economic and Monetary Union 1980',* Marjolin Report, Brussels, March.

Commission of the European Communities (1982), Documents Relating to the European Monetary System, *European Economy,* no. 12, July.

Commission of the European Communities (1990), One Market, One Money, *European Economy,* no. 44, October.

Commission of the European Communities (1995), *Green Paper on the Practical Arrangements for the Introduction of the Single Currency,* Luxembourg, May.

Commission of the European Communities (1998a), Commission's Recommendation Concerning the Third Stage of Economic and Monetary Union, *European Economy,* no. 65, 3-21.

Commission of the European Communities (1998b), Convergence Report (1998), *European Economy,* no. 65, 23-162.

Commission of the European Communities (1998c), Growth and Employment in the Stability-oriented Framework of EMU, *European Economy,* no. 65, 163-210.

Committee for the Study of Economic and Monetary Union (1989), *Report on Economic and Monetary Union in the European Community,* Delors Report, Luxembourg.

Council-Commission of the European Communities (1970), *Report to the Council and the Commission on the Realisation by Stages of Economic and Monetary Union in the Community,* Werner Report, Luxembourg, October.

De Grauwe, P. (1992), *The Economics of Monetary Integration,* Oxford: Oxford University Press.

De Grauwe, P., D. Heremans and E. Van Rompuy (1975), Towards European Monetary Union, *Memo From Belgium,* no. 170, Brussels.

de Larosière, J. (1988), First Stages Towards The Creation of a European Reserve Bank, *Collection of Papers. Committee for the Study of Economic and Monetary Union,* Luxembourg, pp. 177-184.

Delors, J. (1992), *Le Nouveau Concert Européen,* Paris: Editions Odile Jacob.

Delors, J. (1996), *Combats pour l'Europe,* Paris: Economica.

de Schoutheete, P. (1997), *Une Europe pour Tous,* Paris: Editions Odile Jacob.

Dyson, K. and K. Featherstone (1999), *The Road to Maastricht,* Oxford: Oxford University Press.

Eichengreen, B. and C. Wyplosz (1993), The Unstable EMS, *Brookings Papers on Economic Activity,* no. 1, 51-124.

Emerson, M. (1991), The Transformation of Trade and Monetary Regimes in Europe, *Policy Implications of Trade and Currency Zones,* Federal Reserve Bank of Kansas City, Symposium Jackson Hole, Wyoming, pp. 59-76.

Emminger, O. (1977), The D-Mark in the Conflict Between Internal and External Equilibrium, 1948-75, *Essays in International Finance,* no. 122, Princeton.

European Monetary Institute (1995), *The Changeover to the Single Currency,* Frankfurt, November.

European Monetary Institute (1996), *Annual Report 1995,* Frankfurt, April.

European Monetary Institute (1997), *The Single Monetary Policy in Stage Three. Specification of the Operational Framework,* Frankfurt, January.

European Monetary Institute (1998), *Convergence Report,* Frankfurt, March.

Fischer, F. (1994), Modern Central Banking, in F. Capie et al., (eds.), *The Future of Central Banking,* Cambridge: Cambridge University Press, pp. 262-308.

Fratianni, M. and J. von Hagen (1992), *The European Monetary System and European Monetary Union,* Boulder: Westview Press.

Friedman, M. (1953), The Case for Flexible Exchange Rates, *Essays in Positive Economics,* Chicago: University of Chicago Press, pp. 157-203.

Friedman, M. (1968), The Role of Monetary Policy, *American Economic Review,* March, 1-17.

Genscher, H.-D. (1988), Memorandum für die Schaffung eines europäischen Währungsraumes und einer Europäischen Zentralbank, Bonn, Februar.

Giavazzi, F. and A. Giovannini (1989), *Limiting Exchange Rate Flexibility: The European Monetary System,* Cambridge: MIT Press.

Giavazzi, F., Miscossi, S. and M. Miller (eds.) (1988), *The European Monetary System,* Cambridge: Cambridge University Press.

Grant, C. (1994), *Delors: Inside the House that Jacques Built,* London: Nicholas Brealy.

Grilli, V., D. Masciandaro and D. Tabellini (1991), Institutions and Policies, *Economic Policy,* no. 13, 341-392.

Gros, D. and N. Thygesen (1998), *European Monetary Integration,* 2nd edition, London: Longman.

Hagemann, H. (2000), The Post-1945 Development of Economics in Germany, in Coats A.W. (ed.), *The Development of Economics in Western Europe since 1945,* London: Routledge, pp. 119-128.

Howarth, D. (1999a), French Aversion to Independent Monetary Authority and the Development of French Policy on the EMU Project, mimeo, Birmingham.

Howarth, D. (1999b), EMU, Integration Theories and the Annoying Complexities of French Policy-making, mimeo, Birmingham.

Italianer, A. (1993), Mastering Maastricht, in K. Gretschmann (ed.), *Economic and Monetary Union,* Dordrecht: Martinus Nijhoff, pp. 51-114.

Jenkins, R. (1977), Europe's Present Challenge and Future Opportunity, *Bulletin EC,* 10, 6-14.

Köhler, H. and A. Kees (1996), Die Verhandlungen zur Europaïschen Wirtschafts - und Währungsunion, in T. Waigel, (ed.), *Unsere Zukunft heißt Europa,* Düsseldorf: Econ. Verlag, pp. 145-174.

Lamfalussy, A. (1996), Vers la Monnaie Unique: le Rôle de l'Institut Monétaire Européen, *ECU,* no. 36, 3-9.

Ludlow, P. (1982), *The Making of the European Monetary System,* London: Butterworth.

Maes, I. (1991), Monetaire Integratie, *Economisch en Sociaal Tijdschrift,* no. 2, 189-216.

Maes, I. (1998), Macroeconomic Thought at the European Commission in the 1970s: The First Decade of the Annual Economic Reports, *Banca Nazionale del Lavoro Quarterly Review,* no. 207, Dec., 387-412.

Maes, I., E. Buyst and M. Bouchet (2000), The Post-1945 Development of Economics in Belgium, in Coats A.W. (ed.), *The Development of Economics in Western Europe since 1945,* London: Routledge, pp. 94-112.

Magnifico, G. (1971), European Monetary Unification for Balanced Growth, *European Monetary Unification,* 1972, London: MacMillan, pp. 1-42.

Major, J. (1993), Major on Europe, *The Economist,* September 25th.

Maystadt, P. (1998), Peut-on avoir une Union Monétaire sans Gouvernement Économique?, *Bulletin de Documentation,* Vol. 58, no. 1, 1-25.

McNamara, K. (1999), *The Currency of Ideas,* Ithaca: Cornell University Press.

Michielsen, J. (1986), EMU, EMS and ECU: Europese en Belgische Aspecten, *Revue de la Banque, Bank- en Financiewezen,* 27-33.

Monnet, J. (1976), *Mémoires,* Tome 2, Paris: Fayard.

Mortensen, J. (1990), *Federalism vs. Co-ordination,* Brussels: CEPS.

OECD (1999), *EMU. Facts, Challenges and Policies,* Paris.

Padoa-Schioppa, T. (1987), *Efficiency, Stability, Equity,* Oxford: Oxford University Press.

Padoa-Schioppa, T. (1994), *The Road to Monetary Union in Europe,* Oxford: Clarendon Press.

Padoa-Schioppa, T. (1998), *Che Cosa ci ha insegnato l'Aventura Europea,* Roma: Edizione dell' Elefante.

Peeters, T. (1975), EMU and Employment, Price and Income Policies, in CEC, *Report of the Study Group "Economic and Monetary Union 1980",* Marjolin Report, Annex II, pp.125-131.

Pöhl, K.-O. (1988), The Further Development of the European Monetary System, *Collection of Papers. Committee for the Study of Economic and Monetary Union,* Luxembourg, 1989, pp. 129-156.

Pöhl, K.-O. (1996), Der Delors-Bericht und das Statut einer Europäischen Zentralbank, in Waigel T. (ed.), *Unsere Zukunft heißt Europa.* Düsseldorf, Econ Verlag, pp. 193-209.

Rey, J.-J. (1994), Pros and Cons of a Two-speed Monetary Integration, *Essays in Honour of André Szasz,* De Nederlandsche Bank, pp. 31-43.

Rey, J.-J. (1999), Au Coeur de l'Euro, Bruxelles, mimeo.

Sachs, J. and C. Wyplosz (1986), The Economic Consequences of President Mitterrand, *Economic Policy,* no. 2, April, 261-321.

Schönfelder, W. and E. Thiel (1996), *Ein Markt - Eine Währung,* 2 Ed., Baden-Baden: Nomos.

Servais, D. (1991), *The Single Financial Market,* 2nd ed., Commission of the European Communities, Luxembourg.

Stoltenberg, G. (1988), Zur weiteren Entwicklung der währungspolitischen Zusammenarbeit in Europa, Bonn, 15 März.

Swann, D. (1995), *The Economics of the Common Market,* 8th ed., London: Penguin.

Szàsz, A. (1999), *The Road to European Monetary Union,* London: Macmillan.

Tsoukalis, L. (1977), *The Politics and Economics of European Monetary Integration,* London: Allen & Unwin.

Ungerer, H. (1997), *A Concise History of European Monetary Integration,* Westport: Quorum Books.

Van der Wee, H. (1986), *Prosperity and Upheaval. The World Economy 1945-1980,* Harmondsworth: Viking.

Van Rompuy, P., F. Abraham and D. Heremans (1991), Economic Federalism and the EMU, *European Economy,* Special Edition no. 1, 107-163.

van Ypersele, J. and J.-C. Koeune (1989), *Le Système Monétaire Européen,* 3e éd., Luxembourg.

Werner, P. (1991), *Itinéraires Luxembourgeois et Européens,* Luxembourg: Editions Saint-Paul.

Annex 7.1 - A chronology of European integration

1948	The Hague: conference of European federalists
1950	Schuman Plan
1951	Paris Treaty (ECSC)
1957	Rome Treaty (EEC)
1969	Hague Summit
1970	Werner Report
1972	Snake
1973	Accession of UK, Ireland and Denmark
1979	EMS
1981	Accession of Greece
1985	Internal Market Programme
1986	Accession of Spain and Portugal
1987	Single European Act
1989	Delors Report
1991	Maastricht Treaty
1994	Start of phase 2 of EMU
1995	Accession of Austria, Sweden and Finland
1997	Amsterdam Treaty
1999	EMU

Annex 7.2 - The path to EMU

1988	January	Balladur Memorandum
	February	Genscher Memorandum
	June	Hanover Summit: creation of Delors Committee
1989	April	Delors Report
	November	Fall of the Berlin wall
	December	Strasbourg Summit: agreement on IGC for EMU
1990	April	1st Dublin Summit: IGC to start in December 1990
	June	2nd Dublin Summit: separate IGC on political union
	October	German unification
		Rome Summit: 1 January 1994 set as start of the second stage
	November	Committee of Governors submits draft ESCB statute
	December	Start of IGCs
1991	December	Agreement on Maastricht Treaty
1992	June	Danish referendum rejects Maastricht Treaty
	August	Start of crisis in ERM
1993	August	Widening of fluctuation margins in ERM to 15%
	November	Maastricht Treaty comes into force
1994	January	Start of Second Stage (creation of EMI)
1995	May	Commission Green Paper on the changeover
	November	EMI scenario for the introduction of the single currency Waigel proposes Stability Pact
	December	Madrid Summit: changeover scenario adopted, euro selected as name for the single currency
1996	December	Dublin Summit: agreement on Stability and Growth Pact and ERM II
1997	January	EMI Report on The Single Monetary Policy in Stage Three
1998	March	Publication of Convergence Reports of EMI and Commission
	May	Selection of countries for EMU
	June	Creation of ECB and ESCB
1999	January	Start of EMU

Index

Abraham, F. 180
academic economics 71
    debates 35–7, 97–8
    and economics at policy-making
        institutions 120–122, 123
Action Committee for the United States
    of Europe 181
All Saint's Day Manifesto 36, 141
Amato, G. 149
Americanisation 53–4, 55, 70–73
Amsterdam Treaty 1997 179
Anglo-Saxon economic thought 86, 116
Annual Economic Reports 81–104, 112,
    122
    changes in conception of monetary
        policy 94–5
    Keynesian policy conception in first
        reports 90–93
    1980s 114–20, 121
    preparing 85–8
    structure 88–90
    supply-side economics 96–100
Annual Economic Review 89
Ansiaux, H. 181–2
Association for Monetary Union in
    Europe (AMUE) 174
Attali, J. 174

Backhouse, R. 71
Baer, G. 34, 63, 93, 175
balance of payments 7–8, 35–6, 98, 99
    optimum currency area theory 15–16,
        23–4
Balassa, B. 3, 58
Balladur, E. 149
Barre, R. 91
Barten, A.P. 114
Basevi, G. 36, 117, 141

Basle–Nyborg agreement 1987 146
Baumol, W. 71
Belgium 23, 132
    Global Plan for Employment,
        Competitiveness and Social
        Security 158
    role in creation of EMU 180–187
Benelux countries 186
Bertola, G. 17
Blanchard, O. 117, 119
BLEU agreement 186
Bloomfield, A. 136
Bouchet, M. 180
Brandt, W. 30, 61, 136, 181
Bremen Summit 1978 142, 179
Bretton-Woods System 14, 32, 60, 61,
    134, 135, 137
    collapse 29, 31, 62, 83, 139
    European snake in the Bretton-Woods
        tunnel 138–9
Brittan, L. 55
Brugge network 52
Brunner, K. 94
budget, EC 70
budget deficit 161
    Belgium 187
    convergence criterion 154, 163, 164,
        166
    European Community 99, 158–9
budgetary policy 87–8, 90–1, 100, 153–4
Buiter, W. 117
Bundesbank 17, 39, 68, 95, 171, 174–5
    EMS 40, 143–4, 174
business cycle 91
Buyst, E. 180

capital mobility 15–16, 19
Carter, J. 69

central bank independence 176-7
central fiscal authority 19
centralisation, degree of 9, 57
centre of decision for economic policy
    33, 70, 82, 137
CEPS Macroeconomic Policy Group
    111, 117-20, 122, 123
changeover plans, national 177, 184-5
changeover scenario 160-161, 177
Chirac, J. 177
classical unemployment 117-18
Coats, A.W. 56, 70-1, 121
Cockfield, Lord 55, 63
Coddington, A. 34, 91
Cohesion Fund 65, 176, 179
Colchester, N. 63
Comet model 113-14
Commission 17, 50-51, 66, 144, 160
    Convergence Report 163-7
    employment debate with CEPS Group
        117-20
    French and Italian officials 67-8
    functioning and role of economists
        51-6
    macroeconomic thought in first half
        of 1980s 105-27
    macroeconomic thought in 1970s
        81-104
    monitoring and forecasting 112-14
    'One Market, One Money' 66, 173
    policy-making instances 108-11
    structure of the services 51-2, 77
    see also Annual Economic Reports
common agricultural policy 60, 136
common (parallel) currency 36-7, 141,
    183-4
common market 58, 59, 60
communication skills 121-2
Community system for the central banks
    33, 82, 137
Compact model 114
concerted action 84, 96, 97, 119
consensus 121
    in policy objectives 170
continuities 65-70
convergence 41, 92
convergence criteria 68-9, 154, 163
convergence reports 163-7
Cooperative Growth Strategy 108,
    119-20

Corden, W. 16, 21, 35, 36
Council 50-51
Council Decision on the Strengthening
    of the Coordination of Short-term
    Economic Policies 1971 83, 90
Court of Justice 50-51
credibility 17-18
credit mechanisms 143
customs unions 4-5, 6-7, 10, 58
    European Community 60, 136

d'Alcantara, G. 114
De Gaulle, C. 59
De Grauwe, P. 35, 183
de Schoutheete, P. 176
debt ratio 154, 164, 166, 187
deepening 58, 135
deflationary bias 17, 40
Dell, E. 32
Delors, J. 63-5, 109, 134, 167
    role in integration 108, 119-20, 148
Delors Committee 64, 67-8, 151-2, 175
Delors network 52
Delors Report 64, 69-70, 132, 151-2
demand management 91, 92, 96-7
Denmark 30, 157
DG II - Economic and Financial Affairs
    52-4, 85, 86
    economists 53-4, 55
    monitoring and forecasting 112-14
    reorganisation 87-8, 109-11
    staff 78
Directorate-Generals 51-5
    see also DG II
diversification criterion 23-4
divergence indicator 39
Dobson, W. 84
Dornbusch, R. 117, 119
Dornbusch Group 111, 117-20, 122, 123
Drèze, J. 119
Duisenberg Plan 38
dynamics 173-8

ECOFIN Council 185-6
econometric modelling 113-14
economic growth 84, 96, 98, 99, 106,
    107, 177-8
economic integration *see* integration
economic and monetary union (EMU)
    32, 58, 82-4, 131-93

Belgium's role 180-7
business perception of impact 18
Delors Report 64, 69-70, 132, 151-2
EMS *see* European Monetary System
ERM crisis 155-9
feasibility 35-6
final decisions 162-7
first attempt at monetary union 135-41
Hague Summit 60-1
impact on European integration
    process 178-9
long-term structural factors 167-73
Maastricht Process 148-67
Maastricht Treaty *see* Maastricht
    Treaty
path to 193
relaunch of monetary union project
    148-51
second stage 159-62
stages towards 33-4, 62
strong dynamics 173-8
Werner Report *see* Werner Report
Economic Papers 111, 122
economic policy
coordination 92
French and German conceptions
    59-60
organisation of 9, 57
shift from activist to stability oriented
    69-70
Economic Policy Committee (EPC) 88,
    115
Economic Structures and Community
    Policies Directorate 110
economic union 58
economists
participation of non-EC economists
    in study groups 71, 80
role at the Commission 51-6
'economists' 34, 38, 41, 62, 68, 83, 142,
    154
ECU (European Currency Unit) 142,
    174, 184
education 53-4, 55
Eichenberger, R. 71
Eichengreen, B. 19
Emerson, M. 87, 88, 89, 110, 111, 120,
    173
Emminger, O. 139
Erhard, L. 60

euro 184-5
changeover scenario 160-161, 177
Euro Group 162
Eurolink model 113-14
Europa 36, 141
European Atomic Energy Community
    59, 60
European Central Bank (ECB) 17, 150,
    177, 185
European Coal and Steel Community 59,
    134, 135
European Community
international role 172-3
in the early 1980s 106-8
European Community institutions 49-80
change and continuity in economic
    thought 65-70
Commission *see* Commission
historical overview of integration
    58-65
internationalisation influence 70-73
major institutions 50-1
notion of integration 57-8
European Council 51
European Currency Unit (ECU) 142,
    174, 184
European Defence Community 135
European Economic Community 58-60,
    135
European economic government 185-6
European Economy 89
European Fund for Monetary
    Cooperation 34, 37, 144
European integration *see* integration
European Monetary Fund 142, 144
European Monetary Institute (EMI) 154,
    159-61, 162, 187
Convergence Report 163-7
European Monetary System (EMS) 29,
    30, 38-40, 41, 84, 88, 141-7
Balladur Memorandum 149-50
Belgium and 186-7
characteristics 142-4
deflationary bias 17, 40
ERM *see* exchange rate mechanism
feasibility 38-9
Franco-German relationship 174
functioning 144-6
impetus to integration 108, 132
inflationary bias 39-40

Schmidt and Giscard d'Estaing 32, 63, 83, 141
European Movement 134
European Regional Development Fund 178–9
European Reserve Fund 152
European single market 5, 63–4, 66, 108, 148, 173–4
European snake 29, 31, 32, 37, 138–9
European System of Central Banks (ESCB) 64, 152, 153
European Union (EU) 65, 153
Eurosclerosis 106
exchange rate mechanism (ERM) 39, 68, 142–3, 149
   ERM crisis 155–9
   functioning 146, 147, 148
   ERM II 162
exchange rates 72–3, 161, 181
   convergence criterion 154, 163, 166
   effective exchange rates 38
   post-war controversy and optimum currency area theory 14–18, 20–23, 25–6
external shocks 23–4

factor mobility 15–16, 18–19, 26, 36
Feldstein, M. 98
fiscal policy 7, 91
Fischer, F. 170
fixed exchange rates 16–18, 21–2, 25, 26, 61
flexible exchange rates 14, 15, 20–21, 25, 26
Fleming, M. 35
forecasting 98, 112–14
foreign direct investment (FDI) flows 168
Fourcade Plan 37
France
   and central bank independence 176–7
   economic policy 59–60, 69, 108
   EMS 144–6
   French officials at the Commission 67–8, 116
   inflation 93, 94, 139, 140
   new leadership in 1969 30, 61, 136
   planning 59–60, 85–6, 116
   rapprochement with Germany 174–5
   and US 172

Franco–German alliance 134, 171–2
free trade area 58
freedom of factor movements 7
Frey, B. 71
Friedman, M. 94, 170

G7 Bonn Summit 69
GATT 134
Genscher, H.-D. 149–50
Germany 84, 86, 96
   economic policy 59–60, 69
   economic thought and the Commission 115–16
   Franco–German alliance 134, 171–2
   hyperinflation in 1920s 134–5
   inflation 93, 94, 139, 140
   new leadership in 1969 30, 61, 136
   rapprochement with France 174–5
   unification 152, 157, 176
   and US 172
Giavazzi, F. 39, 66
Giersch, H. 106, 119
Giovannini, A. 66
Giscard d'Estaing, V. 30, 136, 139, 174
   EMS 32, 63, 83, 141
'golden sixties' 82–4
government finance *see* budget deficit; debt ratio
Grant, C. 52, 68
Great Depression 134
Greece 30–31
Grilli, V. 170
Gros, D. 40, 146
growth, economic 84, 96, 98, 99, 106, 107, 177–8

Haferkampf, W. 92
Hague Congress of European Federalists 1948 134
Hague Summit 1969 29, 30, 60–61, 82, 135
Hall, P. 84
Hanover Summit 1988 64, 150, 151
Hansen, A. 91
Harrod, R. 115–16
Heller Report 90–91
Heremans, D. 180, 183
Hicks, J.R. 91
Howarth, D. 150, 176
hyperinflation 134–5

'impossible triangle' 148
industrial policy 70
inflation 31, 69, 84, 98, 99, 146
    Annual Economic Reports 91-2, 93
    convergence criterion 154, 163, 164,
        165
    early 1980s 106, 107
    France and Germany 93, 94, 139,
        140
    hyperinflation in Germany 134-5
    optimum currency area theory 15,
        16-17, 20
    and unemployment 35-6
inflationary bias 39-40
Ingram, J. 16, 36
integration
    chronology of European integration
        12, 79, 192
    defining 57-8
    economic thought at European
        Community institutions 65-70,
        73
    historical overview of European
        integration 30-32, 58-65,
        133-6
    impact of EMU on European
        integration process 178-9
    increasing degree of economic
        integration 167-9
    increasing political will 171-2
    monetary integration debates in 1970s
        29-45
    optimum currency area theory and
        European monetary integration
        13-28
    origins of European monetary
        integration process 133-5
    state and market in post-war
        integration theory 3-12
    strategy of monetary integration 67-9
    tension with sovereignty 66-7
    see also economic and monetary
        union; European Monetary
        System
interest rates 154, 155, 163, 164, 166
internal market programme 5, 63-4, 66,
    108, 148, 173-4
international economic integration 8-10
international institutions 69, 134
international role of Europe 172-3

internationalisation 53-4, 55, 70-73
intra-industry trade 24, 167, 169
Ireland 30
Ishiyama, Y. 21
Italy 67-8

Jenkins, R. 32, 83, 141
Johnson, H. 26, 35

Kees, A. 176
Kenen, P. 23-4, 25-6
Keynesianism 115-16, 170
    Annual Economic Reports 90-93,
        96
Klamer, A. 71
Koeune, J.-C. 37
Kohl, H. 69, 148, 150, 171, 177
Köhler, H. 176
Kolm, S.-C. 71
Konstanz Seminars 94-5
Krugman, P. 24

labour market rigidities 119
labour mobility 15-16, 19
Lamfalussy, A. 160
language 71, 72
Larosière, J. de 151, 177
Layard, R. 117, 119
Leijonhufvud, A. 91
Lipschitz, L. 60
Llewellyn, J. 112
Louis, J.-V. 57, 58
Lucas, R. 94
Ludlow, P. 32, 83, 108, 111, 141, 143

Maastricht Process 148-67, 193
Maastricht Treaty 57, 68-9, 132, 153-4,
        159, 179
    pillars of the EU 65, 153
    referenda on 157
    securing agreement on 175-7
MacDougall Report 70
Machlup, F. 3
macroeconomic policy coordination,
    failure of 69
Macroeconomic Research and Policy
    Directorate 87, 89-90, 110
Madrid Summit 1995 161, 184
Maes, I. 8, 25, 29, 58, 91, 116, 119, 170,
        180

Magnifico, G. 35, 36, 141
Major, J. 172
Malinvaud, E. 116
Marjolin, R. 85, 86, 116
Marjolin Report 34, 62, 93, 139
market 40–41
  internal market programme 5, 63–4,
    66, 108, 148, 173–4
  and state in post-war integration
    theory 3–12
Marris, S. 56, 121, 122
Masciandaro, D. 170
Massé, P. 86
Mayer, T. 60, 71
Maystadt, P. 162, 185
McKinnon, R. 8, 20–23, 25–6, 98
McNamara, K. 170
Meade, J. 5–8, 10–11, 18–19, 36
medium-term policy orientation 96–100
Metric model 113–14
Michielson, J. 184
Mingasson, J.-P. 110
Mitterrand, F. 108, 144–5, 148, 150,
  176, 177
monetarism 181–2
Monetarist counter-revolution 94–5,
  170
'monetarists' 34, 37, 41, 62, 67–8, 83,
  142, 154
monetary integration *see* integration
Monetary Matters Directorate 110
money 16, 21–2
money illusion 21
money supply targets 95
monitoring 112–14
Monnet, J. 60, 181
Monti, M. 119
Mortensen, J. 64, 85, 109, 142
multi-speed strategy 183
Mundell, R. 8, 14–19, 25–6, 36

national changeover plans 177, 184–5
National Economies Directorate 110
national policies 93
nationality of economists 52, 53, 54
negative integration 9
Netherlands 23, 186
Neumann, M. 95

OECD 71, 86, 91, 116

oil price shocks 31–2, 62–3, 93, 96
'One Market, One Money' 66, 173
Oort, C.J. 38
openness 20–21, 22, 23, 169
Optica Reports 36
optimum currency area theory 13–28
  Kenen 23–4, 25–6
  McKinnon 20–23, 25–6
  Mundell 14–19, 25–6
Ordnungspolitik 115
Ortoli, F.-X. 109, 111
Oxford model 113–14

Padoa-Schioppa, T. 63, 68, 120, 135,
  152
  DG II 68, 87, 101, 109–11, 116,
    122
  Werner Report 34, 93, 175
Pagano, M. 39
parallel currency 36–7, 141, 183–4
parallel progress 34, 62, 68, 83
parallelism 181–2
Paris, Treaty of 59
Parliament 50–51
Peeters, T. 180
Pfeiffer, A. 109, 120
Phillips curve 35, 91, 140–141
pillars of the EU 65, 153
Pinder, J. 59
planning 59–60, 85–6, 116
Pleven Plan 135
Pöhl, K.-O. 17, 142, 151, 152
policy making
  at the Commission 108–11
  debates about monetary integration
    among policy-makers 37–8
  economics at policy-making
    institutions 120–122, 123
  economists and 56
political will 171–2
Pompidou, G. 30, 61, 136
Portes, R. 71, 120
Portugal 31
positive integration 9–10
price stability *see* inflation
Prometeia model 113–14
public finance *see* budget deficit; debt
  ratio

Quest model 114

rational expectations hypothesis 94
regional cohesion 178-9
regional policy 36
research 120, 122, 123
Rey, J.-J. 175, 183
Rome Treaty 5, 135
Rompuy, E. Van 183
Rompuy, P. Van 6, 57, 180
Rosanvallon, P. 60, 85-6, 116
Russo, M. 109

Sachs, J. 144
Schiller, K. 115
Schmidt, H. 32, 63, 69, 83, 141, 174
Schönfelder, W. 150, 152, 187
Schor, A.-D. 59
Schubert, L. 109, 120
Schuman Declaration 1950 59, 135
Schumpeter, J. 120-121
Scitovsky, T. 18-19
Second World War 58, 133-4
Servais, D. 148
single currency
    Belgian approach to launch 184-5
    changeover scenario 160-161, 177
    fixed exchange rates vs 16-18, 21-2,
        26
Single European Act 1986 64, 148
single market programme 5, 63-4, 66,
    108, 148, 173-4
snake, currency 29, 31, 32, 37, 138-9
social market economy 115-16
sovereignty
    tension with integration 66-7
    transfer of 14, 29-30, 40, 57-8
Spain 31
spillover effects 9, 57
Stability and Growth Pact 161
stagflation 84, 116-17
state 29, 41
    and market in post-war integration
        theory 3-12
    public finance *see* budget deficit; debt
        ratio
structural factors 167-73
Study Group on Economic and Monetary
    Union 36
subsidiarity principle 6, 57
supply-side policies 96-100, 118-19,
    170

Swann, D. 179
Sysifo model 113-14
Szàsz, A. 174-5

Tabellini, D. 170
target zones 38
Thatcher, M. 30, 69
Thiel, E. 150, 152, 184
Thorn, G. 109
Thorn Commission 108
Thygesen, N. 40, 146
Tinbergen, J. 8-10, 10-11, 57
Tindemans report 183
trade-creation 4-5
trade-diversion 4-5
trade interdependence 167, 169
trade policy 7, 9
transaction cost 17
Trezise, P. 38-9
Triffin, R. 181
Tripartite Conference on Employment
    and Stability in the Community
    1976 92-3
Tsoukalis, L. 62, 68, 83, 138, 139

unemployment 106, 107
    debate between the Commission and
        the CEPS Group 117-20
    and inflation 35-6
    optimum currency area theory 15,
        16-17
Ungerer, H. 144
United Kingdom (UK) 69, 71, 83, 140,
    172
    request for budget contribution
        reduction 30, 106
United States (US) 19, 106, 172

Van Den Bempt, P. 110
Van der Wee, H. 134
Viner, J. 4-5, 6, 10-11
Vines, D. 6

wage moderation 119, 163
Waigel, T. 161
Wegner, M. 83, 85, 109
Werner Report 30, 31, 32-5, 41, 69,
    82-3, 131, 136-8
    blueprint for economic and monetary
        union 61-2

parallel progress 34, 62, 68, 83
political importance of EMU
    178
stages towards economic and
    monetary union 33–4, 62
weaknesses 34–5, 62, 93, 175

'White Paper' 1985 63
widening 58, 135
'worm' 186
Wyplosz, C. 144

Ypersele, J. van 37, 39